SOME MODERN AUTHORS

SOME MODERN AUTHORS

BY

STUART P. B. MAIS

" Perhaps the best test of a man's intelligence is
his capacity for making a summary."
Lytton Strachey.
" It is not sufficiently considered that men more
frequently require to be reminded than informed."
Doctor Johnson.

Essay Index Reprint Series

BOOKS FOR LIBRARIES PRESS
FREEPORT, NEW YORK

First Published 1923
Reprinted 1970

INTERNATIONAL STANDARD BOOK NUMBER:
0-8369-1836-3

LIBRARY OF CONGRESS CATALOG CARD NUMBER:
73-128276

PRINTED IN THE UNITED STATES OF AMERICA

TO

MY WIFE

PREFACE

In earlier volumes of literary essays I disclaimed any
pretensions to be thought a literary critic. I wrote of
men and women whose books I liked, for two reasons :
one, I liked writing about them ; two, I wanted to
enlarge the number of their readers. Then by that
curious irony which certainly governs my life I became
a professional book reviewer, and now those who use
terms loosely imagine that I really am a literary critic.
In truth, I am further from being one than ever I was.
For what does it entail to be a book reviewer ? It
means to open parcels all day long, to dip into as many
as seventy books in as many hours, not casually, but
to make sure that they have or have not what is called
in Fleet Street news - value. It is an amusing job,
but as far removed from literary criticism as breaking
stones. This book is no collection of criticisms that
have appeared in a newspaper. It is a holiday that
I have thoroughly earned. I am master of my own
space. I need exercise no news sense. I do not have
to think in inches. I can use my own judgment. I
write as I like. I do not mean that I have voluntarily
turned my back on literary criticism. As a novelist
I have with some difficulty created a technique of my
own which only about two critics have had the ability
to discover. My true business in life is creative. The
function and technique of criticism have up to now been
hidden from me. I have got as far as the discovery
that the critic is one who appreciates, who tries to
follow the craft of the author, who tries to see how far
the artist has carried out his own intention. I do not

abuse him because his way is not my way. In other
words, I realise that criticism is as much an art as
painting. I wish I could acquire it. It is very far
removed from the log-rolling or the too brilliant
vituperation that now passes for criticism. I plead
guilty to neither of these vices. It is hard to know
exactly under what category these papers of mine fall.
They are not academic. I have not let myself run riot
as I used to in fulsome eulogy. My gusto in the
past has done some harm to those I sought to praise.
I have kept silence about those whose work calls up
no sympathetic response in me. I have moderated
my transports about the objects of my admiration. I
have striven to interpret the personal impression made
upon my mind by reading a few of my contemporaries.
And here a word of warning. There is of course no
finality in criticism any more than there is in the
physical sciences. But when we judge of poets dead
and gone we do attempt a summary of their whole
achievement. To do this of living authors is to anticipate their obituary notices. Who knows what the
next phase of such a novelist as Compton Mackenzie
may be? He leaves his attractive buffoonery and
more attractive chorus girls for a melancholy treatise
on Mother Church. His next novel may well be an
attempt to out-Conrad Conrad on the subject of
Eastern Seas. It would be absurd to give a final
verdict on a man's capability half-way through a race.
On the other hand, it is fun to take snapshots while he
is in mid career : to notice with joy how neatly Arnold
Bennett takes (in *Mr Prohack*) the hedge of Humour;
to writhe in agony as we watch him flounder (in
Lilian) in the sticky morass of sex. In the year
1922, 10,842 books were published; 1931 of these
were novels. It is fairly obvious that the general

reader, the man or woman who reads for intellectual entertainment, cannot sample every one of these. I am employed as a Taster. It is my privilege to give here some indication of the merits of a few of the better vintages—that is all.

CONTENTS

PART I : SOME MODERN NOVELISTS

II

PART II: SOME MODERN CRITICS

PART III: SOME MODERN AUTO-BIOGRAPHERS

PART IV: SOME MODERN POETS

PART V: SOME MODERN DRAMATISTS

CONTENTS

PART I

SOME MODERN NOVELISTS

SHERWOOD ANDERSON
STELLA BENSON
EDWARD BOOTH
ERNEST BRAMAH
GILBERT CANNAN
JOHN GALSWORTHY
WILLIAM GERHARDI
JOSEPH HERGESHEIMER
A. S. M. HUTCHINSON
VICENTE BLASCO IBAÑEZ
SINCLAIR LEWIS
WILLIAM McFEE
KATHERINE MANSFIELD
SOMERSET MAUGHAM
JOHN MIDDLETON MURRY
J. C. SNAITH
HUGH WALPOLE
VICTORIA SACKVILLE-WEST
E. H. YOUNG

I

SHERWOOD ANDERSON

THE more I read of Scott Fitzgerald the more I like Sherwood Anderson. Scott Fitzgerald is, I believe, a best seller. He knows how to choose a title. *The Beautiful and Damned* is not so good as it sounds. It is a very long account of a rich New York idler married to a very beautiful and self-willed girl who lulls his mind to sleep. They are extravagant, drink far too much, and quarrel realistically. When the war snatches him away he has a brief affair with a Southern girl (it is typical of her that she wears lilac organdi) and returns to his wife. He is first cut off by his Prohibitionist grandfather and then reduced to complete beggary. His attempt to write popular short stories, like his attempt to do office work, is unavailing. In the end he disputes his grandfather's will, wins his case and thirty million dollars, and goes mad. This book has caused what is called a sensation in America on account of its merciless indictment of the Smart Set. To us it all seems very far away. It is by no means a bad book. It is only when we put it into contrast with one of Sherwood Anderson's that we dismiss it as clever and realistic, but not what we want. It photographs, but it does not interpret.

Sherwood Anderson is the interpreter of the new America. He is as fresh as Walt Whitman. He has got hold of something entirely new. He has a subtitle for *Winesburg, Ohio* : it is *Intimate Histories of Everyday People*. That word " intimate " is significant. He cares not at all what his characters do, nor how they behave. He is solely concerned with their inmost thoughts. He begins by giving us a picture of an old writer in bed before whose eyes pass a procession of

grotesques: he got out of bed and wrote about them.
He evolved a theory which was this : "In the beginning, when the world was young, there were a great
many thoughts, but no such thing as a truth. Man
made the truths himself, and each truth was a com-
posite of a great many vague thoughts. All about in
the world were the truths, and they were all beautiful.
. . . There was the truth of virginity and the truth of
passion, the truth of wealth and of poverty, of thrift
and of profligacy, of carelessness and abandon. . . .
It was the truths that made the people grotesques.
The moment one of the people took one of the truths to
himself, called it his truth, and tried to live by it, he
became a grotesque, and the truth he embraced became
a falsehood."

When an author begins like that we can settle down
with a contented sigh. Not for him the shibboleths,
not for him indictments against the Sins of Society,
the Vice of Wealth and all that. This man, we feel,
has something to say which will disturb us and shake us
if we only have the patience to get used to his method.

His very first story, "Hands," is quite unforgettable.
In Winesburg lived Wing Biddlebaum, called Wing
because his nervous little hands were always restless
like the wings of an imprisoned bird. He was the town
mystery. One friend he had, young George Willard,
reporter of *The Winesburg Eagle*, who was exercised
about the strange activity of those hands which had
once picked a hundred and forty quarts of straw-
berries in one day. There came a time when the old
man put his hands on the boy's shoulders and told
him to forget all he had learned, to begin to dream.
He became first inspired, then frightened, and walked
abruptly away. The secret of his hands was this: in
early years he had been a schoolmaster, a magnificent
rare type of man who ruled by gentleness. He
caressed his pupils, and under the caress doubt and
disbelief fled from them and they began to dream.
Then a half-witted boy became enamoured of him,
blurted out terrible imaginings as if they were facts,

accused his master. Men came to hit him, to hang him; threw sticks and mud at him. He escaped to Winesburg, striving to conceal those hands which had been so much to blame. " Keep your hands to yourself," they had roared at him. He tried to; but he was hungry to express himself, and he expressed himself through his nervous, ever-moving fingers.

The second story is ''Paper Pills.'' An old doctor spent his time filling his pockets with scraps of paper on which he had written his thoughts. He scrunched these scraps into little hard round balls and threw them away. When he was forty-five he married a tall dark girl who came to him because she was going to have a child. She had two suitors: one talked of virginity until it seemed to be a greater kind of lust; the other said nothing, expressed his passion for her and went away. She married the doctor and died. He continued to write down his little truths on scraps of paper and then threw them away.

There is a poignant study of George Willard's mother, who hated her husband because he wanted his son to be ambitious. She prays that he shall escape the defeat that,had been hers. " If I see him become a meaningless drab like myself I shall come back. . . . I will take any blow that may befall if but this boy be allowed to express something for us both." When she meets her son she is awkward with h́im, but she rejoices that he is not a dull clod, all words and smartness. The thing that was killed in her is alive in him. She hears her husband trying to implant seeds of ambition in the boy's mind and nearly decides to kill him with her sewing scissors. The boy comes in to her and tells her that he can't expect her to understand, but he wants just to go away and look at people and think. She can't express her thankfulness. "I think you had better go out among the boys. You are too much indoors," is all she can say. ''I thought I would go for a little walk," is all that the unsuspecting boy can reply.

Among the men with whom George comes into
contact is the philosopher doctor Parcival, who strives
to make the boy realise the virtue of being contemptuous. A child had been run over and he refused to go
down to its help " . . . in the end I shall be crucified,"
he says. " Remember this : 'Everyone in the world
is Christ and they are all crucified.' " In the next
chapter we hear of George's escapade with Louise
Trunnion. " I'm yours if you want me," had been
the sole content of her letter to him. " She hasn't
got anything on me. Nobody knows," was his sole
comment to himself when he left her.

The next story, " Godliness," concerns a fanatic who
could master others but could not master himself. He
looked upon himself as a man of God and a leader
among men of God. He worked day and night to
make his farms productive, but his energy was longing
to express itself in slaying unbelievers and building
temples. The rise of industrialism turned him from
the will to serve to the will to power. He wanted to
make money fast. Instead of a longed-for son, he had
to put up with a daughter, Louise, neurotic and over-
sensitive, who married John Hardy, of Winesburg.
She got hold of him as the other Louise got hold of
George by writing to him : " I want someone to love
me and I want to love someone. If you are the one
for me I want you to come into the orchard at night
and make a noise under my window. It will be easy
for me to crawl down over the shed and come to you.
. . . If you are to come at all you must come soon."
The age-old desire of woman to be possessed had taken
possession of her. She became first his mistress, then
his wife. When her son David was born she was not
interested. " It is a man child and will get what it
wants anyway. Had it been a woman child there is
nothing in the world I would not have done for it."
David goes to stay with his grandfather Jesse, who
conceives the idea of sacrificing a lamb to God and
putting the blood on David's head. The boy is so
terrified that he hits his grandfather with a stone on

the head and runs away. "It happened because I was
too greedy for glory," says Jesse.

They are unforgettable, these men of Winesburg—
Joe Welling, the volcanic little man in and out of
season flooding conversation with his ideas; Edward
King wearing through the sleeve of his coat because
he always scratched his left elbow with his right hand
when he laughed.

One of the most convincing stories is that of Alice
Hindman, a clerk in Winney's Dry Goods Store.
When she was sixteen she gave herself to Ned Currie,
a fellow-reporter with George on the *Eagle*. "Now we
will have to stick to each other, whatever happens,"
said Ned, and went to Chicago and forgot her, while
she grew more and more lonely, saving up money
against her lover's return. At last she faced the fear
which had held her and became more and more
passionately restless. She wanted to be loved, to have
something answer the call that was growing louder
and louder within her. She had mad desires to run
naked through the streets. Only after nearly forcing
herself on to an old and deaf man does she realise the
fact that many people must live and die alone, even in
Winesburg.

Not all the stories are devoid of incident.

"Respectability," for instance, is melodramatic.

Wash Williams, the ugly telegraph operator in
Winesburg, was solitary and dirty, save for his hands.
He was a man of courage. He hated all women. He
pitied all men. To George Willard only did he tell the
reason. In his eyes his wife [yes, he had a wife] was
dead—a living-dead thing like all women. ". . . I tell
you there is something rotten about them. My wife
was a thing sent to make life unbearable to me. . . .
I would like to see men a little begin to understand
women. They are sent to prevent men making the
world worth while." He had been virginal in his
youth and adored the young girl he married. He
found after two years that she had acquired three
other lovers. He just sent her back to her mother and

said nothing. Later, in answer to a letter from her
mother, he went to see her, aching to forgive and forget.
Her mother sent her in to see him—naked. "I didn't
get the mother killed. I struck her once with a chair.
. . . I won't ever have a chance to kill her now."

"Tandy" takes only five pages of print and yet is
one of the most impressive of all the sketches.
A drunken stranger prophesies over an agnostic's
child. "I know about her," he said, "although she
has never crossed my path . . . out of her defeats has
been born a new quality in woman. I have a name for
it. I call it Tandy. . . . It is the quality of being
strong to be loved. It is something men need from
women and do not get. . . . Be Tandy, little one.
Venture anything. Be brave enough to be loved."

There is a queer story called "The Strength of God,"
in which a Presbyterian minister is tortured by the
temptation to look through a corner of his window at
a woman lying in bed. He discovered that at night
she lay in bed and read. After a colossal fight to
conquer his desire he gave way to it more and more,
until one night he saw her throw herself naked beside
her bed and pray. With a cry of joy he recognises
that what he took for a trial of his soul was only a
preparation for a more beautiful fervour of the spirit.
This girl is Kate Swift, the school teacher, silent, cold
and stern to her pupils, and yet at times oddly happy.
She was very beautiful. She used to tell them stories
of Charles Lamb and Benvenuto Cellini. In her heart
she was eagerly passionate. The object of her passion
was George Willard. "You must not become a mere
peddler of words," she said. "The thing to learn is to
know what people are thinking about, not what they
say." How well Sherwood Anderson has learnt Kate
Swift's lesson. George was more dense. "It will be
ten years before you begin to understand what I mean
when I talk to you." A passionate desire swept over
her to make the boy understand the import of life.
She had an equally passionate desire to make him
love her. One moment she is in his arms; the next

she is beating on his face with her little fists; the next the Presbyterian minister is describing her as an instrument of God bearing a message of truth. In George's eyes all Winesburg appeared to have gone suddenly crazy.

There is the story of Enoch the lonely who tried mixing with artists until he found that their feverish eternal talk led nowhere. "He did not want friends for the quite simple reason that no child wants friends." He was always a child. He married and for a moment delighted in the game of producing citizens. He then felt choked and walled in. He left his wife and children and went back to his room, where he was happy until a woman came into his life and drove him out. He tried to make her understand, and when he found that she did he was submerged, drowned out. She took all his phantoms away with her, and Enoch went back to loneliness in Winesburg.

George Willard's education goes through a further stage of development in his " awakening " with Belle Carpenter, who was really in love with a strong bar tender who suffered from lack of words, but had a good enough fist to settle George's hash when the boy thought that Belle was about to surrender to him.

Another stage in George's development is caused by Elmer Cowley, who, in his determination not to let George think him "queer," rains blows on him suddenly, leaving him half unconscious. He had previously threatened to shoot a "traveller" who was trying to sell patent fasteners for the same reason. "I ain't so queer—I guess I showed him I ain't so queer. I'll be washed and ironed. I'll be washed and ironed and starched." How well I know Elmer. He has his double in every village in England.

The whole of life's irony is summed up in "The Untold Lie."

Ray and Hal were two farm hands. Ray had got a girl into trouble and married her. "Tricked, by Gad! that's what I was; tricked, by life! and made a fool of," he said to his friend. Hal in reply says: "I've got Nell

Gunther into trouble. Shall I do it, or shall I tell her
to go to the devil?" Ray knew that there was only
one thing to tell him, but he couldn't say what he
knew he should say. He goes home, and the beauty of
the night makes him want to hit his wife. He starts
running. "I didn't promise my Minnie anything,
and Hal hasn't made any promise to Nell. She went
into the woods with him because she wanted to go.
What 'he wanted she wanted. . . . Why should anyone pay? I don't want Hal to become old and worn
out." He runs to catch Hal and tell him not to.
"They are the accidents of life, Hal," he wanted to cry.
"They are not mine or yours. I had nothing to do
with them." When he meets him he loses his nerve.
Hal tells him that he has decided to marry the girl.
"I want to settle down and have kids." "It's just
as well," said Ray to himself. "Whatever I told him
would have been a lie."

Another person who learns things is Tom Foster,
who spent all his time in silence loafing. Once and
once only he got drunk and pretended that he had
been making love to Helen White. "It was like
making love. It hurt me to do what I did and made
everything strange. It taught me something . . .
that's what I wanted."

In "Death" we meet George's mother at forty-one
remembering her girlhood's passionate longings for
adventure. There had been one lover who cried out
in the moment of his passion over a hundred times:
"You dear! You dear! You lovely dear!"

She escapes once more for a moment with the local
doctor, who had told her not to make love, which is
"the divine accident of life," definite.

"Love," he had said, "was like a wind stirring the
grass beneath trees on a black night . . . if you try
to be definite and sure about it, the long hot day
of disappointment comes swiftly."

She had had half-a-dozen lovers before she married
her husband, but she had never entered upon an
adventure prompted by desire alone. "Like all the

women in the world, she wanted a real lover. Always there was something she sought blindly, passionately, some hidden wonder in life." It hadn't been a husband she wanted, but marriage. There came a time when she wanted to get out of town, out of her clothes, out of her marriage, out of her body, out of everything. " I wanted to run away from everything, but I wanted to run towards something too." When she confides all this to the doctor he takes her in his arms, muttering, "You dear! You lovely dear! Oh! you lovely dear!" but a clerk dropped an empty box on a pile of rubbish in the hall and the spell was broken. " The thing that had come to life in her as she talked to her one friend died suddenly," and she was left to go along the road of death, seeking, hungering. And when at last she died George her son looks on her dead face and sees that it is unspeakably lovely. " The dear, the dear, oh, the lovely dear!" says the boy.

After his mother's death George crosses the line into manhood, the sadness of sophistication comes to him, he realises that he must live and die in uncertainty. He wants, most of all, understanding. He feels the need of Helen White. He tells her that he is going away, that he wants her to develop into a beautiful woman, different from all other women. Together they go out in the darkness of the night : they kiss, but the impulse to kiss passes. George reverences her and loves her, but does not at the moment want to be confused by her womanhood. These two oddly sensitive human atoms held each other tightly and waited. They embraced eagerly. Mutual respect grew big in them. Suddenly they dropped into the animalism of youth. They ran races. They took hold for a moment of "the thing that makes the mature life of men and women in the modern world possible."

The next morning George left Winesburg without seeing Helen, his mind occupied with the recollection of little things, carried away by his growing passion for dreams.

I have been at pains to analyse nearly every story in *Winesburg, Ohio*, because I am convinced that it is one of the most significant books of our generation. How flat, stale and insipid by comparison are the works of Scott Fitzgerald. Even *Main Street* made no such impression on me as this book did. It explains itself. Its artistry is perfect.

The Triumph of the Egg is flavoured slightly differently. It is not quite so coherent. *Winesburg* is really a novel. It is the history of the development of George Willard's soul in the earlier formative years. *The Triumph of the Egg* is a group of isolated short stories. The first "I Want to Know Why," is one of the best. It is about some Kentucky boys who ran away to a race meeting helped by a nigger, Bildad Johnson. "You can trust them. They are squarer with kids. I don't know why." The story is told by one of the boys who is crazy about thoroughbreds. "It's in my blood like in the blood of race-track niggers and trainers." We get the boy's point of view perfectly. "Nothing smells better than coffee and manure and horses and niggers and bacon frying and pipes being smoked out of doors on a morning like that. It gets you, that's what it does." For six days these truants from home stayed at Saratoga . . . but there was one thing that stuck in the boy's gullet; gave him, as he says, the fantods. It was this. There was a horse, Sunstreak, that the boy loved with a love that extended to its trainer, Jerry Tillford. "I liked him that afternoon even more than I ever liked my own father." After the racing that night "I was just lonesome to see Jerry, like wanting to see your father at night when you are a young kid." He found him drinking and bragging in a house full of bad women, ugly, mean-looking women. "A nigger wouldn't go near such a place." Jerry began looking at an unclean woman with a hard ugly mouth, and his eyes began to shine just as they did when he looked at Sunstreak in the paddock. "Then, all of a sudden, I began to hate that man. I wanted to—kill him. And Jerry's eyes kept shining—

and he went and kissed that woman and I crept away.
. . . At the tracks the air don't taste as good or smell
as good. It's because a man like Jerry Tillford, who
knows what he does, could see a horse like Sunstreak
run and kiss a woman like that the same day. What
does he want to do like that for? It gives me the
fantods. What did he do it for? I want to know
why." That, I think, is one of the great short stories
of the world.

In the second story, "Seeds," he reverts to his
theory of grotesques. An old psychoanalyst tells the
narrator not to expect definiteness in love. "The
lives of people are like young trees in a forest. They
are being choked by climbing vines. The vines are
old thoughts and beliefs planted by dead men. I am
myself covered by crawling, creeping vines that choke
me. And that's why I want to run and play. . . . I
am weary and want to be made clean."

There was a woman who came from Iowa to Chicago
who became alarmed whenever a man approached her,
yet she would stand naked in her bathroom facing
the hall where the men passed up and down, leaving
the door slightly ajar. In the end she was turned out
by the landlady. She ran down to the doctor's room
and knelt at his feet. "Take me," she said, "take me
quickly. There must be a beginning to things. I can't
stand the waiting. You must take me at once." Her
life had been so utterly devoid of men that she had
become sex personified. The doctor did not become
her lover. It would have settled nothing. "She
needed a lover, and at the same time a lover was not
what she needed. She needed to be loved. . . . We all
want to be loved, and the world has no plan for creating
our lovers. . . . I cannot be a lover. I am paying old
debts. Old thoughts and beliefs—seeds planted by
dead men—spring up in my soul and choke me."

In "The Other Woman" a young husband who is
in love with his wife tells of his sudden desire for a
tobacconist's wife ten years older than himself, who
came to him for two hours just before his marriage.

Her faith in her own desires and courage in seeing things put him into a truer relationship with his wife. The story of "The Egg," which gives its title to the book, would have pleased the heart of Jonathan Swift. It is told by a boy of his ambitious parents. They began catastrophically on a chicken farm. "One hopes so much from a chicken and is so dreadfully disillusioned. Small chickens look so bright and alert, and they are in fact so dreadfully stupid. They are so much like people they mix one up in one's judgments of life. If disease does not kill them they wait until your expectations are thoroughly aroused and then walk under the wheels of a wagon—to go squashed and dead back to their maker."

Failing on the chicken farm, the boy's father starts a restaurant and conceives the idea of amusing his patrons. One night a young man came in and the father tried all sorts of tricks with eggs to entertain his customer, who was bored, and imagined his host to be slightly mad. He had to submit to the inspection of freakish chickens in bottles, "terribly deformed birds floating in alcohol," and then to a futile attempt to make an egg go through the neck of a bottle. The egg broke, the father got angry, threw one at the laughing man and took another up to his wife's bedroom, where he broke down and wept. "I wondered why eggs had to be, and why from the egg came the hen who again laid the egg."

The triumph of the egg! What a masterpiece of quiet irony on the futility of life. I can't imagine how Swift missed his opportunity. He could not have done it better. But it is in a vein unlike Sherwood Anderson's usual vein. *The Man in the Brown Coat* is more typical. In this sketch an author, the writer of three hundred, four hundred thousand words, laments that he cannot get out of his brown coat. "My wife and I sit together in the evening, but I do not know her. I cannot shake myself out of myself. My wife is very gentle, and she speaks softly, but she cannot come out of herself. I have heard the voices of her mind. I heard the voice of fear crying when she was first overtaken by passion and crawled into my arms—but why, in all our life together, have I never been able to break through the wall to my wife? Already I have written three hundred, four hundred thousand words. Are there no words that lead into life?"

This is a *cri de cœur* if ever there was one.

In another story there is an old, half-crazy man who claimed intimate relationship with everyone whose name cropped up in the newspapers. "The whole story of mankind's loneliness, of the effort to reach out to unattainable beauty tried to get itself expressed from the lips of a mumbling old man, crazed with loneliness."

There is power in "The Door of the Trap," in which a mathematical master tries to solve his agitation about life by walking, running away from it. He made friends with one of his pupils, Mary Cochran, while his wife goes on interminably reading Stevenson's novels. "Damn it all!" he suddenly breaks out. "What makes you want to read about life? What makes people want to think about life? Why don't they live? Why don't they leave books and thoughts and schools alone?" In the end he kisses Mary and sends her out of his life. "She will be imprisoned," he thinks, "but I will have nothing to do with it. She will never belong to me."

But in some ways the most significant of all the stories is the longest and the last, "Out of Nowhere into Nothing." The theme is that love is destroyed by contact.

"I want you as a lover—far away. Keep yourself far away," was the refrain running through the mind of Walter Sayers, thinking of Rosalind Westcott, who had gone home to tell her mother that she proposed to give herself to a man already married. For six years Rosalind had been working in Chicago, while at her home in Willow Springs a hawk-like lover of hers, Melville Stoner, has been waiting for her return. He

tells her that he wants to express himself in writing.
"I would have but little to say about what people do.
In what way does it matter? You will eat supper
with your father and mother. Then your father will
go up town ... your mother will speak of her intention
to can fruit ... your father will pump a pail of water ...
a little of the water will be spilled. It will make a soft
little slap on the kitchen floor——" Rosalind suddenly
stops him. "By a recital of a few commonplace facts
he had suddenly invaded her secret places." This is
exactly what Sherwood Anderson himself does. "If
I wanted to write I'd do something. I'd tell what
everyone thought." "Understanding need not lead
to weariness," thinks Rosalind.

In Chicago she was always hungry—hungry for
companionship. She wanted to possess something,
a man, to take him on jaunts, to own him. All the
books cried: "Sex—it is by understanding sex I will
untangle the mystery."

But it was not that at all. "One grew tired of the
subject." She had found out something.

"If the sex impulse within my body had been
gratified, in what way would my problem be solved?
I am lonely now. It is evident that after that had
happened I would still be lonely."

She had become secretary to Walter Sayers, whose
idea of love was a fragrance, the shading of a tone over
the lips, out of the throat. Rosalind was happy in his
office. They both wanted to be lovers, but Rosalind
before offering herself to him had felt the call to go
home to her mother and tell her. When she got
there she found the two conflicting spirits: Melville
Stoner, bold, cunning, unafraid, knowing too much
of the dark, stupid side of her life; and Walter
Sayers, gentle, a man of understanding. The sudden
death of Melville Stoner would bring sweet silence.
Life in his figure had her in its grip, invading her secret
thoughts. She forced herself to put him out of her
thoughts, and dwelt lovingly on the white wonder of
life that would come through her physical love for

Sayers. "I shall willingly sacrifice everything else on the chance that may happen," she thought. Her mother implored her not to do what she proposed. Sex was a sin. The stars did not sin. They did not touch each other. "There is no such thing as love. The word is a lie," said her mother.

Rosalind ran out into the night. She met Melville Stoner. "With him she had established the thing beyond words, beyond passion—the fellowship in living, the fellowship in life." They parted, and she began to run. "She had thrown off the town and her father and mother as a runner might throw off a heavy and unnecessary garment." She wanted to be naked, new-born. Her body tingled with life. She did not know how she was going to meet the problem which she had come home to solve. She only wanted to run on for ever.

And this is how Sherwood Anderson, the man with the trumpet, urges us to make temples to ourselves. It is clarifying, salutary and ennobling. It fulfils one splendid requisite of modern life. It urges us back and back and back again to first principles. No one who takes the trouble to read Sherwood Anderson intelligently can doubt that here is a clarion call to a new sweet philosophy. We can make something of life once the old beliefs are dead.

Young America is better than old Russia.

Here is a literature of vitality. It means something.

II

STELLA BENSON

ALL too rarely this far too little known authoress swoops down from her eyrie and leaves us dazzled with the colour and the beauty and the magic she has gleaned in her flight. First there was *I Pose*, in which she danced her way into our hearts on the wings of a gossamer humour that was absolutely fresh ; it was followed by *This Is the End*, in which we realised that the polish of her wit was much more than glitter. The realism was paving the way for real sympathy when the shams had been dispelled. Third on the list came *Living Alone*, containing in many respects the most beautiful ideas of any of her books. There followed a three years' silence, broken only by *Twenty Poems*, which attracted none of the attention they deserved, and now in *The Poor Man* she has struck out in an entirely fresh venture and interpreted for us with extraordinary reality the character of a deaf, pimply-faced, ineffective, hesitating, cocktail-loving " poor fish," for whom the world is too difficult and too beautiful to bear. In anyone else's hands Edward Williams would have become either a scarecrow or an object for the slushier sort of commiseration. In Stella Benson's hands he is always interesting : through his eyes we see America and China anew ; we become one with him even when we are laughing at him, most of all one with him when we want to kick him. We begin in San Francisco, in a colony of highbrows, where music is being played.

" Music to Edward Williams had no connection with words or rules or understanding. He could not have been at all musical, for he never thought of saying : ' You know Scriabine is clean, my dear, clean like a scrubbed olive,' or ' It has been wittily said that Moussorgski is the spiritual son of Ouida and Charlemagne,' or any of the things sounding rather like that, that we expect to hear from musical people as the Victrola falls silent. Edward Williams was a person of no facts at all; probably he was the only person in the world so afflicted, or at any rate the only man. Music to him was always anticipation, even when it was over."

This music is being played in the rooms of Miss Rhoda Romero, an insolent, handsome and contented (except for the fact that she was rich) Bolshevik artist who shared her flat with Avery Bird, a Russian Jew. " They had once married in a moment of inconsistency, but had since divorced each other in order that they might live together with a quiet conscience." Others present were Mrs Melsie Stone Ponting, who lived mainly to be kissed, and Emily, the girl with the fierce eyes, for whose sake Edward was prepared to chase half over the globe. Unfortunately for Edward's chances Emily was already in love with someone else's husband. More unfortunately, " Emily was always much affected by the skins and shapes of men and women. The last hour had been made almost unbearable to her by the fact that Edward had red spots all over his forehead and chin."

Edward gives a party in order to get to know Emily better, and confides his condition to Rhoda. " Can't you see how it is with me ? " he says. " I'm not stupid. I'm not even slow, though I'm deaf. But God is against me, and you are all against me. If I could even once come into a room and have people look up and say, ' Hurrah, here he is at last,' I'd be a different man. I've never heard that. I hardly dare to be alive against so much opposition. My own voice is terrible to me because there is no one who wants to hear it. Rhoda, if I could be sure of myself for one minute, it would be worth while to be alive." He conceives the idea of not only being host to a crowd of guests, but of making everyone recite some of his or her

C

own poems. Edward rather fancied that his own poetry
was good. We are given not only samples of the verse,
but Avery Bird's comments on them. " That," he
says of one, " is as full of meat as a unicorn's belly in
springtime." One which he stigmatised as " callow,
but then so are the chickens of ostriches," proved to
be a private letter sent in by mistake and read aloud
by Rhoda as a piece of *vers libre*.

Edward is on the point of having the satisfaction
of hearing his own poem read out when a passing fire
engine distracted and broke up the party. No wonder
Edward always wears his spirits at half-mast. He
never has any luck. He goes on a camping expedition
and comes back to San Francisco for an operation.
When he recovers he finds that Emily has gone to
China with the McTabs (Tam McTab was her lover).
As soon as he was fit Edward started to try to earn
enough money to follow her. He tried to find buyers
for *Milton for Our Boys*. " It was not, of course, ' in
poetry.' Poetry is unhealthy for children, unmanly
for Our Boys." He found much discomfort and rude-
ness, but no buyers. He goes out into the country
with a " typical young woman of the Wild West. She
had no interest or recreation whatever, apart from
flirtation. Englishmen were all nearly lords in her
democratic imagination. They were therefore laughable, but worth charming." So Maure Weber started
to charm Edward by taking him out to her Pop, the
retail merchant of Calistoga, " who called his house
not a house, but a ' home.' We who can live in houses
and can see the word Mother in print with dry eyes, or
hear the glugging of someone else's baby over its food
in a cafeteria without vicarious domestic ecstasy,
must seem very coarse to Americans."

Edward spent two nights at the Weber homestead,
having to endure brother Cliff with his " S'matter with
Ed's chin—'s all pimples ? " and Pop with his
accurate spitting and inaccurate vision of England,
and Maure's attempts to make a " beau " of him.
Then he rode away on Cliff's " loaned wheel " and tried

to sell *Milton for Our Boys* to the inhabitants of the
"World's Egg Center." He sold the borrowed bicycle
(Edward has no false shame about money) and got
back to San Francisco, where Avery Bird greets him
with "For Christ's sake get off this side of the world,
you—gopher." Eventually he gets to China in his
quest of Emily. Japan had meant no more to him
than a country packed with colour and little hills. At
Hong-Kong he woke up to the fact that the sky was
the colour of fire. "Edward could almost hear the roar-
ing of the fire in the sky . . . mists like snakes writhed
between the islands." He suddenly remembered
that he did not know Emily's surname. He studied
hotel registers : "Miss Framlingham, Delhi, India.; Miss
Wherray, London ; Miss Burnett, Canterbury—they
all sounded like thin women with withered necks and
little green veils hanging from the backs of their hats,
not like Emily." He decides to go on to Peking.
He cannot afford the fare and so tries to earn it by
teaching a class of fifty boys, half Eurasian, half
Chinese, "all ordinary English subjects."

Miss Benson's description of his inability to cope
with singing, ragging boys is quite unforgettable.
"Oh, silence—oh, silence—oh, silence—I can't stand
this," he shouts. There is the good boy with his
"Last Monday we have finish Matthew—holy-gospel
—according to twenty-four chapter." There is the
interested query : "Excuse me, sah, what does it
mean, virgin ? "

There is too the mirthful screaming of the women
teachers in the interval.

Edward stayed at the school for a month, with
blackboards overturned on his head, boys with their
arms round his neck, feebly trying to keep up some
semblance of dignity. "A joke's a joke . . . oh, come
now, go easy "—that sort of thing.

He saved money and was turned out for being
drunk. He went to Tientsin on an indigo boat. Sacks
of indigo were disgorged at Chefoo. Edward wandered
about the town thirstily with the abstemious captain.

" Outside one of the mission gates a thin boy, quite naked, tortured a yellow lizard. There were yellow scarred hills round the harbour. They trailed a silken hem of white sand into the sea, and, behind the town, a green scarf of orchard land was thrown upon the shoulder of a low hill. The Yellow Sea was really yellow. It was more like a desert than a sea. The eye would have found a string of camels crossing the sea no anomaly. The Pei-ho river was yellow too. The ship entered the river between low mud forts. Salt was stacked on a broad streaky plain to the north. Primitive windmills, like merry-go-rounds at English fairs, whirled among the stacks of salt. The villages were of yellow mud. A little girl in dark strawberry-red—an exquisite colour for a dweller in golden mud—watched a ragged yellow camel from a dark doorway."

Stella Benson has as fine a power of bringing home to us the essential colour of China as Somerset Maugham has.

Edward found Peking in the dawn.

" A great gate cast its mountainous, tented shadow to his feet. The curves of the roofs above the gate were high and ample and optimistic—there was an open space ; low trees splashed shadows on white dust and wet grass."

Edward found the names of Emily and the McTabs in the hotel register. They had gone on some weeks ago and left behind them Mrs Melsie Stone Ponting's thirteen-year-old son, whom Edward took in hand. Together they explored the Imperial City with its rose-red wall and golden roofs. " The guard-houses are like jewels having many facets. The elaborate horizon of the roofs is like a thread on which are strung fantastic jewels—red and gold and green and turquoise blue. Dragons and strange fishes and curling waves and plumes are strung upon the fringe of the pale sky."

Stone Ponting was wealthy. Edward had no qualms about borrowing from him to buy a cream-coloured ready-made suit which made him look like an unsuccessful dentist. "You look like thirty cents," said the callous infant on seeing him.

They embarked on a wide, sunny little steamer for Ichang. They ran into brigands who fired at them. Later, Edward and Stone watched the corpses floating like dead spiders down the river. They ran into a civil war. They ran into the McTabs; but Emily had again flown—now to Shanghai. Tam takes Edward and Stone across to Chung-King for a night's entertainment—to watch some killing among the soldiery, and to discuss Emily. In the intervals of telling Edward that Emily had been his mistress Tam had to stop every few minutes to watch the fun. In the end they joined the soldiers. In the intervals of the rifle fire Edward learns that Emily had always laughed at him, always loved Tam. In the end Mrs McTab had thrown her out. At this point Edward gave way to a fit of weeping. "You poor thing," says Tam, "you poor—thing."

Edward telegraphed to Emily at Shanghai. He finds her among a group of Indian Civilians. She takes him to her room and in a frenzy of weeping tells him of her misery in having to live without Tam.

"I can never be alone. That's the dreadful part. I can't get away from myself. I am horrible to myself."

"If you leave me alone," she says later, when he has asked her to marry him at once, "I shall never stop crying. Can't we go to some happier place?"

She is pretending that he is Tam—for a minute at any rate he achieves ecstasy: then reality breaks in on her. She pushes him away from her and runs to the inner room and locks the door. He implores her to come back. She does.

"Leave me alone," she shouts harshly and hideously. "Can't you leave me alone? I can't bear you. I couldn't bear to touch you—you poor, sickly thing." Then she hits him again and again in the face and bursts once more into tears. "You must believe it now," she sobbed. "You—poor—thing."

Then she finally leaves him.

It is a ruthless and finely worked out ending to a very memorable book.

Stella Benson has every gift. Her poems at the heads of each of her chapters are jewels of rare beauty. Her descriptions of California and China are vivid, full of colour, remarkable for the originality of the vision they call up, her characters are clearly and humorously delineated, and the main theme—that of the feckless Edward pursuing a vain chimera of beauty, knowing himself doomed to failure—is magnificently conceived and carried out. Everyone will recognise something of himself in the indeterminate, colourless ass who tries all the time to make his presence felt, to make others realise that he matters, who wallows in an ocean of self-pity when things go wrong. Edward represents that side of us which enjoys hurting itself.

He is an amazing study of a poor devil ridden with an inferiority complex.

III

EDWARD BOOTH

A S the author of *The Cliff End* and *Fondie* he
was known as E. C. Booth: as the author of
The Tree of the Garden he becomes Edward
C. Booth on the cover and Edward Booth on the title-
page. It is all rather disquieting. He has many gifts
and more faults, this author of the uncertain name.
He takes a very long time to write a book, which is
accounted, in England, a sign of genius. He writes
very long books; he has an amazing command of the
Yorkshire dialect; he is grotesquely sentimental. He
opens *The Tree of the Garden* with the worst sentence
I have ever come across in a novel: "Wrapped in her
unaccustomed garments of bereavement, the widow
of John Openshaw stood one morning before his
massive roll-top desk in the comfortable smoke-room,
misnamed a study, holding in her reluctant fingers
the key which—to the shrinking susceptibilities of
such recent sorrow—felt as if it had been purloined
from the dead."

After such woolly wordiness we feel that whatever
compensation there may be to make up for that gross
slovenliness of style, it will have to be something very
much out of the common. I cry for the pruning-
hook.

The story is that of a boy, spoilt by his widowed
mother, falling in love with a farm girl, leaving her with
the promise that he will come back to marry her, and of
course having an accident which prevents him from
keeping his promise. His lawyer goes in his place and
seduces the girl to keep her quiet, and by the time
that the hero catches up with her again she is on the

streets. It makes me angry even to have to describe
such a plot.

If there is one subject done to death, it is this *Adam
Bede* business of rich young men robbing village girls
of their virginity—which only goes to prove once
more that it is the treatment that matters, and nothing
but the treatment.

The Tree of the Garden is worth reading because
Booth dwells so lovingly on the life of the country-
side. Guy Openshaw, the hero, may be—is, in fact
—an unmitigated fool, but Thursday Hardrip, the
slatternly bastard heroine, is a joy because of her
complete naturalness : she is of the earth earthy,
and the beauty of earthiness is really the subject of
all Booth's song. Guy is sent to Whinsett as a boy
to recover from a fatuous mother . . . he rescues
Thursday when she falls out of a cart as the result of
a blow from her drunken grandfather. She loves him
at once. He goes away, to return after five years as a
camper-out. The girl comes to his tent the first night
he gets there. Like all Booth's heroines, Thursday
has great physical beauty, soft, smooth skin, velvety
lashes, coils of dark hair, firm limbs, deep, dark eyes
—but it is a shame to paraphrase Booth when he is
describing the natural delights of the human form,
or of scenery.

Let us take the moment in the cow-shed at dawn
when Guy realises for the first time how lucky he is to
have such a goddess pining for his love :

" Lit by the morning sun, he realised that her flesh
was almost fair. The hair, too, that he had so long
accounted black, was in reality a deep rich brown,
overshot with an auburn shimmer suggesting hidden
strands of bronze and gold ; and the seeming darkness
of the girl's eyes derived from the heavy lashes fringing
them, for their irises were of a deep reticulated grey,
verging on violet. The hollow under her throat
caught the sun sideways, and held a little shadow-pool
of blue-purple ; under her lower lip was just such
another pool, deepening the smile that curled it. Her

chin was rosy; her cheeks slightly flushed; her glance liquid bright, as though, like this morning's flowers, the eager dew lay in it." Booth has time to look his last on all things lovely every hour—and, like all last looks, his is a long one. He waxes lyrical on Thursday's skill as a milkmaid: "She had the rapt look of a harpist, plucking music from the tremulous strings of milk that quivered in alternate spurts into the pail between her knees. At times the rinsings rang loud and martial against the metal with a hint of cymbals; at times they cleft the rising froth with a deeper note." Thursday's beauty is sufficiently provocative at all times, but Guy is a poor, cold fish . . . even when she tries to teach him how to milk he merely shrinks in horror when his gaze slips to the profound depths of her unguarded bosom. It is lucky that she is such a trier, for never can a man have shown fewer signs of reciprocating love than this incredible Guy. On his last night she takes him for a walk over the cliffs where couples lying with laced arms all over the fields should have acted on him as exemplars: a storm comes on and they shelter in a low embankment hung over with bryony and honey-suckle: she implores him to lie by her. "Lig beside me. Say you're not vexed wi' me. Say ye care for me. Do ye? Say you'd sooner be laid oot here wi' me than wi' anybody else, for all it rains."

After incredible assault his outworks are taken. He surrenders himself to a kiss, so vehement and long drawn-out that he is staggered. . . . Having begun, Thursday casts aside all pretence. "There's naught I wouldn't do for ye. There's naught ye cared ti ask me . . . that I should say 'no' to. Try me! Gi'e me a chance ti show how fond I is of ye. Aye, do!" But he didn't. Only when he was alone in his tent did his fingers chafe to touch her, to trespass in the tresses of her hair; only then did she steal into remembrance through his nostrils—"like the beseeching breath of bruised wild roses or wounded honeysuckle."

How was this son of Mrs Openshaw, breaks out his

creator, to divine the glorious truth that flesh is
heiress of the Kingdom of God ? After pages of talk
Guy at last asks Thursday to become his wife.
" Dean't ask it o' me," she says weakly. " Ask me
summut else. Ask me summut easier. Nay . . .
if you want me as you say ye do, tek me. Tek me
wi'oot asking. Do aught ye like wi' me. But don't
talk o' wedding me. . . . It'll only mek trouble for us
both. Let's mek believe we're wed, us two. Neabody
need know, an' it'll hurt neabody."

After more talk—they all talk far too much—
Guy goes, having promised to write. And then
comes the inevitable descent into melodrama. Guy
breaks his arm. Thursday waits for the postman
in vain. Then the lawyer comes. Guy's letters
have been diverted by Charlotte, the *tertium quid.*
The lawyer, a quite impossible villain, took in the
loveliness of Thursday at a glance and decided to
accept what Guy had refused. This led to apathetic
resignation on Thursday's part, followed by the
sort of sordidness that one associates with the
youngest decadents. In the end Guy meets her again
as a harlot. He goes with her and she gives him her
history. " I let him [the lawyer] have his way wi' me.
It seemed easiest. . . . After that he used to come an'
stop wi' me at nights. . : : I left him." Follows her story
as general servant : " too pretty to be let sleep alone."
Guy stays with her and she at last has the sense to tell
him what a fool he has been with his talk of marrying :
had he only been content to take her she would have
been faithful to him and to him only, and not got to
the state of " sleeping with men for half-a-sovereign."

I have seldom read a book which has made me so
angry as *The Tree of the Garden.* All the characters
are " fond." Mrs Openshaw is a " fond " mother
indeed to spoil her son ; Guy is a " fond " young man
to resist the call of beauty ; Thursday is " fond " to
let herself care for such an anæmic idiot as Guy . . .
and the characters who are not " fond " are incredibly
villainous.

There ought to be a close season in the novel world for intercepted letters and rape. *The Tree of the Garden* would have been a good book had Thursday's love for Guy been given full play, had Guy consummated it carelessly, and learnt afterwards how little a part the sexual really plays in life. As it is, Thursday alone interests us, and she has scarcely begun to live at the end of the book. There is one passage (where Mrs Openshaw trusts that Guy " behaved in the way that a true gentleman would always behave before a lady—even in the dark ") which is so crude as to make us wish to deny any literary merit in Booth at all. But when Thursday has allowed the lawyer to take her without a struggle—" Tell him," she says, " I gi'ed you what he never troubled ti ask for " — yes, that is credible; the agony of her hunger for Guy is credible; but Booth's power lies almost wholly in his power of describing scenery.

" From the telegraph wires torpid buntings reiterated their rusty phrases; tireless swallows skimmed the surface of the road, with the velocity of thought; blackbirds lulled themselves to sleep with the drowsy sweetness of their own music; industrious yellow-hammers tinkled tiny notes on golden anvils; the cuckoo, its song already suffering change, stuttered with the over-protestation of a schoolboy asserting innocence. And withal, the sleeping silence of the sulphur-coloured corn, brimming up to the level of the dusty hedgerows; the ripening grasses in the meadows; the soft blue sky spread overhead like a silken canopy. . . . Not a flower that grew along the roadside but seemed instinct with Thursday's similitude; not a crane's-bill or pink campion or umbel of white-elder or bank of golden bedstraw but breathed the name of Thursday Hardrip: spoke to him with the sweetness of her lips." Yes, that is why we read Booth. He has a wonderful gift for bringing out the sweetness of the East Riding coast scenery. In *The Cliff End* he showed himself capable of writing a first-rate romance: his heroine was a joy. In *Fondie* he gave a powerful picture of a decadent parson's daughter and her downfall.   In *The Tree of the Garden* he has failed altogether to give his hero verisimilitude but as in the other two books, there is, in the girl, something that pulls the fat out of the fire, and redeems Booth from the commonplace.

IV

ERNEST BRAMAH

TWENTY years ago a few keen readers found *The Wallet of Kai Lung*. Keen readers always wish to share their discoveries. For twenty years Ernest Bramah's circle of lovers has been gradually increasing. At last, after too long a silence, he has written a successor, *Kai Lung's Golden Hours*. The original book, as Hilaire Belloc says, " was meant to produce a particular effect of humour by the use of a foreign convention, the Chinese convention, in the English tongue. It was meant to produce a certain effect of philosophy and at the same time it was meant to produce a certain completed interest of fiction, of relation, of a short epic."

Kai Lung's Golden Hours does this and more, far more. It is an exquisitely humorous narrative based on *The Arabian Nights* model.

We meet Kai Lung, relater of imagined tales, by the roadside, attracting a very beautiful maiden, Hwa-mei, with honeyed words. Unfortunately he manages to annoy Ming-shu, the secretary of the Mandarin of Yu-ping, who hales him off to prison. The story develops into a duel between Ming-shu, who wishes to see Kai Lung dead, and Hwa-mei, who wishes to see Kai Lung married to her. She gains access to him and warns him how to conduct himself before this Mandarin on his trial. On the first day, just before he is to be condemned, Kai Lung manages to whet the Mandarin's appetite to hear "The Story of Wong Ts'in and the Willow Plate Embellishment." Wong Ts'in had a " secret process of simulating the lustrous effect of pure gold embellishment on china by the application of a much less expensive substitute." Unfortunately

45

his workmen struck work. "In place of one tael every man among us shall now take two, and he who before has laboured eight gongs to receive it shall henceforth labour four." "My hand itches to reward you in accordance with the inner prompting of a full heart," is Wong Ts'in's cryptic reply, "but——" "May the All-Seeing guide your footsteps," he says as they go out dissatisfied, and then adds softly, "into a vat of boiling sulphur."

One workman alone did not join the other strikers. He was Wei Chang, who loved Fa Fai, the daughter of his employer. To him as he worked alone came Fa Fai with a scheme for defeating the strikers. She produced a plate of translucent porcelain, combining in its design a simplicity with picturesque effect. She explains that the house in the design is her father's; the three figures on the bridge are three of the strikers on their way to consult the oracle that dwelt beneath an appropriate sign. They are positioned as crossing the river to a set purpose, and the bridge is devoid of a rail, in the hope that on their return they may all fall into the torrent and be drowned. The willow-tree is capable of holding the chief strikers' weight, if a reliable rope should connect the two.

Fa Fai and Wei Chang become so engrossed in each other that Fa Fai loses sight of the Willow plate. "It was somewhere near the spot where you——" He arose "with the unstudied haste of one who has inconvenienced a scorpion." In his excitement he sat down on another bench on another undecorated plate, rose to find that he had imprinted an exact replica of Fa Fai's Willow pattern thereon, followed up the suggestion by sitting on ten more plates in quick succession, and found thereby a means of confounding the strikers who "providing themselves with knives and axes, surrounded the gate of the earth-yards and by the pacific argument of their attitudes succeeded in persuading others who would willingly have continued at their task that the air of Wong Ts'in's sheds was not congenial to their health. Towards Wei Chang,

whose efforts they despised, they raised a cloud of
derision, and presently noticing that henceforth he
invariably clad himself in lower garments of a dark
blue material (to a set purpose that will be as crystal
to the sagacious), they greeted his appearance with
cries of 'Behold the sombre one! Thou dark
leg!' so that this reproach continues to be hurled
even to this day at those in a like case, though few
could answer why."

Wei Chang and Fa Fai were happily married, and
centuries elapsed before it was discovered that it was not
absolutely necessary to sit upon each plate to transfer
the porcelain embellishment. The chief striker was
pushed into the river by a devout ox and dragged out
by a rope cast over the lower branch of the willow-tree.

This excellent tale, which is quite as worthy of immortality as Charles Lamb's story of the roast pig, had
the effect of deferring Kai Lung's punishment for a day,
but Ming-shu now gets vindictive and more wily. At
his next trial Kai Lung learns from Hwa-mei that he
is to be implicated and condemned without appearing.
Luckily the Mandarin has dreamed a dream three
times, the meaning of which no man was able to discover. Hwa-mei tells her lover the substance of the
dream and Kai Lung seizes the opportunity to post-
pone his doom by telling "The Story of Ning, the
Captive God, and the Dreams that mark his Race,"
showing how the Mandarin's dreams showed his
affinity with the gods.

After many attempts on his life which Kai Lung
frustrates through the help of Hwa-mei and his own
fertile brain the two lovers at last are united.

Mr Bramah's proverbs are shrewd, witty, and
picturesque:

"He who lacks a single tael sees many bargains."

"When two men cannot agree over the price of an
onion, who shall decide what happened in the time of Yu?"

"In three moments a labourer will remove an
obstructing rock, but three moons will pass without
two wise men agreeing on the meaning of a vowel."

"Though you set a monkey on horseback yet will his hands and feet remain hairy."

"He who believes in gambling will live to sell his sandals."

"Beware of helping yourself to corn from the manger of a blind mule."

"Those who are unmoved by the threat of a vat of flowing sulphur in the Beyond, rend the air if they chance to step on a burning cinder here on earth."

"Do not burn down your house in order to inconvenience even your chief wife's mother."

"Better an earth-lined cave from which the stars are visible than a golden pagoda roofed over with iniquity."

"The lame duck should avoid the ploughed field."

"However high the tree, the shortest axe can reach its trunk."

This kind of thing, to be met with at least once on every page, is attractive enough, but there is more attraction still to be found in the banter and the irony with which the book is filled. "Shen Heng soon disposed of the returned garment for two thousand taels to a person who had become prematurely wealthy owing to the distressed state of the Empire." Thus ends a delightful story of a crafty servant outwitting his lord in the matter of a burial robe.

This passage again is refreshing after the commonplaces of the ordinary prose writing of to-day :

"Is the smile of the one referred to," asks a character, "such that at the vision of it the internal organs of an ordinary person begin to clash together, beyond the power of all control ? "

"Not in the case of the one who is speaking," replied the grandfather of Chang Tao, "but a very illustrious poet, whom Shen Yi charitably employed about his pig-yard, certainly described it as a ripple on the surface of a dark lake of wine, when the moon reveals the hidden pearls beneath ; and after secretly observing the unstudied grace of her movements, the most celebrated picture-maker of the province burned the implements of his craft, and began life anew as a trainer of performing elephants."

There is something of the same sparkle in Sun Wei's defence: " Until driven to despair this person not only duly observed the Rites and Ceremonies, but he even avoided the Six Offences. He remained by the side of his parents while they lived, provided an adequate posterity, forbore to tread on any of the benevolent insects, safeguarded all printed paper, did not consume the meat of the industrious ox, and was charitable towards the needs of hungry and homeless ghosts."

" These observances are well enough," admitted Leou, ". . . and with an ordinary number of written charms worn about the head and body they would doubtless carry you through the lesser contingencies of existence. But by, as it were, extending the five-fingered gesture of derision from the organ of contempt, you have invited the retaliatory propulsion of the sandal of authority."

" To mark their sense of your really unsupportable behaviour it has been decided that all seven shall return to the humiliating scenes of their former existences in admittedly objectionable forms. . . . Sun Chen, your venerated sire, will become an agile grass-hopper ; your incomparable grandfather, Yuen, will have the similitude of a yellow goat ; as a tortoise your leisurely minded ancestor Huang, the high public official——"

To avoid such indignities Sun Wei is prepared to do anything, and is recommended by Leou to seize the person of one of the gods and hold him to ransom.

" ' Ho Tai, requiring a light for his pipe, stretched out his hand towards the great sky-lantern,' " quoted Sun Wei.

" Do not despise Ching To because his armour is invisible," retorted Leou. " Your friends in the Above are neither feeble nor inept."

How admirable is this dialogue : how delicious the telling of the ensnaring of Ning, the high god. Sun Wei owned 'a young slave " of many-sided attraction," who " was disporting herself in the dark shades of a secluded

D

pool," after her day's work, when a phœnix flying overhead dropped a wonderful pearl into the stream. Hia, the slave girl, picked it up and put it in her mouth, and was about to get out of the water when she saw a stranger regarding her with pleasure from the bank. "Without permitting her glance to be in any but an entirely opposite direction, Hia was able to satisfy herself that the stranger was a person on whom she might prudently lavish the full depths of her regard if the necessity arose . . . when he spoke his voice resembled the noise of arrows passing through the upper branches of a prickly forest. . . . He began to sing of two who, as the outcome of a romantic encounter similar to that then existing, had professed an agreeable attachment . . . and had without unnecessary delay entered upon a period of incomparable felicity. Doubtless Hia would have uttered words of high-minded rebuke at some of the more detailed analogies of the recital had not the pearl deprived her of the power of expressing herself clearly . . . nor did it seem practicable to her to remove it without withdrawing her hands from the modest attitudes into which she had at once distributed them. Thus positioned, she was compelled to listen to the stranger's well-considered flattery, and this (together with the increasing coldness of the stream as the evening deepened) convincingly explains her ultimate acquiescence to his questionable offers . . . upon receiving from Hia a glance not expressive of discouragement he at once caused the appearance of a suitably furnished tent . . . rich viands, rare wine and costly perfumes . . . a retinue of discreet elderly women to robe her . . . and all the accessories of a high-class profligacy." The Delilah-like Hia makes him give her the sheaths from off his nails, amethyst, ruby, topaz, ivory, emerald, white jade, iron, chalcedony, gold and malachite . . . when he woke the next morning Hia had disappeared, and Ning "who had been a god was indistinguishable from the labourers of the fields."

Little wonder that the incomparable Hwa-mei was unable to resist so peerless a weaver of tales. After all, what girl could resist a man who, in describing her charms, talks in such a lyrical strain as this : " Her matchless hair, glossier than a starling's wing, floats like an autumn cloud. Her eyes strike fire from damp clay, or make the touch of velvet harsh and stubborn, according to her several moods. Peach-bloom held against her cheek withers incapably by comparison."

This is a book to be dipped into, sipped slowly, and ever to be remembered. As Hilaire Belloc says : " Rock stands and mud washes away." *Kai Lung* is rock all right.

V

GILBERT CANNAN

GILBERT CANNAN in his early books, *Old Mole*, for example, was always looking for a way of escape, for that something which he knew was round the corner. Now he has seen round the corner and found that he was right. He withdrew from England, which he has always cursed, and wandered through Europe, America, the Near East and the entire length of Africa and found—himself. He is now radiant with the discovery, everything for him is simple: he is mellow and more tolerant of many things, but he cannot realise that we poor, besotted English have not had his advantages—consequently we find it hard to understand exactly what it is that he has found. Sherwood Anderson has interpreted it more clearly. Sherwood Anderson is not confused by having too much brain.

Cannan cannot even now forgive us for our habit of starving, deriding, scandalising, bullying and spying upon the few sensitive and passionate men and women we produce. In *Annette and Bennett* we see Cannan at his best, rounding off the Lawrie saga. It is the story of tragic comedians. Cannan himself is of their company. He lashes us because we cannot think straight and yet loves us with a sweetness that is all the stronger for his suffering.

We are in this final volume concerned with Stephen's great-aunt, Mary the governess, the woman who had the talent of being in the wrong place at the right time in perfection, who was strong enough to realise the unimportance of emotions which most of us ruinously exaggerate. She had learnt, as Cannan has learnt, to suspect all institutions in proportion to their success.

Abroad she had learnt to think clearly (Cannan's first requirement in his heroes and heroines), to feel swiftly and to enjoy. She came back from abroad to see her tired, helpless brother Jamie, frightened by the agony on his face caused by the furious enmity of Catherine his wife. It was Jamie who voiced what is one of Cannan's fundamental beliefs, that the game of Greatness had run its course, that the human mind was changing, that men and women were cowering deeper and deeper into their homes for protection against the storm and to hide away from each other their own nakedness and poverty of soul. Jamie had adopted his grandson Stephen, the child of the feckless Annette and his son Bennett, whose married love is beautifully portrayed in this book. Jamie was kept going by his love for the boy and his determination to hand on to him some of the philosophy he had himself come by so hardly. He was fond of drawing a picture of humanity climbing up an endless ladder leading out of nowhere into nowhere, so that nobody looked to the right or the left, and each man saw nothing but the boots of the man above him, which, in desperate affection, he licked, knowing also that if he did not do so he would be kicked in the guts and thrown down. Jamie thanks God that he had been thrown down long ago. " When the ladder breaks—and it is cracking now—I shall be the only man left, the only man able to crawl away."

Bennett was having a terrible struggle to get money. He cared for nothing in the world but Annette. "Every possible moment he had to be with her to miss no word that she said, no note of her laughter, no drop of the tenderness with which her presence surrounded him, no throb of the thrill when he touched her," and yet he turned to the ritual of religion. Annette was a child with her children, a divinity to her husband, and never a woman at all. She never worried about money. She went on having children and still more children. If only, she thought, Bennett were not so gnawed by his hankerings after the Church and respectability and rigidity, and could lose his dread for his family—the family.

Cannan has a good deal to say about the family. "The chemistry of the family should be the paramount study of the twentieth century for, properly understood, the energy of its hatred might be turned to some good purpose. It might be persuaded to turn its corrosive powers upon the horrors of life and away from its natural prey, love and spontaneity and good humour," three things that came to Annette as naturally as breathing. Bennett had faith in God, faith in Annette and no faith at all in Thrigsby. He loathed nature only a little more than he detested machinery. He got into the hands of a Jew money-lender and soon had to find £300.

Annette guessed his troubles, but never got anything definite out of him till the night he pulled a loaded pistol out of his pocket and told her. Jamie had always said: "If you ever have to choose between money and anything else in the world, choose—anything else. It may lead somewhere. Money eats its own tail . . . a good joke goes a long way . . . a damned sight longer than anything else. People like me are paid in jokes. The good we do is subtle and invisible and there is no price on it." He inoculated Annette with this doctrine. "What does being short of money matter?" she asks. It certainly seemed to matter to the religious Bennett. When he told Annette that he had to find £300 she went off into peals of laughter. When he says that he will become bankrupt, she replies: "The best thing that could happen to you." "There isn't a woman in the world," she goes on, "who wouldn't give her eyes to have been to you what I have been." She goes secretly to Jamie for help. "You two young things," he says, "though I don't know that anyone is old enough to live in this beastly world. . . . I'll have to stir myself . . . a man can only be honoured in dishonour among such people." He goes to his sister Mary and gets the £300 from her. When he gets to her he begins to outline his schemes for the grandchild whom he is educating: "When Stephen is a man and knows how life and mind and thought have changed he will understand, and he will be able to act where I have been able only to endure. . . . Do you want the young to be more helpless in the world than we have been, to find no life, to collapse of disappointment in their middle years? . . . I will have things true and full, or not at all. If all that I could have on those terms was misery—very well then, I would have misery . . . we have to bridge the failure of our generation and the collapse of the next." He makes his sister realise that he had brought his world crashing about his ears to be free of it; not to evade responsibility, but to meet it.

After making his request for the money Jamie goes for a solitary walk over the Lake hills. "Lonely! Good God! What needs a man to be lonely when he has eyes in his head and a heart to feel? What if excess of feeling does drive away men and women? There are still trees and clouds and birds . . . there was always happiness in the world, too much . . . there was nothing that this heavenly world could not yield if it were wooed aright; no need that it could not satisfy."

But Cannan feels that this is too much himself speaking. He has had a vision in the wilds of Africa. "Ecstasy is out of fashion. What has it to show for itself? Nothing but its possessor's keen appreciation of the boon of living, than which there is nothing more fruitful, nothing more precious, nothing that more liberates the purpose of the soul."

At any rate this was a grand day up in the hills, yielding him the capacity for solitude and the life that only begins when that is grasped, fullness and fertility, knowledge and desire begetting love, related to nothing and no one, absolute. He descends from his Mount of Transfiguration refreshed in spirit, uplifted as men have been from the beginning of time after contact with high places. He even brings himself to talk complacently about his routine-mad wife. "A

life-work to let her have her way with me, to understand her, and in a way to love her. The world is what
a woman will have it, and here are these factories and
offices to keep us all safe and reliable so that they can
know where we are from nine to five."

When Mary tells him that he thinks too much he
retorts : " Why this dread of thinking ? . . . the
thought in a man's brain is stronger than himself. It
is not the man who thinks the thought, it is rather
the thought that thinks the man." She gives him the
money and he goes.

There is one other character in the book who voices
the Cannan wonder about the future.

" I want to know what our nephews and nieces are
going to do when we have spent the money which we
have done nothing to earn, for we shall leave them
nothing else—no faith, or philosophy or thought, or anything to remember us by. We shall be just a kind of
blur, a fog of mindlessness getting in their way. . . .
One wants something else in life besides a lot of habits."
It might be Sherwood Anderson speaking. This is the
voice of that young America about which Cannan waxes
so eloquent. Cannan is the apostle of hope. He has
got out, he has done with being bitter. He sees a new
world : the break-up of the old means a new heaven
and a new earth.

VI

JOHN GALSWORTHY

JUSTICE! That is always the first word that springs to the mind when one recalls the work of Galsworthy. No modern writer strives so hard to maintain the balance of the scales so exactly. Always he strives, like Mark Sabre, to see both sides of a question, and nearly always he succeeds. We think of the excellence of that balance in *Strife*, in *Justice*, in *The Silver Box*, but a fallible being will fail somewhere, and there is one glaring example of failure which cannot be overlooked. On *The Forsyte Saga*, if his dedication of it is to be taken literally, Galsworthy would probably prefer to be judged, " believing it to be of all my work the least unworthy of one [his wife] without whose encouragement, sympathy and criticism I could never have become even such a writer as I am."

" The very simple truth," he says in the preface to this long novel, " which underlies the whole story [is] that where sex attraction is utterly and definitely lacking in one partner to a union, no amount of pity, or reason, or duty, or what not, can overcome a repulsion implicit in Nature."

Irene refuses to compromise with life herself and so she hands on the ban and prevents her only child from ever attaining happiness, thereby giving her whole case away. Soames's sense of property which Galsworthy condemns in the harshest possible terms is nothing like so evil a vice as Irene's self-centredness. Excuse her how he will, Galsworthy cannot escape from the fact that the heroine with whom he sympathises so deeply is almost grotesquely selfish. Galsworthy has painted in unforgettable colours the passing of a period, but he expressly disclaims that his book is the scientific

57

study of that period. He defines *The Forsyte Saga* as " an intimate incarnation of the disturbance that Beauty effects in the lives of men. The figure of Irene never present, except through the senses of the other characters, is a concretion of disturbing Beauty infringing on a possessive world." He forestalls obvious criticism when he suggests that readers pity Soames " in revolt against the mood of his creator " by saying that he " too pities Soames, the tragedy of whose life is the very simple, uncontrollable tragedy of being unlovable."

With regard to the final, almost too painful, result of this long drawn-out agony, the separation of Jon and Fleur, he suggests that " the facts determine Jon, not the persuasion of his parents," which only shows how wrong, how pig-headed a creator can be about his own characters. What facts ? The fact that Fleur is the daughter of his mother's hated husband ? Would that count for much against real love ? Let us rather say the concatenation of circumstances, his father's letter (persuasion), his father's death, the direct result of disclosing the facts (persuasion again), his mother's dreadful " Don't think of me, think of yourself " (most insidiously persuasive of all), the obvious anguish of the self-centred Irene (implicit persuasion all the time). No, no ; Jon is coerced. Happiness lay with Fleur. Duty called him to obey Irene . . . and obey her he did against all the laws of love and common sense. Irene in her ruin must needs drag down with her the only thing she cares about—positive proof indeed of her cardinal sin. This is the blot on one of the finest novels of the age, that Galsworthy for once has allowed his feelings to run right away with him and only at the end puts forward the lamest of excuses to defend himself. For a great book *The Forsyte Saga* undoubtedly is, our age seen from above by a fastidious, keenly observant, sensitive and very human critic. It needed just such a spirit to interpret the passing of the aristocracy and the rise of a " democratic, dishevelled, hurried, noisy, apexless " England

where manners, flavour, quality are " all engulfed in one
vast, ugly, shoulder-rubbing, petrol-smelling cheerio,"
to depict the dying of " the Forsyte age and way of
life when a man owned his soul, his investments and
his woman without check or question." Into all this
hugger-mugger was the exquisite Fleur born—" to-day
with its Tubes and cars, its perpetual smoking, its
cross-legged, bare-necked girls visible up to the knees
and down to the waist if you took the trouble . . .
with their feet, too, screwed round the legs of their
chairs while they ate, and their ' so longs,' and their
' old beans,' and their laughter—girls who gave Soames
the shudders whenever he thought of Fleur in contact
with them ; and the hard-eyed, capable, older women
who managed life and gave him the shudders too."
    It is for this reason that we get so much of the beauty
and the loving in a world fast running God knows
where that *The Forsyte Saga* stands out, for its exquisite Fleur, with her dark chestnut hair, her dark hazel
eyes, Fleur in her Goya dress, white muslin on head, a
fichu round her back neck over a wine-coloured frock,
fulled out below her slender waist, with one arm akimbo,
the other raised, right-angled, holding a fan which
touched her head ; Fleur spilling out her exquisite love
for Jon, " a vintage full and sweet with sunset colour
on the grapes " ; Fleur and Jon in the great beech temple
on Chanctonbury Ring while the morning dew was on
the ground and the larks were singing ; Fleur's " Oh,
Jon ! " as he looks up at her with adoring eyes when
she comes to exhibit her grape-coloured dress ; Fleur
holding the carriage door to prevent intrusion on the
way to Reading ; Fleur's determination to hold her
lover at any cost ; Fleur's victory over Soames : " It's
our lives, not yours "—why in heaven's name couldn't
Jon make that point clear to Irene ?—Fleur's eyes
at her wedding, fluttering like a caged bird's wings ;
Fleur's final " Daddy ! " to Soames before she gives
herself to young Mont . . . how one's heart goes out
to this exquisite girl : at the thought of her our
very senses ache. How dared Galsworthy throw her

into the arms of so ordinary a man as Mont when the sensitive, generous, loving Jon was so obviously her soul's mate ?

It is a judgment on Galsworthy's whole scheme that in *To Let* it is hard to summon up any interest in Irene. Our heart is given to Fleur and we really care very little what happens to the others so long as she can gain her happiness. Because that is frustrated we lose all our sympathy for Irene. We feel more kindly disposed towards Soames because he did at least make a bid on behalf of Fleur, and sinks his own private prejudices in order to further the interests of the daughter who (he felt) failed to love him as he ought to be loved. Irene's dark brown eyes and golden hair may have caused Soames a lifetime of frustrated desire, but they leave us cold. Her silence, passivity and graceful perversity, her affair with Bosinney do not endear her to us. A stronger man than Soames would have whipped her into satisfied docility, but the Forsytes, the middlemen, the commercials, the pillars of society, the corner-stones of convention " don't hold " with primitive measures. Irene wanted an Ethel Dell hero as lover : she got instead a fastidious gentleman, a suicidal architect with hungry eyes, and a dotard with a weak heart.

Irene was not of those who have the " guts " to make the best of things : she always made the worst of them, giving way to that indefinable malaise, that unease which is the mark of all weak characters who fail to get exactly what they want. " A good beating," said Soames, " is the only thing that would bring you to your senses." What a pity he had not the courage of his convictions. When he accepts the decision of the barred door he sits down on the stairs and buries his face in his hands ; he is lost from that hour.

The type of wife who answers the query, " Where have you been ? " with " In heaven—out of this house ! " deserves corporal punishment. To pass by such a thing is comparable to an ineffectual school-master allowing the beginning of a " rag." But

Galsworthy is emphatically against corporal punishment: he labels it "an extremely mean action." Surely there are circumstances in which a husband must take direct action if he wishes to remain husband and not become cuckold. Unconsciously we are driven to compare Irene's treatment of Soames with Winifred's attitude to her scapegrace husband, Monty, who returns to her "dead to the world" after racketing all over the globe with a multitude of women. "Go and have a hot bath," she says. "I'll put some clothes out for you in the dressing-room. We can talk later." This to the "selfish, blatant clown" who had never really cared for her and who had done her down at every turn. The way of the world? Perhaps, but she makes Irene cut a poor figure by comparison.

All that Irene can say is, "God made me as I am" —how well we know the excuse—"wicked if you like— but not so wicked that I'll give myself again to a man I hate."

Not so wicked is good. So this time she marries young Jolyon in March and gives birth to Jon in May. Soames' daughter by his new French wife was born in November.

Is it just chance that Jon calls his mother Guinevere?

It is good in *To Let* to get away from Irene—on the rare occasions when she appears she is merely shrewish in her hatred of Soames and like a hen-mother in her jealousy of Jon—and let oneself dive into the very heart of Fleur—Fleur writing to Cherry about seeing "the air sort of inhabited" and feeling "dancey and soft . . . with a funny sensation—like a continual sniff of orange-blossom—just above your stays"; Fleur making no effort to hide her love of Jon; Fleur angry at Profond's "small bit" fondness for her mother; Fleur putting on her "freak" frock of gold tissue out of "caprice"; Fleur with the green parasol forcing Jon to marry her quickly before he hears the truth about the family feud; Fleur giving way to a paroxysm of tears after her wedding just for one moment before stiffening her lips for ever. What

power was there in Jolyon's letter to conquer the
Juliet-like love of such a girl as this? "The man who
once owned your mother as a man might own a slave"
—words, words, empty words . . . but they did the
trick, because Jon was too young . . . a treacherous
beastly letter.

"Jon—I love you!" says the too-fond Fleur.
"Don't give me up! If you do, I don't know what——
I feel so desperate. What does it matter—all that
past—compared with *this*?" She speaks truly—what
does all that past matter? It matters everything
because of the subtle poison that Irene pours into her
son's ears. "You are a giver, Jon; she is a taker."
Taker? What term ought such a mother to apply
to herself?

"Oh!" cries Fleur in despair when Soames has to
tell her that he too has failed, "what did you—what
could you have done in those old days?"
That is the point. What did he do? He loved and
his love was not returned. A heinous offence surely to
be visited on him thus.

And we part from Irene on the harshest possible
note: she sees Soames, waves almost gaily to him with
her grey-gloved hand and smiles. She can afford to.
Has she not won all along the line? And for Soames
. . . what was left? "He might wish and wish and
never get it—the beauty and the loving in the world."

It is the highest possible tribute we can pay to
Galsworthy that we care enough about his characters
to get really angry when he tries to elicit our sympathies for an unsympathetic, undeserving character.
Galsworthy himself has given us the phrase to apply
to Irene. "Bone-egoistic" he calls Mrs Noel's curate
husband in *The Patrician*. "Bone-egoistic" is precisely the epithet for Irene. It explains her exactly.

VII

WILLIAM GERHARDI

GERHARDI (pronounced like the Christian name Gerard with a " y " at the end) is an Oxford undergraduate who in his one novel, *Futility*, shows extraordinary promise. The book is dedicated to Katherine Mansfield and has a striking preface by Edith Wharton, in, the course of which she says (what most of us have felt) that in Dostoievsky, Tolstoy, and the rest we acknowledge the reality of their theme but altogether fail to know " which way the master is seeking to propel us," while in the English and French novelists who have, since the war, " undertaken to translate the Russian soul in terms of our vernacular " we hunt for enlightenment altogether in vain.

" Then," she continues, " I fell upon *Futility* . . . on the second or third page I met living intelligible people, sons and daughters of somebody, as Russian, I vow, as those of Dostoievsky or Goncharov, and yet conceivable by me because presented to me by a mind open at once to their skies and to mine. I read on, amused, moved, absorbed. . . . This, it seems to me, is the most striking quality of Mr Gerhardi's book: that he has . . . enough of the true novelist's ' objectivity ' to focus the two so utterly alien races to whom he belongs, almost equally, by birth and up-bringing—the English and the Russian—to sympathise with both, and to depict them for us as they see each other. . . . One wonders at the primness of the hand which has held together all the fun, pathos and irony of the thronged sprawling tale. . . . Mr Gerhardi's tale is extremely modern; but it has bulk and form, and a recognisable orbit, and that promise of more to come

which one always feels latent in the beginnings of the
born novelist."

Mrs Wharton's claim for it is no extravagant one.
" The laughter, the tears, and the strong beat of life "
in it make *Futility* a remarkably fine achievement.

We are first introduced to the Bursanov family
through the medium of Andrei Andreiech, an Englishman with a Russian name, who is in love with Nina,
one of the three daughters of a feckless, ineffective
father whose main trouble was to keep his mistresses
quiet. Andrei regards the household as normal until
they take him to see Tchehov's *Three Sisters*, when he
is made to realise how true to Russian life that play of
futility is.

" How can there be such people ? " asked Andrei of
Nina's father, Nikolai. " They can't do what they
want. They can't get where they want. They don't
even know what they want. They talk, talk, talk,
and then go off and commit suicide or something."

" It's all very well," replied his host, " to *talk*. Life
is not so simple . . . Tchehov is a great artist."

Andrei asks Nina what the trouble is and discovers
that the woman they live with, Fanny Ivanovna, is not
their mother. Fanny and Nikolai were like cat and
dog, he taunting her with her incompetence in speaking
Russian, she giving back as good as she got. Fanny
(who is German) is always confiding in Andrei, and
gives us some idea of the complicated affairs of the
family.

She met Nikolai, who was rich and had large mining
concessions in Siberia, when she was starring in musical
comedy. He had promised to get a divorce from his
wife, who had run away with a penurious Jew dentist
called Eisenstein. Nikolai could not get his divorce
without losing his children . . . so for eleven years
Fanny lived with him as his mistress. He then (at the
time of the story, at the age of fifty-three) decided
that he wanted to marry Zina, a girl of sixteen, a fellow
school friend of his youngest daughter, and when asked
what he wanted the rest of his family to do, replied,

"Live on as we have been living. . . . What if I am married to Zina ? I can still come home every night to you and the children. It changes nothing."

Fanny's idea is that no one will ever leave him because of his gold mines in Siberia and house property in Petrograd, whereas in truth the mines pay nothing, and the houses are mortgaged. When Fanny's long drawn-out story of her suffering is over Andrei discovers that she tells it in confidence at least once a fortnight ; instead of being as he thought the born confidant of strange women, he was merely the victim of a tedious autobiography.

Immediately there are complications of a really comic kind. Eisenstein comes to plead with Nina to use her influence over her mother, who now wishes to leave him.

No sooner has he been dismissed after proclaiming that Vera, one of the supposed three sisters, is his daughter and not Nikolai's, than the girls' mother, Nikolai's original wife, who ran away with and now wants to run away from Eisenstein, tries to gain access to Fanny, and failing to do so makes a confidant of Andrei. We are then shown Nikolai happy, and ten years younger, smarter, taller, better, because of his sixteen-year-old Zina. Andrei goes with the loving couple to see Zina's people, and it is there that we meet Uncle Kostia, who is perhaps the best drawn of all the characters.

"Uncle Kostia was a writer. Yet, though he had attained middle age, Uncle Kostia had never published a line. His two departments were history and philosophy, and everyone . . . thought him very clever. . . . He would wake up extremely late and would then sit for hours on his bed, thinking. . . . Uncle Kostia rarely dressed and rarely washed. When at length he parted with his bed he would stroll about through all the rooms in his dressing-gown, and think. . . . At length he would settle down at a writing-table near the window in his brother's study, and then for a long time Uncle Kostia would rub his eyes. In a languid manner he would dip his pen into ink, and his hand would proceed to sketch diagrams and flowers on the margin of his foolscap, and Uncle Kostia would stare long at the window. . . . Uncle Kostia would grow very still . . . and one by one the members of the family would leave the room on tiptoe, and the last one would shut the door behind him noiselessly. For Uncle Kostia was writing. What he wrote no one knew. . . . From what I could make out no one had ever seen a line of his writing. But that he thought a good deal there was no question. His life was spent in contemplation. But what it was he contemplated, equally no one knew." Such was the family to which Nikolai extended his protectorate. The paradox of his position was that he had fled from his many family responsibilities to this engaging flapper precisely because of the intolerable burden of so many responsibilities—and had incurred additional ones.

Everyone in the book having now muddled things, it becomes Andrei's turn. He works out a scheme by which they can all be happy, and unfolds it optimistically to Nina, who surprises him by laughing at him, asking him what business it all is of his, and then calling on the whole of the family to come and look at the chart and diagram which he had prepared. Nikolai takes it as a joke in the worst possible taste. In the end Andrei loses his temper and shouts at them all : " Do you silly people realise how utterly laughable you all are ? O my God ! Can't you see yourselves ? " (I could not see myself.) " But can't you see that you have been lifted out of Tchehov ? . . . What's there to prevent some mean, unscrupulous scribbler, who cares less for people than for his art, from writing you up ? . . . I feel I am almost capable of doing it myself. . . . It's so easy. You just set down the facts. The only handicap that I'm aware of is that you are all of you so preposterously improbable that no one would believe that you were real. This is, in fact, the trouble with most modern literature. No fiction is good fiction unless it is true to life, and yet no life is worth relating unless it be a life out of the ordinary; and then it seems improbable like fiction." He parts from Nina and the family with, as he thinks, dignity, in high dudgeon. When he steps into his victoria in the street his horse decides to retreat. At the window stood Sonia, Nina, Vera (the three sisters), Fanny, Nikolai, lovers and hangers-on looking down and laughing.

He goes to Oxford; at the outbreak of war joins the navy, and just before the revolution is sent out to Russia on a special mission. He finds the family exactly where they were when he left them, except that Fanny, in order to save herself from being sent back to Germany, has been married off to Eberheim, an elderly German with cancer. Otherwise—there were the three sisters always sitting on the backs of sofas and chairs, fox-trotting and waltzing, Nikolai never in the house, the revolution going on quite inconsequently. In Part III." . . . The Admiral and I, and a few others . . . travelled to Siberia, where we engaged in a series of comic - opera attempts to wipe out the Russian revolution. . . . I cannot but remember it, not merely as an adventure in futility, as admittedly it was, but as an ever-shifting, changing sense of being alive."

There is a glorious General Bologoevski, who has two English phrases which he uses all the time: " It is a damrotten game, you know," and " I give dem h-h-hell."

Andrei, of course, runs into Nikolai at Vladivostock, all his entourage with him—his wife, Magda, Zina, Fanny, his daughters and their hangers-on. Not only had they all followed him from Petrograd like ducks their leader, but " when I had to go over to Japan just for a fortnight on a matter of business—they all followed me there. . . . You see, they are, so to speak, economically dependent on me. . . . They simply have to be where I am if they are to get money out of me—Russia being what she is to-day."

There is a splendid description of a ball given in

Vladivostock, at which the General repeats to Andrei over and over again, apropos Nina: "What eyes! What calves! What ankles! Look here, why in heaven don't you marry her?"

Life in Siberia seemed to be a round of dances, dinners, concerts and garden-parties. The most farcical episode in the book, and the best told, is that of Nikolai's attempts to get a coupé in his train to Omsk, followed by his unexpected success and the trek of the well-fed and mostly drunken party through a country of half-starved refugees. Dismal forests stretch over hundreds of versts, while Uncle Kostia talks about the sense of accomplishing something that comes over a man as he travels. "I look out of my window and my heart cries out: 'Life! Life!'" and Fanny divulges her domestic worries, her autobiography to yet another listener, and the drunken General worries about the existence of God. ". . . I felt indeed I was on the summits of existence. Why should *I* be treated to such stupendous depths of irony? There beyond the clouds the gods were laughing, laughing voluptuously."

There is a gruesome picture of the fighting between the Whites and the Reds at Omsk.

"When I entered the station I saw piles of dead bodies lying on the steps, on which rich red blood trickled down all the way; and on top of all that handsome boy, with the back of his scalp blown off. They were shot at by machine-guns as they were being driven down the stone staircase in the station, and their boots had been removed and appropriated by their executioners. One man three hours afterwards was still breathing heavily. He lay on the steps, bleeding, and covered by other bleeding bodies. Another man in the pile was but slightly hit. He lay alone in the pile of dead, with a curious mob and sight-seeing soldiery walking about him, shamming death. After three hours he rose and walked away, but was caught and shot."

After a desultory love campaign with Nina, Andrei the Russo-Englishman came back to Oxford "with its sham clubs and sham societies," so like " a doll's house, a thing stationary and extinct of life," left it again on his adventure in futility, made up his mind this time to make Nina marry him, and hurried to Vladivostock, where she tells him that she never loved him. When he tells her that he has been travelling three months on purpose to see her she replies that he must have been moving very slowly : when he persists in declaring his passion she tells him that he has a smut on his nose. At dances he was reduced to being a " wall-flower." " It was idiotic to have travelled sixteen thousand miles to do this sort of thing." Nina asked him to give up pursuing her. She was completely indifferent to him. This time the Nikolai family is the one to go— to Shanghai : he sees " the three pretty kittens, each lovelier than the other, and quite irresistible together," go, and then celebrates the occasion of his soul's release. " I felt as if I was being freed from prison."

Gerhardi is the first man (with the possible exception of Goncharov in *Oblomov*) to show us the Russian through his weakness humorously. He has the merit of brevity and wit ; he never descends to grotesque caricature and yet he never allows himself to take his characters too seriously. He may not have found much use for Oxford, but it obviously taught him accuracy and a commendable economy of phrase.

VIII

JOSEPH HERGESHEIMER

NO one was likely to deny power to *The Three Black Pennys*, no one was likely to be anything but disappointed with some of its successors. No one denied the beauty of his style, no one denied that he was for ever getting lost in a snowdrift of sentimentalism.

In *Cytherea* he not only comes back to his own, but links himself up with Sherwood Anderson and Sinclair Lewis as an interpreter of the new spirit of revolt in America.

Lee Randon, the hero, " at worse than forty-five," fell in love with a doll, " Cytherea," that he had bought on Fifth Avenue, beautifully dressed in the belled skirt of the eighteen-forties, of plum-coloured silk, with a bodice and wide short sleeves of pale yellow. He was attracted by " the wilful charm, the enigmatic fascination of the still face. The eyes were long and half closed, under finely arched brows; there was a minute patch at the right corner of a pale scarlet, smiling mouth : a pointed chin marked an elusive oval beneath black hair drawn down upon a long slim neck, hair to which was pinned an odd headdress of old gilt. . . . Never in life, he told himself, had he seen a woman with such a magnetic and disturbing charm."

As an escape from his rather too serious wife, Fanny, who adored him, he found Cytherea more and more attractive. There was nothing tangible or definite to explain her charm, but she stood for the satisfaction of his essential desires. He cherished in secret and jealously guarded his restless searching after perfection. Earlier in life, before he joined the Magnolia Iron Works, he had been interested in poetry, read much, and at intervals found a woman with whom he could sweep into an æsthetic emotional debauch, a debauch which usually had an ugly and humiliating end. Then he played for safety, married the practical Fanny, who saw that the pipes were inspected and the flues cleaned, who never wore underclothes of coloured crêpe de Chine, but of fine white cambric, whose dressing was faultless and severe, as her love for him was "old-fashioned and ark-like," completely virginal. Fanny regarded the mechanism of nature with distaste, passionate she had never been. Lee was not so tranquil: marriage had not killed the vague longings of his youth. So restless does he become that Fanny suggests that he should learn repose from the doll Cytherea, the cause of all his disturbance. "Fanny hadn't noticed her smile, the long half-closed eyes, the expression of malicious tenderness . . . the pale seductiveness of her wrists and hands. . . . He tried to imagine a woman like that, warm, no—burning with life." All the men he knew had more or less his own feeling of restlessness: "he could think of none, even half intelligent, who was happy." The big men of commerce were broken in mid-life; Lee and his friends escaped by way of the country club dances and cocktail parties: it was at one of these that he met Mina Raff, the cinema star who was working such havoc in his friend Peyton's life. Mina realises the power of the doll. "No common infidelity could be half as dangerous." It is Mina who lets him into the secret that all women are either prostitutes or mothers.

She herself is an artist, but she robs Claire, Peyton's wife, of her husband. "It's her blonde, no bland, charm and destructive air of innocence," says Claire of Mina. "I envy him: it will be a tremendously interesting experience."

In spite of all, Claire loves Peyton: Lee goes even so far as to remonstrate with his friend, "Mina loves you now, and to-morrow she'll love a Belgian violinist, a great engineer, a Spanish prince at San Sebastian." He goes to New York to plead with Mina. It is here

that he meets Savina, Mrs Loyd Grove; forty-one or
forty-two in years, thin, eyes of dark blue, pale skin;
Savina, whose still, intent face, pointed chin and long
throat, the suspended grace of whose wrist was vaguely
familiar to him.   She takes him to a dance.   ".It has
been surprisingly nice," she says, at the end of the
evening.   He meets and argues with Mina, and certainly disturbs her by showing how domestic Peyton
is at heart.   He returns to Savina Grove, suddenly
discovers that she is passionately in love with him, and
at the same moment realises with a spiritual shiver
that she is Cytherea come to life.   For a moment or so
they argue : she accuses him of being contented and
satisfied.   " I'm not safe at all," he ultimately cries
out.   " I don't want to be safe," she whispers—and
then their flame-like and intolerable passion swept
them off their feet.   Savina's emotion was too great
for life.   They spend one day together, in which she
is far more fully surrendered to the situation than he
is.   " Savina was far out in a tideless deep that swept
the solidity of no land.   She was plastically what he
willed ; blurred, drunk with sensation, she sat clasping
rigidly the edge of his coat.   The possession of the
flesh wasn't what primarily moved him . . . they
exchanged endless kisses.   ' I am a part of you,'
confesses Savina.   ' It would kill me if I weren't.' "

The difference between them was that the woman was
immersed in her passion while a part of him stood aloof,
" like a diminutive and wondering child he had by the
hand."   Late that night she came to him.   The next
day he goes home.   Fanny begins to suspect and begins
to nag.   At any rate his mission to New York was
successful.   Peyton stays with his wife, who confesses
that her triumph is not great.   " Neither of us is very
much excited about it . . . he is too much like a ball
on a rubber string . . . they shouldn't have hesitated,
Lee : that was what spoiled it, in the end beat them."

As time passed Lee's want of Savina grew ; he
wanted the touch of her hands, her clinging body,
her passionate abandon, with every sense.   " His

entire being was saturated with a longing that was at once a mental and physical disturbance." He lost his love for Fanny absolutely while Fanny continued to love him. "It was a detestable situation."

Husband and wife bicker and quarrel—it all becomes sordid. Yet he had no regret—only a sharp gladness— in his adultery with Savina: "it had filled him with an energy, a mental and nervous vigour, long denied to the sanctified bed of marriage." He became first indifferent to, then bitter against, his wife. He becomes refinedly brutal, ingeniously cruel. "A mirror would shut you up quicker than anything else—you look like a woman of sixty; go somewhere and fix your face." "You haven't any idea of marriage except as a bedroom farce." "You're so pure that you imagine more indecencies in a day than I could get through with in five years. . . ." After a little of this sort of thing she hits him hard with a paper-cutter. He shakes her until. her neck nearly breaks. The blow kills— both of them. He tells her that he will have to go.

"I can't talk," she replies, "the words are all hard like stones down in my heart—you'll have to go."

He goes—straight to Savina: they escape to Cuba, the blinkers off at last, both radiantly happy. "I want to empty and exhaust myself," says Savina. She does: she dies of a weak heart, suddenly, after two weeks of bliss, killed by happiness.

Lee begins to realise the mystery of Cytherea. "I had made the mistake of thinking that I, as an individual, had any importance. In my insane belief that a heavenly beauty, a celestial chorus girl, was kept for me, I pictured myself as an object of tender, universal consideration. . . . Magnifying our sensibilities, we had come to demand the dignity of separate immortalities . . . and so I left the safety of a species, of Fanny and children, for the barrenness of Cytherea. That's her secret, what she's for ever smiling at—her power, through men's vanity, to conquer the earth. She's the reward of all our fineness and visions and pleasure . . . the privilege of escaping from slavery into impotence. . . . We made her out of our longing and discontent, an idol of silk and gilt and perverse fingers, and put her above the other, above everything. . . . She was stronger than I, Savina was the goal and I was only the seeker . . . in absorbing me she was content."

He is not content. We leave him doubtful of his next move. He is as likely to commit suicide as anything else. The only thing that is certain about him is that he will not return to Fanny. "The amazing fact is that, since I have acquired a degree of wisdom, there is nothing for me to do, nowhere to go. The truth, I have always heard, will make you free. . . . What is it the truth will make you free for except to live in the solitude of public hatred ? "

The end of all is atrophy. Hergesheimer is artist enough to avoid moralising. He is a valuable witness to the general unrest, for Lee, Fanny, Savina, Mina, Claire and Peyton—all the six of them—ring true.

He is not so easy to read as Sinclair Lewis: he is a far more conscientious workman ; his not to photograph, but to select with extreme care only the incidents and peculiarities that advance his action.

IX

A. S. M. HUTCHINSON

THE first and most obvious thing that strikes one about A. S. M. Hutchinson's work is its inherent goodness and sincerity. He writes always from the heart, never from the head. All his main characters go through great tribulation, and no reader can possibly suffer with them as their creator suffers.

"You that have tears to shed, prepare to shed them now," he cries when, in *This Freedom*, Rosalie's only daughter, Doda, dies under an illegal operation. It is a *cri de cœur*; almost as if Hutchinson were speaking of some appalling thing having overtaken his own, only daughter. "Or if," he continues, "you have no tears, but for emotion only sneers, do stop and put the thing away. It is intolerable to think to have beside that bed, beside that child, beside that Rosalie, your sneers. It's not for you, and you do but exacerbate the frightful pain there's been in feeling it with them."

"The frightful pain"—yes, it's really true. One's first feeling on reading that passage is one of extreme annoyance at the arrogance of the novelist in daring to dictate to us just what we shall and what we shall not feel. It is a blazing indiscretion, almost unforgivable in an artist. But that begs the question. Is Hutchinson an artist at all? He is certainly a good spinner of yarns. He is at pains to tell a story full of action; there is too much rather than too little incident in his novels.

But these eternal repetitions: Mr Fletcher, the gardener in *Once Aboard the Lugger——*, with his "It's 'ard—damn 'ard. I'm a gardener, I am; not a wind-shaft"; "It's 'ard—damn 'ard. I'm a gardener, I am;

75

not a blood-hound " ; " It's 'ard—damn 'ard. I'm a gardener, I'am ; not a dog-muzzle "—there are dozens of them.

Mr Marrapit with his " Adjust that impression—I am Lear—I am Sinbad—I am Wolsey " ; are these things artistic, or merely the vain repetitions that the crafty hunter after popular taste puts in to placate the vulgar palate ?

On the music hall one " Search me," or " Here we are then," raises a smirk ; repeat the phrase ten times and the sides of the audience shake ; repeat it twenty times and you are in a fair way to become " The World's Greatest Mirth-Provoker."

But this sort of repetition may be allowed ; the sort of repetition that is certainly inadmissible is the repetition of phrases like " Strike on " in every page of the latter part of *This Freedom*; the seven times repeated " On the spot " on one page of *Once Aboard the Lugger——*. This kind of thing, like the cruelly inverted sentences that he so often uses, becomes a habit, then a disease. In his later work it jars, it mars, it permeates whole books, it becomes an evil fungus.

There is a queer superstition extant that only with *If Winter Comes* did Hutchinson become one with Nat Gould, Charles Garvice, Miss Barclay and Ethel Dell.

Once Aboard the Lugger—— (his first novel), published in 1908, immediately ran into four editions, and now has reached a tenth.

There are still readers who prefer it to any of his later work. It is a novel that would have appealed to Fielding. It is hard to give it higher praise.

The Thackerayan interruption of the author on the stage is wholly delightful, the irrelevant chapters among the best. The first appearance of the heroine, Mary Humfray, shot into the arms of the hero, George, out of a hansom, is in the best possible Hutchinson vein. " ' Mercy ! ' she cried, and came like a shower of roses swirling into George's arms." All Hutchinson's heroines are like a shower of roses. They are essentially fragrant, pure, beautiful, simple-minded, romantic, but

made to suffer terrible things. Mary's father is killed
while hunting; her home is sold; alone in London
she suffers every sort of indignity before she joins
the Chater household, with its inevitable Amazonian
drinker. Hutchinson simply cannot leave the bottle
alone. From Mrs Major and her "Old Tom," to
Keggo and her "medicine," every one of Hutchinson's
weaker characters is a victim of the same vice, just as
all his heroes and heroines obey the Marlowe principle
of falling violently in love at first sight, and most of his
heroes prefer a good scrap with plenty of blood-letting
to any other sport.

There is much light shed on the simple pieties
believed in so wholly by Hutchinson in Mary's love-
letter to George.

"... I suppose clever people would laugh at the
religion my mother and father lived in, taught me,
died in, and now is mine. I believed—and I believe
—in what I have heard called the Sunday School
God; the God who lives, who listens, and to whom I
pray. ..."

I cannot conceive life in the Hutchinson circle to be
complete without family prayers.

Almost alone among modern novelists he stands true
to the simple faith that inspired *The Pilgrim's Progress*.

"No man, nor book, nor thing can be touched
without virtue passing thence into you." The sentiments, not the language, are the sentiments of Milton.
"We are not living if we are not working. We cannot
have strength but we win meat to make strength. . . .
Material treasure is not ours. We but have the enjoyment of it while we can defend it from the forces that
constantly threaten it. . . . Cultivate the perception of
beauty, the knowledge of truth; learn to distinguish
between the realities of life and the dross of life; and
you have a great shield of fortitude of which certainly
man cannot rob you, and against which sickness,
sorrow or misfortune may strike tremendous blows
without so much as bruising the real you. Either we
are reading the thoughts of men whose thoughts heap

a priceless store within us, or we are reading that
which—though we are unaware—vitiates and puts
further and further beyond our grasp the Truths of
Life. . . ."

Sentiments like these abound—no wonder such a
man could have the supreme audacity to hold an
English audience spell-bound by listening to Owen
Nares declaim the Psalms from the stage. Certainly
no other living dramatist would have dared to do such
a thing. Hutchinson's faith subdues mountains.

But Hutchinson is a humorist. *Once Aboard the
Lugger——* is merely the story of a rare cat stolen
from its owner and restored to him.

These are the ingredients of farce—and there is
much that is farcical in this sprightly novel.

" I damn well shall die," cries Mr Fletcher, urged on
by Mr Marrapit to search the grounds for the missing
cat, " if I go creepin' and crawlin' and hissin' much
longer. It's 'ard—damn 'ard. I'm a gardener, I am ;
not a cobra."

There is humour, tinged with the nearest approach
to bitterness that Hutchinson ever allows himself,
in the character of the famous novelist, Mr Vivian
Howard, the loss of whose cat provides him with
just the sort of publicity he appreciates.

" This man had an appreciation of the position he
had won. This man stood for English literature. . . .
The talents that were his belonged to the nation ; very
freely he gave them to the people. This man did not
deny himself to the crowd as another might have
denied himself. Of him it never could be said that he
missed opportunity to let the public feed upon him.
This man made such opportunities. Where excitement was, there this man, passing between his novels,
would step in. If a murder trial had the public
attention this man would write upon that trial—
nothing was too small for this man.

" Walking the public places he did not shrink from
recognition ; he gladly permitted it. Not once but
many times, coming upon a stranger reading one of

his novels, he had announced himself; autographed the copy."

This passage sheds a valuable light on Hutchinson's own character. It is hard to imagine any man as well known as he is really dreading the limelight as he dreads it. He certainly never has made and never will make himself a motley to the view.

Asked to take a call at the fall of the curtain on the dramatised version of *If Winter Comes* he would probably say: "Mice and mumps! No. It's 'ard— damn 'ard. I'm a novelist, I am; not a rotten-egg gatherer."

Four years after the appearance of *Once Aboard the Lugger*—— came *The Happy Warrior*, another novel that has gone into ten editions in ten years. In this book he soars—or descends—to the melodramatic for the first time; he has never let go. Nothing could be more in the Lyceum vein than the rejection of Audrey (the real Lady Burdon) by the false Lady Burdon and her consequent death in child-birth. The real heir is brought up with the false heir and, of course, falls in love with the same girl. Why on earth has not this book been dramatised and put on the films years ago? Surely here is the plot of all great successes on the sentimental stage, calculated to draw tears from even the most sophisticated cinema-goers. Hutchinson is among the world's best tear-compellers. His cry is from the heart to the heart. Reason and intellect have no more place in his scheme of things than verisimilitude. He is Dickensian in many things—in none more than his sentimentalism.

But there is a saving strain in him: a longing at times to escape into the open air.

It is Japhra and Ima, the gypsies, who save not only the happy warrior, Percival, but also the reader's interest in *The Happy Warrior*.

Japhra is true-bred, a proper beagle, a believer in *Robinson Crusoe, The Pilgrim's Progress* and the Bible. "They are the books for a questioner—and they are the books of a fighter."

We make no cavil at Percival's fighting qualities; the description of his bare-knuckled fight with "Foxy" Pinsent is in epic vein, by far the finest description of a fight that I have ever read.

It is as good as Ima's starry eyes and Dora's dull-gold hair, as strong as Ima's devotion to Percival, and Percival's love for his "Snow-White and Rose-Red" Dora. But before we reach the historic fight we have to wade through deaths. Hutchinson is as careless as Nature in his death-dealing capacity. There are still some of us who like to see economy exercised in this particular. If we novelists were really to hold up the mirror to Nature we should cease to be artists. Nature is wasteful and has no respectable ideas on the art of selection. The artist cannot afford to be wasteful, and must select all the time. All is most decidedly not grist that comes to his mill. Having created characters he ought not to be prodigal in littering his stage with their corpses. Hutchinson can never resist the easy tear-compelling call of a death-bed.

It is one thing, and a good thing, to emphasise the littleness of life. "The way of the mighty men in whom the spirit rebuketh life and increaseth, and at death goeth shouting back." "Reck nothing how life assaileth . . . hold on only to thy spirit . . . here's happiness,-here's content." These sayings are good, but the sudden tragedies fulfil no moral or artistic purpose. They are a sop to the lovers of the morbid, as bad as the love scene between Dora and Percival (comparable with that between Lucy and Richard Feverel in its idyllic reticence) is good. But the best part of *The Happy Warrior* is the description of the "tough life, the quick life, the good life" of the open road in Japhra's booth, with its culmination in the three-minute rounds with the "raw-'uns" between "Foxy" and Percival. There is, as I said, nothing in literature like the account of this fight, this sort of thing : "Blood-fierce went that foxy one when he see that blood, an' in he goes, fierce after blood, for to finish it . . . he muddy soon goed back to craft again, foxy! That quick-boy shook his head an' run back; an' draws a breath an' meets him; and throats him one an' staggers him; an' draws a breath an' follows him; an' pastes him one an' grunts him; an' tic-tac! tic-tac! tic-tac! an' follows him, an' follows him, an' follows him. Like a wops he was, like a bull-tarrier he was"— pages of it like that, and then the finish " . . . like a bull-tarrier . . . that quick-boy lep' at him. *One!* he smash him an' heart him, an' I see that foxy one glaze in his eye an' stagger with it. *Two!* that quick-boy drive him an' rib him. . . . *Three!* that quick-boy smash him an' throat him, an' back he goes that foxy one! and crash he goes! an' flat he lies . . . an' my life! to hear the breathing of him! There was never a knock-out like it, never no one as quick as that quick-boy when first along he come tic-tac! tic-tac! tic-tac! left-right! left-right! left-right!—never his like! One of the rare ones, one of the clean-breds, one of the true-blues, one of the all-rights, one of the get-there, stop-there, win-there—one o' the picked!"

That fight represents the high-water mark of Hutchinson's genius. He has never quite climbed there again. It is an inspired passage, written at white heat. After that all is anticlimax. The dreadfully inadequate villain, Egbert Hunt, with his incessant talk of " tyrangs," has to be trailed across the pages to give our Percival his chance of dying a hero's death, to give point to Japhra's philosophy, to give Ima a chance of holding her beloved in her arms and to free Dora from the disagreeable necessity of betraying one of the two men she had sworn to marry.

It is this sort of rounding off a book which has isolated passages of greatness in it that makes some of us swear never to write a novel with a happy ending — *The Happy Warrior* ceases altogether to have life when Hutchinson remembers that there are groundlings who must be served. We watch the creaking of the machinery in motion, and stand aghast. A Hutchinson novel—and machine-made! It seems incredible. Alas! 'tis pity—but 'tis true.

F

Followed in 1914 his third, *The Clean Heart*, the least successful of the five to judge from the number of editions printed.

But in the character of Mr Wriford he has done something that he has not done elsewhere. Here is a successful novelist and journalist beset by obstinate questionings; clever, lucky, rich, a demon for work, thinking nothing but work, breathing nothing but work, utterly broken by work, nervy, self-centred, sick of it all, throwing himself into the Thames, running madly to escape the shadow of himself that pursues him as relentlessly as the Hound of Heaven until he meets the fantastic counterpart to Japhra, Mr Puddlebox (addicted to whisky, of course) who chants—until he drowns himself to save his " loony " companion—a succession of variants on one verse of the Psalms, " O all ye loonies of the Lord, bless ye the Lord ; praise Him and magnify Him for ever."

" You think too much about yourself, boy," says Mr Puddlebox. It is true ; we all do. Mr Wriford is very near to Everyman ; he is real.

Under the tutelage of Mr Puddlebox, Wriford ceases to care about anything. He lets himself go.

" A week ago," he soliloquises, " I was an editor in London and afraid of everything and everybody. Now I've been in the river, and I've stolen a ride on a wagon, and I've had a devil of a fight with a wagoner, and I've kicked a policeman head over heels bang into a ditch, and I've nearly been burnt alive, and I've broken out through the roof of a barn and fallen a frightful buster off it, and I've slung a chap into a pond, and I've nearly killed a chap, and half-drowned him in milk, and I've nailed a man to the floor by his night-shirt, and I've jumped out of a high window, and been chased for my life, and I've stolen a ride in a motor car. . . ."

Not bad for one week's vacation. But even George Borrow didn't pretend that he had done all that. Why for the salvation of Mr Wriford's soul was it necessary to make his redemption so utterly removed from the actual ? Mr Middleton Murry's hero in *The Things We*

Are also escapes from life by walking to Barnet, but
he meets with no such untoward accidents by flood
and field; surely verisimilitude isn't a crime, even in
fiction. But once launched on his sea of extravagances
there is no stopping Hutchinson. The wretched Wriford now has to go to prison, to get as obsessed with
the necessity for tramping ever onward in the cold and
the wind and the rain as erstwhile he had been obsessed
with the necessity for continuing his work out of
season—" There's no being happy that way and never
will be," pleads Mr Puddlebox. " Think of someone
else, boy. For God Almighty's sake, think of someone
else, or you're beat and mad for sure ! "

But poor Puddlebox has to go to his death, trying
to rescue Wriford from a rising tide under the Cornish
cliffs, before Wriford can learn his lesson. Wriford
has to escape to an amazing preparatory school (the
headmaster of which, of course, drinks) and learn to
make small boys happy before he learns his own lesson.
And lastly, he has to meet the wonderful Essie, the
plumber's daughter, and bring her within an inch of
death before he can learn his lesson. It is all too hopelessly far-fetched. Hutchinson wants as stern a lesson
in realism as it is possible to administer. Surely, outside Dotheboys Hall there never was such a school as
Mr Pennyquick's Academy at the Tower House. Then
immediately on the top of that absurdity comes the
innocent, frankly-loving, laughing Essie, and we forgive
him all.

But why, why, in the name of heaven, did Hutchinson
play so false with his characterisation as to suggest that
Wriford was the sort of man to indulge in free love with
" the dayspring from on high " ?

" What, live in sin ? " cries Essie.

Wriford was a fairly mad sort of person, but he would
never have made a mistake like that. No—it is just
Hutchinson's craving for melodrama at any price. He
must have another fantastic cliff accident, a repetition
of the long drawn-out agony inseparable from each of
his characters to make Wriford realise his lesson. " To

see with others' eyes, to judge from their outlook upon life, to estimate life in terms of those upon whom life presses and not in terms of self—that is the secret of happiness, that is the thing in life that I have missed," cries the stricken Wriford.

But we must have the happy ending. Essie is spared to him—in a bath-chair.

" What, are you crying, too ? " says Essie. " Aren't we a pair of us, though ? "

Crying because they hear a psalm sung through an open church door.

There comes the war—a silence of seven years—and then the world acclaims the author of *If Winter Comes*; and now everyone is trying to account for its astounding popularity. With that book we lose count of editions. Here, say the fuddled critics, we have the portentous sign—a good book and a best seller—how is it done ?

But was *If Winter Comes* a good book ? It started off by being modern enough—an idealist, Mark Sabre, a man who always sees both sides of every question, is unhappily married to a mean and nagging wife who objects even to his harmless jesting, his nicknames for the servants, High Jinks and Low Jinks, is out of sympathy with his work, and breaks with him when he befriends a girl who is an unmarried mother. Up to this point it is undoubtedly good, but Hutchinson cannot escape his besetting sin. The latter part of the book is a trough of piled-up horrors.

One suspects Hutchinson of never being happy unless he is acutely miserable. When he can play upon your emotions to the extent of making you flinch as at a touch on an open wound, then he is happy. Having got Mark Sabre well down in the mire, he proceeds to make him rub his nose in it and undergo exquisite torture. Effie, the only really sympathetic character in the book, the direct descendant of Mary Humfray, Ima and Essie, must needs be driven to commit suicide ; Mark, to add to the horror of losing her companionship, must needs be thought to be her murderer—nothing is spared us to bring him to his knees. I for one was prepared to see him die wrongfully convicted on the scaffold. There comes a point when one simply doesn't care how much punishment is dealt out. Hutchinson, with his interest in and knowledge of boxing, should have known that we are too tired and lacerated at the end to worry about his reunion with Nona.

He is too far gone to be patched up. Like Lear, he has been stretched upon the rack too long. He might as well die. And this is the book over which the world raved, and is still raving. What is the reason? Is it that the modern reading public, steeped in sentimentalism, demands that it shall wallow vicariously in torment, or that it recognises with delight the eternal trait of the soulless, practical, uncompromising wives of to-day in Mabel? All these have, I think, combined to sell the book, but the outstanding reason for its success lies in the author's fundamental goodness. *If Winter Comes* was a shattering counterblast to the monstrous regiment of " highbrow " novels with which the market has of late been flooded. Nearly all modern novelists are clever; the British reading public (mainly composed of women) suspect cleverness; they find themselves bored with books that depict them as material-minded, without standards of conduct. *If Winter Comes* was a refuge—a chance to get back to " Mummy's knees," family prayers, simple faith, untarnished 'scutcheons, high ideals, asceticism.

The Puritan strain in the race, which is after all latent even in the " sensationalists " of to-day, is roused. *If Winter Comes* is the first sign of our palinode against the licentiousness of this latter-day Restoration period. Those who prophesy an early national religious revival may well take heart from the popularity of this book.

Readers are beginning to liken themselves to Christian wandering through the wilderness of this world with a heavy burden borne cheerfully on back: they see themselves, one and all, in Mark Sabre.

That is why *This Freedom* fell comparatively flat. Men and women who have been screwed up to high tension in their emotions find it something of an anticlimax to read about the tragedy of the married business woman. They scent an inherent falsity in the argument that no mother can afford to run a home and a business. The lie direct is given to that in nearly every working-class family.

Rosalie suffers for her passion for Lombard Street by seeing her elder son convicted of fraud, her only daughter die under an illegal operation, and her younger son done to death by his own hand.

Yet there is much that is good in *This Freedom.*

Rosalie's earliest years in the country rectory, where her father dominated everything (wonderful father, showing his children how to eat a herring, how to sharpen a pencil), are excellently described, though Hutchinson as usual cannot resist the chance of making one of Rosalie's sisters commit suicide. Rosalie's school days are equally vivid, in spite of the inevitable drunken schoolmistress, Keggo. Rosalie's life in the boarding-house (always two husbands with wives and three men without wives) is also delightfully done, until we come to the absurd incident of Miss Salmon and her " You could get dozens and dozens of men to love you, but you have taken mine, and I never, never can get another." Then comes the conflict.

" They don't issue return tickets to women. For women there is only departure—there is no return."

It is chivalrous of Hutchinson to enter the lists on behalf of women, but he happens to be fighting for a false cause. It is not true that all men are free, and all women everywhere bound in chains. Triumphs have been won ere now in the theatre, in the world of painting, literature and business by women who were also model mothers.

It isn't every woman who has Rosalie's ill-luck to marry a man so bloodless that his fiercest oath is " Mice and mumps." The lack of responsiveness in her children is due to something in their nature and in hers, and has nothing to do with her penchant for finance. The fact that Miss Prescott brought them up as rationalists is simply an accident. Yet Rosalie (woman

only in her unreasonableness) dares to say that no
father ever sacrificed himself for his children; only
mothers do that. And Hutchinson believes this
staggering misstatement. "It's why women are so
much more bitter than men." But they aren't;
mothers certainly aren't.

The children drift further and further away from
home; not because, as Hutchinson thinks, Rosalie is
too tied up with her business to look after them, but
because both their parents are amazingly dull and out
of touch with them.

We are made to suffer so with Rosalie and her
anæmic husband (he, a success at the Bar? Never!)
that in the end of all we have to be given the sop of
Doda's illegitimate child on Rosalie's knees. "Lessons,
lessons! on mother's knees! on mother's knees!"

She is given her second chance, like the characters
in *Dear Brutus*, and we can guess that the influence of
Bagehot and the romance of commerce will now become
as an evil nightmare, never to be thought of without a
shudder.

But the lover of Hutchinson will close the book with
a sigh. "Go back, go back," he will cry. "Give us
more of *Once Aboard the Lugger——*. Leave it to the
herd to write the problem novels. Get you back to the
simple delights, the primitive beliefs; avoid realism,
and avoid these gross extravagances of style, these
vain repetitions, these over-stressed torturings of the
mind. Like your own Japhra, raise your eyes to the
hills, from which emanated *Robinson Crusoe*, *The
Pilgrim's Progress* and the Bible; keep your mind
intent on these things and we will listen to you till
the crack of doom. . . ." But Hutchinson is now a
successful man, and the way of the successful is hard.
We look with trepidation on his future.

X

VICENTE BLASCO IBAÑEZ

IT is a fatal thing for any author to invite comparison with the Bible. There is a passage in the sixth chapter of the Revelation of St John the Divine that runs: "And I saw, and behold a white horse: and he that sat on him had a bow: and a crown was given unto him: and he went forth conquering, and to conquer. . . . And there went out another horse that was red: and power was given to him that sat thereon to take peace from the earth, and that they should kill one another: and there was given unto him a great sword. . . . And I beheld, and lo a black horse; and he that sat on him had a pair of balances in his hand. . . . And I looked, and behold a pale horse: and his name that sat on him was Death, and Hell followed with him. And power was given unto them over the fourth part of the earth, to kill with sword, and with hunger, and with death, and with the beasts of the earth."

I have recently seen *The Four Horsemen of the Apocalypse* on the films, where an egregious ass declaimed a prologue which contained the words: "The third is Famine, and he rideth upon a horse that is black, for he bringeth agony unto little children." I had not before this understood quite how hideous the words "agony" and "children" can be made to sound when mouthed by an inferior reciter got up to look like Augustus John and to speak like an illiterate revivalist paid thirty shillings a week to rouse men's cheapest emotions. I am uncertain whether Ibañez is responsible for the travestied words: I should say that he was capable of it if the film story approximates to the original novel.

It sounds absurd to criticise a novelist after seeing his work on the pictures without having read his book, but I take it that I am but setting a fashion which will come more and more into vogue as the cinema gets more popular. Everyone knows *The Four Horsemen of the Apocalypse* : it is at least as well known as *If Winter Comes* : but I doubt whether one per cent. of those who have seen it filmed have read the book. For my part I dare not face it. Ibañez represents a new order of writer. The law of supply and demand is queer. A new race of men and women have sprung into existence to meet the demand for the " cinema face." All men now demand that women, to be attractive, should be thin — all women are in consequence thin. The cinema demands perfectly regular features and suave movements in one sort of " hero "—and we get Rodolph Valentino and Ivor Novello, both extremely attractive-looking men ; in another sort it requires a man who can dive about two hundred feet, mount horses and cars at top speed, be possessed of prodigious strength and cat-like litheness—and we get Douglas Fairbanks, the reincarnation of Robin Hood.

So Ibañez is called into being by the demand for a crude story brimful of action, which lends itself to dramatisation on the cinema. *The Four Horsemen*, judged by any standard, is a completely ridiculous story, but it gives film audiences a chance to gloat over prairies, untimely deaths, baths of solid gold, low life in the tango land of Buenos Aires, gay life at tango teas in Paris, artists' studies, seductions both of rich men's wives and poor men's daughters, the sacking by the Germans of French castles, the burning of villages, and ever, like the tom-tom in Eugene O'Neill's play, there is the added treat of guns and bombs.

They have all the joy of the din of battle without having to endure its concomitant anguish. They are even permitted to watch blood trickling out of the mouths of dying soldiers, and orphans tugging at the cold breasts of murdered mothers.

As for the story, who cares ? There isn't time in a passing kaleidoscope to do more than shudder and gloat at the " realism," to admire Rodolph Valentino, and fall in love with the tear-compelling Alice Terry. What does surprise us is that Ibañez should use so many words. *The Four Horsemen* ought not to occupy a greater space than they occupy in the Bible — Ibañez is much too wordy. To those who like bulk, his later novel, *The Enemies of Women*, a variant on *Love's Labour's Lost*, with its five hundred and forty-seven closely printed pages, will appeal. For my part I look forward to seeing these " graphic " pictures of lustful Paris, lecherous Monte Carlo, Nihilist Russia interpreted for me by Valentino. I find it tiring to read many pages of this kind. I must in justice to Ibañez give you a sample.

It is a duchess who speaks ; her audience is a prince : we move in the best circles with Ibañez.

" ' I know what is the matter with you. . . . What you need, after several months of living alone like a maniac, is a woman. . . .'

" The Prince smiled bitterly at the suggested remedy. He had often thought of it. The censor that he kept within had repeated the same advice : ' Find a female and it will all pass away immediately. . . .'

" He had frequented the Casino with the resolute air of a slaughter-house man about to choose his prey from the flock. He would glance over the troop of girls in the gambling-rooms; only once, with the desperate energy of a patient gulping down a disgusting medicine, he had followed one of these beautiful animals, and shortly afterwards he felt disgusted with his baseness and ashamed of his backsliding."

On the next page the Prince " had thrown both his arms around her [the Duchess's] shoulders, mastering her, drawing her breast forward, pressing it against his own. . . . Finally the moan of protest ceased. Both heads remained motionless. . . . She spoke in a tone of surrender . . . she forgot everything around her.

Her eyes were still open, but the vision of the sea, the golden sunset in the sky, and even the pine boughs forming a canopy above their heads, had disappeared from her gaze."

Can't you see that already on the pictures ? What a wonderful " close-up," or whatever they call it. How Mr Rex Ingram and Mr D. W. Griffith must revere the genius of men who can write like this for over five hundred pages. And then the ending : " The aim of life is to live. Life is an endless springtime, and covers everything it touches with the eager moss of pleasure, with the swiftly creeping ivy of dreams. . . . The earth and sky know nothing of our sorrows. And neither does life."

I have had some harsh things said of my own novels, but at least I have avoided that kind of ending. On the films, such a paragraph is taken to be the fitting climax to every long reel. At all costs let us be moralists. The audience must be sent away in thoughtful mood, so that the life of the streets outside may strike them as crude, inartistic and inferior.

Ibañez' latest novel, *The Mayflower*, shows his peculiar gifts to their best advantage. It is a wild dramatic story of Valencian fisher-folk, a novel with scarcely any conversation, filled with thrilling, picturesque and passionate scenes, perfectly adapted for the film.

Its very brevity is its greatest charm. It is extremely easy to read, if unnecessarily gruesome. Here is a passage which would give the cinema man some fun to reproduce :

" Tio Pascualo was hardly recognisable. His body was swollen, green, the belly inflated to the point of bursting. The decaying flesh was gnawed away in places by hungry little fishes, some of which, loath to let go their prey, were still clinging to it by their teeth, wriggling their tails and giving an appearance of disgusting life to the horrible mass."

Pascualo, the bold sailor, left his widow, Tona, in the

direst penury—with nothing in the world except the wreck of his boat. To make a living she sawed a hole in one side of it and made a door and a small counter : it became a paying gin-store, and kept her and her two sons alive. The elder of these, Pascuale, grows into a stout, full-bellied, moon-faced man, the image of his father. "He looked like a seminary student specialising on the Refectory," and he earned the title of "The Rector "; eight years his junior was Tonet, "a child of feline shrewdness, who treated everybody with imperious petulance, as unsteady but brilliant as 'The Rector' was stable and plodding."

Tonet was a "lost soul," a "waster," but he could swim like a fish, and had no fear or respect for anyone.

The mother met a young policeman, Martinez, when she was thirty-six and he was twenty-four. Into her passion for him she put all the vehemence of a woman whose youth is sloping toward sunset. Martinez let himself be caressed, until about two months before the infatuated woman was due to bear his child, and then he disappeared. The child turned out to be an untamable wild cat of a girl, Roseta, who grew up to hate Tonet, whose attention was then occupied by the shameless Dolores, in whose home he spent most of his days.

Tonet (what a part for Rodolph Valentino) was blindly adored by another girl, Rosario, who, after trying for him for long enough, managed to secure him as husband, when Dolores had taken advantage of one of his absences to marry his elder brother, the Rector.

Tonet's life in the navy had made him look like an aristocrat to the girls of the Cabañæ, with his palish-dark face, his carefully curled moustache, his hands clean and well manicured, his hair sleek (I cannot get Valentino out of my mind—nor can Ibañez). He returned proud in the possession of a wife who believed in him as she believed in God—but the charms of such wives quickly fade to such men as Tonet. He began to spend all his spare time with his first love, his brother's wife, Dolores. " Four years after her marriage Dolores was at last able to announce the coming of an heir to the Rector's fortune ; and the Rector, with a silly smile on his moon face, advertised the auspicious event on every hand — and all his acquaintances were delighted, though they smiled with a sly wink he did not notice. No one really knew to be sure. But funny, wasn't it ! That rather deliberate decision of Dolores corresponded strangely with the time Tonet had become a less frequent visitor to the café, and had begun to spend more of his time in his brother's house."

That ought to go very well on the films.

The Rector makes a pile of money out of one big smuggling expedition which nearly ends disastrously. If they can stage that wild cutter-evading, tobacco-running business as well as Ibañez describes it *The Mayflower* will be one of the world's super-hyper-par-excellence-beat-the-band films. But there is a tit-bit before we get to that. Dolores and Rosario, Tonet's mistress and wife, now have a glorious " scrap " in the streets of Valencia. It is at this point that we recall most vividly the fact that they are fishwives.

In language they out-Masefield Masefield. Dolores opened the battle in characteristic style.

" She turned squarely around, and bending slightly registered a resonant slap on the pair of spacious hips that trembled under her calico skirt with all the elasticity of her firm flesh.

"'Look, Rosario ! Don't talk to me ! Talk to this ! "

The witticism was wholly successful. As she looked round to see the effect her blow had had, a handful of sardines struck her full in the face.

The fun then grows quickly.

" Rosario's fingers had closed over one of those pearl ear-rings that had been the admiration of the Fish-market. She had torn it out. The pretty girl began to sob, pressing her torn ear under both her hands, while blood streamed through her fingers."

I am longing for the obvious film to be released.

Here is a chance for realism to do its worst. We have hardly time to recover from the thrill of seeing two pretty girls tear one another's hair out, and ears off, than we are off on the *Garbosa,* "Yo, ho ho, and a bottle of rum," from Valencia for Algiers. Excellent indeed is the picture of the captain and crew eating their dinner "under the shade of the sail, scooping with their spoons in the same spot, drinking deep draughts from the wine jug to cool their parched throats, their shirts open in front, sweating in streams, panting from the lifeless sultry calm. . . . After their meal the men walked about on deck lazily and with heavy eyes, drunk with sunlight rather than with wine." The picture of Algiers too is quite wonderful. "The women! Little Moor girls, their cheeks all painted up, their finger nails stained blue, and queer tattooing on their breasts and backs": Tonet's description that is—of course.

Out come the bales of contraband, piled high on the old boat "till barely a foot of smokestack was visible over the top." She crawled away like a mud turtle or a torpedo boat, so low was she sitting in the water. There is a gorgeous chase by the cutters, escape and anchorage in an island pool, a rising wind—and the "pot-bellied numskull" Rector's determination to get on. "Anyhow in the other world every day is Sunday. . . . Die young, and the lobsters eat you: die old, and it's the worms." After a wonderful battle before the gale, the Rector cuts a reef out of the sail, "the *Garbosa* spurted like a race-horse, showing her keel," and he ran straight on shore, to be broken to bits as soon as ever the bales had been got free. Out of the twelve thousand *reales* that he made over that the Rector built himself a great new ship, which Roseta christened *Flor de Mayo—The Mayflower.*

That was a clever trick on Ibañez' part. When the mighty super-film is ready the public will flock to see their Pilgrim Fathers setting out from Plymouth.

They won't be disappointed, but they will be cozened none the less.

Roseta, of whom we have heard but little, has grown up into a peerless beauty of tangled golden hair, dreamy sea-green eyes, exquisite white skin, regarding her half-brothers, the scamp, Tonet, and the pudding-head Rector, with superb contempt.

Cinematographic effects come out well in the christening, but better still in the next chapter, where Roseta, for sheer devilry, upsets the apple-cart by rousing the Rector's suspicions. She acts Iago to his Othello with complete success, and eggs him on to murder Tonet. There is a jolly interlude in the ceremony of wishing the fishing-fleet godspeed. This is done by insulting the men who are going away.

"As the boats cast off, atrocious witticisms flew back and forth between deck and shore—all in good humour, of course . . . and it was a test of brains to . . . say just the right words to those husbands whose eyes would be snugly plugged with wool, and come home in blessed ignorance of all their wives had been up to meanwhile." A jolly ceremony! This sort of thing: "I know where the curate is going to stay to-night. Johnnie will take good care of her, don't worry, my lad! Moo-oo! Moo-oo!"

So when the Rector goes they shout at him: "Tonet is with Dolores! Tonet is with Dolores! Cuckold! He's leaving a happy home to-night! But Tonet will be there! No vacation for Dolores!"

Another picture when the fishing fleet returns of the market and the golden harvest for the Rector.

Another picture when Rosario, Tonet's deserted wife, adds the finishing touch to the job so neatly begun by Roseta. She shows the Rector the bruises Tonet gives her for venturing to remonstrate with him over Dolores. She tells him if he wants proof to look closely at his son. "He looks like Tonet—eyes, shape, build and complexion." Somewhat naturally the poor cuckold is at last seized with "a mad instinct to kill, to destroy." He rushes home, waits for Tonet to emerge, misses him, goes off to get drunk (here the film speeds up), and puts to sea for the last time.

The Mayflower is struck by a tornado (a wonderful super-film effect here): "she veered like a shot, sank into a great yawning chasm between two smooth but almost perpendicular walls, and she had her stern to windward just as the next huge breaker came "—there is a lot of that. There is a splendid picture of wild, wailing women on the shore—the rain biting at their faces, the gale washing their skirts about, and whistling in their ears while some of the fleet goes down before their eyes.

"One by one the boats rounded the breakwater, cheered by the crowd, and greeted by sobs and cries of joy. . . . The harbour entrance had turned to a veritable hell of wind and wave and whirlpool. Three boats were still in sight and for an hour . . . they backed and veered in the hurricane, struggling against the dread currents that kept sweeping them down the coast. At last they too got in . . . then a boat was (seen) driving shoreward in mad career though a mere shred of canvas was visible at the foot of the bare pole. . . . That straggler would be the blood-offering to the sea. . . . An hour passed. A sight to turn your hair white!" Barrels crush sailors to pulp against the mast, eddies of water sweep "the mangled headless torso against the hands and faces of other men, and washed blood and bits of flesh around over the planking " . . . and in the end even the Rector gave a great cry of terror. "*The Mayflower* was at the bottom of a great gully in the sea. From behind a huge roller of black shining water was curling : and a back wave just as high was rushing the other way. . . . With a horrible crunching . . . *The Mayflower* went down into a great boiling cauldron, and when she came to the surface again her deck was as level and clean as a scow's."

A fitting film climax is provided by the picture of the Rector insisting on Tonet giving his life-belt to the son whose paternity was now no longer in doubt.

The last scene of all shows us Dolores kneeling over the body of her drowned son, Rosario, the deserted childless wife standing by, forgiving all.

What a film !

All aspirants for fame on the cinema must read this best of all models of how it should be done.

XI

SINCLAIR LEWIS

I FOUND *Main Street* dull. When I first read Jane Austen I found Jane Austen dull. I did not find *Babbitt* dull, because I had learnt to share the fury that seizes on any sane man when he has to put up with months and years of this sort of conversation:

"Just been making a trip through the South. Business conditions not very good down there."

"Is that a fact ? Not very good, eh ? "

"No; didn't strike me they were up to normal."

"Not up to normal, eh ? "

"No; I wouldn't hardly say they were."

"Yump, not hardly up to snuff."

It is good that there should be an observant, infuriated child wandering about, taking notes and photographs. We see Babbitt, the prosperous real-estate agent in Zenith; the city that manufactures more condensed milk and evaporated cream, more paper boxes and more lighting-fixtures than any other city in the United States; the city that stands second in the manufacture of package-butter, sixth in the realm of motors and automobiles, and third in cheese, leather findings, tar roofing, breakfast food and overalls; the city where there is one motor car for every five and seven-eighth persons. In this stupendous city Georgie Babbitt, aged forty-six, rebels, domestically, spiritually, sensually, civically—every way. He is married, has three children; looks unromantic, but has dreams of a fairy child who waits to rescue him from his wife and friends. Lewis is at pains to show us the Babbitt *ménage* from every conceivable point of view. It lacks only one thing to make it ideal : it isn't a home.

And yet it is very like a great number of homes. Father Babbitt cursing because his family are always cursing and scrapping like a bunch of hyenas; father Babbitt saying: " Seen the morning paper yet ? " to his wife, who in twenty-three years of married life had seen the paper before her husband sixty-seven times; father Babbitt making strenuous resolves to stop smoking, laying out plans, expounding the virtues of it, doing everything—except stop smoking. This is home in reality.

Yes; Sinclair Lewis has gone a long way to reincarnate Everyman in Babbitt—Everyman in business. Babbitt trains himself to speak at Boosters' Club Luncheons. He had vision: in other words, he could guess which way the town would grow and therefore make money on real-estate broking. He was virtuous: he advocated, but naturally did not practise, prohibition; he praised the laws against driving too fast, even if he never obeyed them; he lied, but he regarded men who profited by lying as worthy of being shot; he made about eight thousand dollars a year. He was fond of his youngest daughter and Paul Riesling, his oldest friend.

" How's the old horse thief ? "

" All right, I guess. How're you, you poor shrimp ? "

" I'm first-rate, you second-hand hunk o' cheese."

Thus do they greet one another, with a love far passing the love of women, after three days' absence. Paul is no more—rather less—happy with his wife than Babbitt is with his.

" After twenty-four years of that kind of thing " (" Paul, will you kindly call the manager ? "), " you don't expect me to fall down and foam at the mouth when you hint that this sweet, clean, respectable, moral life isn't all it's cracked up to be, do you ? . . . You're so earnest about morality, old Georgie, that I hate to think how essentially immoral you must be underneath. . . . About ten times as many people find their lives dull, and unnecessarily dull, as ever admit it, and I do believe that if we busted out and admitted it sometimes, instead of being nice and patient and loyal for sixty years and then nice and patient and dead for the rest of eternity, we might make life more fun."

Not until we get a particularly dull conversation among these " city folks with punch and pep " about the dullness of small-town, Main Street burgs, do we realise how vitriolic is Sinclair Lewis's pen. These athletic clubs, country clubs, dinner-parties, Rotarian club speeches; the letting of poor friends slide, the being let slide by friends who regard you as poor; the sermons of Monday, the pugnacious revivalist, and of Dr Drew, the Presbyterian poet; the most efficient advertising side of the Sunday school journals; the lovely midge in the sun, Eunice Littlefield, the movie-mad lover of the motor-mad son of Babbitt—who whenever she came to the house discussed with pleasant intimacy the fact that she had been forbidden to come to the house—Graff, fired from the office, having " words " with Babbitt:

" Babbitt, old dear, you're crooked in the first place and a damn skinflint in the second. . . . I've been going crooked, but now I'm going straight, and the first step will be to get a job in some office where the boss doesn't talk about ideals. . . ."

Yes, we get full measure all right. I suppose that is Lewis's chief merit. He is quite merciless: his object is to see and to record. There is a ghastly scene in which Babbitt rounds on Paul's wife: " You're a fool: a scolding old woman. . . . Who the hell are you that a person like Paul should have to ask your permission to go with me ? You act like you were a combination of Queen Victoria and Cleopatra." But we are made to realise how much everybody concerned enjoys the row. To Zilla, Paul's wife, torturing husbands to see how sore she can make them is a game. She gets shot for that—and nearly dies. Paul has to go to a penitentiary for three years for shooting her. Babbitt wandered home after visiting him " and found his wife radiant with the horrified interest we have

in the tragedies of our friends." "Of course," she
exulted, "Paul isn't altogether to blame, but this is
what comes of his chasing after other women instead
of bearing his cross in a Christian way."

Deprived of his greatest friend, Babbitt gets more
and more restless. He goes up to his daughter's room
to see if she has any books he might care for. He finds
Conrad, Cabell, Vachel Lindsay, H. L. Mencken.
" He liked none of these books. In them he felt a
spirit of rebellion against niceness and solid-citizenship.
. . . He noted a book, *The Three Black Pennys*, by
Hergesheimer." Expecting to find an adventure story
about counterfeiting he began to read it—not for
long. "There it was again : discontent with the good
common ways."

He began himself to think. "It was coming to him
that perhaps all life as he knew it and vigorously
practised it was futile : that heaven as portrayed by
the Rev. Dr John Jennison Drew was neither probable
nor very interesting : that he hadn't much pleasure out
of making money : that it was of doubtful worth to
rear children merely that they might rear children who
would rear children. What was it all about ? What
did he want ? "

It wasn't wealth, position, travel, servants only—
they mattered, but only incidentally. He wanted his
friend Paul, who was now spiritually dead to him in
prison : he wanted the fairy girl of his dreams—in
the flesh. He thought of his stenographer. He
tried — " nothing doing." He thought of Lovetta.
He tried—nothing doing. He found a manicurist, who
quickly made him realise that he was an old bore
who had to be endured as the penalty attached to
eating a large dinner. He found a Mrs Tanis Judique,
who asked him to find a flat for her, and having found
it, asked him to come and see her in it ; which he
did—and stayed. He became completely faithful to
Tanis. His wife revolted him. He was " borne on a
current of desire and very bad whisky and all the
complications of new acquaintances," ever meaning to

stop drifting, never able to. His new friends were certainly no less intolerable than the old ones. Sinclair Lewis is at pains to prove that the dullness of virtue is only less dull than the dullness of vice. Babbitt's wife puts up a fight for the first time : " Don't you suppose I ever get tired of fussing ? I get so bored with ordering three meals a day, three hundred and sixty-five days a year, and ruining my eyes over that horrid sewing-machine, and looking after your clothes and Rosie's and Ted's and Tinka's and everybody's, and the laundry and darning socks, and going down to the Piggly Wiggly to market . . . and everything. . . ." Mrs Babbitt's revolution is listening to lectures on " Cultivating the Sun Spirit." Babbitt gets ruder to his wife, throws off Tanis, tells his wife that it is her fault that he ever had to go out in search of other women. He gets ruder to the more stable citizens of Zenith. He tries to be independent, but he hears whisperings—whisperings about his backing the revolutionary element in the town, whisperings which only ceased when his wife had to be operated on for appendicitis. Then all the staunch conservatives weighed in with books and fruit, and the Tanis section left him severely alone. Babbitt ceased to be a domestic revolutionist and became a member of the Good Citizens' League. He sank back in his cage, caught : he went on playing for safety. We leave Babbitt exactly where we found him, sympathising with his son because he has had the good sense to marry Eunice without asking anybody's leave. " I've never done a single thing I've wanted to in my whole life ! I don't know I've accomplished anything except just get along. I figure out I've made about a quarter of an inch out of a possible hundred rods. . . . I do get a kind of sneaking pleasure out of the fact that you knew what you wanted and did it. Well, those folks in there (the rest of the family) will try to bully you, and tame you down. Tell 'em to go to the devil ! Don't be scared of the family. No, nor all of Zenith. Nor of yourself, the way I've been."

Yes, that is Babbitt: the man who was scared of himself; Babbitt, as Walpole says, " own brother to our Mr Polly, Uncle Ponderovo, Denry of the Five Towns, the Forsyte family and even Mr George Moore." This nimble merchant, whose mission in life it is to sell houses for more than people can afford to pay, is given to us in such perfect detail that we accompany him in feeling as well as in the body through all his processes of damning wet towels in the bathroom, using very modern loose-leaf pocket-notebooks to enter memoranda which were always forgotten; looking on his car as the poetry and tragedy of his life, his office as his pirate ship; getting cranky and tired; human, always human—in his hypocrisy and compromise most of all.

Sinclair Lewis, like Sherwood Anderson, expresses the new American revolt against materialism. He is, however, a long way behind Anderson in that he expends all his energy in purely destructive criticism. On the other hand his vitriol takes effect. His books are bound to shake even the richest " thick-skin."

XII

WILLIAM McFEE

WITH his third book, *Command*, Mr McFee ought to establish his reputation permanently. In *Casuals of the Sea* and *Captain Macedoine's Daughter* he got himself talked about as another Conrad, presumably because he wrote of the sea and the East and knew the Merchant Service from within. But we might as well credit the magazine writer Frankau with being a second Surtees because he takes hunting for his theme. Mr McFee can be compared with Conrad without loss of dignity to himself or Conrad, but the comparison is not helpful. The very first page of *Command*, with its alert, humorous description of the modern girl, is something quite outside Conrad.

" These dark-haired, grey-eyed, stylish, highly strung, athletic, talented girls . . . go everywhere by themselves, and to men whom they dislike they are sheathed in shining armour. They can dance, swim, motor, golf, entertain, earn their own living, talk music, art, books and china, wash a dog and doctor him. And they can do all this, mark, without having any real experience of what we call life. They are good girls, nice girls, virtuous girls, and very marriageable girls, too, but they have a superficial hardness of texture on their character which closely resembles the mask of experience. They are like the baggage which used to be sold in certain obscure shops in London with the labels of foreign hotels already pasted on it."

This is poles removed from the Conrad way of writing. It was this type of girl to whom Reginald Spokesly, second officer, had got himself engaged. We are, luckily, spared the ordeal of having to meet Ada. There is a far more attractive girl waiting in the Near East.

104

Evanthia Solaris, with her brilliant amber eyes, is not easily forgettable. Certainly not by Spokesly. Excellent indeed is the drawing of the character of this Balkan adventuress, who at eighteen could make fine lace, cook, fight and speak six languages without being able to write or read at all. She ran away to find the world at war at Salonika, and to imbibe some queer notions about European politics. This "velvet-soft being of sex and sinuous delicacy, of no country and no creed, a thing of indestructible loveliness and problematic utility," was mainly occupied when Spokesly finds her in trying to reach Smyrna and a lover with whom she had become infatuated. She simply used Spokesly, who was easy to use, for her own ends. She realised how necessary it was to have some man to help her achieve her object. "Women, in her experience, were like expensive automobiles. They were always owned by somebody, who drove them about and sometimes ill-treated them, and even rode them to destruction, and who lost them if they were not carefully guarded . . . nobody ever thought less of them because they were costly to run."

Extremely simple in her personality, she trusted that God would take care of her and "it was rather disconcerting to reflect that God did. Evanthia all her life never thought of anybody but herself, and all things worked together to bring her happiness and to cast her lines in pleasant places. . . . She was afflicted with none of the complex psychology which makes the Western woman's life a farrago of intricate inhibitions. Love was an evanescent glamour which came and passed like a cigarette, a strain of music, a wave of furious anger. Evanthia remembered the hours . . . forgetting the persons." For Fridthiof alone her feeling was different. This clever, vital, careless, amusingly irreligious, unfaithful lover of hers had her completely in thrall, and she has no compunction whatever in leading Spokesly on to believe that she will marry him so long as she can get him to smuggle her away to Smyrna.

When eventually Spokesly comes to claim her he is staggered at the trust she has in him. All the time she plays up to him when he stows her away on board, even to the extent of letting him believe that she was his for the asking. Spokesly is very credulous even for a man who is such a fool as to put his trust in systems of memory training. He finds that he is "running a cargo" in war-time for the enemy when he thought that he was employed on a job completely above-board. True, his Levantine employer, Dainopoulos, was crafty enough to outwit not only the unsuspecting Spokesly but the French and English officers, who were less gullible. Dainopoulos was one of those who won the war for themselves : he needed no little books of the London School of Mnemonics to teach him how to be a success. He knew that the trick lay in getting other men, of the Spokesly breed, to work for him. Spokesly nearly dies in his service. First he is torpedoed on the *Tanganyika*, and excellent indeed is Mr McFee's description of that accident of war; then he is rammed on the *Kalkis*, while he had Evanthia on board, his captain at the time—Ronnie of the downcast eye, interminable grouse and plum-coloured silk handkerchief—being one of the most successfully drawn characters in the book.

Evanthia amuses herself on the voyage in thinking of the amiable, faithless lover she means to rejoin, and laughs quietly at Spokesly's love-making, his promise of marriage when they get ashore, and so on.

Once she is touched to the point of burying her teeth in his wrist. But on their arrival at Smyrna the Aleman Giaour who had so infatuated her arrives, and she gives Spokesly his *congé*. There is something very attractive in the character of the Herr Leutnant and his philosophic nihilism and his wit. "A nation of mongrels who think of nothing but thoroughbred horses and dogs " is his description of the English to Evanthia. He is of those who look forward to an age when the yellow men from Asia and the blacks from

Africa will overrun Europe. "And in the end humanity will cease to exist."

Spokesly returns to find Ada married and his own pleasure in England gone. He takes a harbour-mastership in the West Indies. Evanthia meanwhile is deserted by her lover, and lives with Dainopoulos's invalid English wife in great style, murmuring, "Je deteste les hommes!" as she lies in a silken hammock in the great houseboat by the breakwater, listening to the sweet strains from the disc concealed in a cabinet shaped like a huge bronze shell.

Mr McFee has the novelist's main qualities: he can tell a rattling good story, and his characters are real. It was clever to make Spokesly no sensualist, but a man who experienced a difficulty in having any spiritual life apart from women. "He could do with a minimum of inspiration, but such as he needed had to come from them." It was an excellent idea to make such a man the Sir Galahad for Evanthia.

Mr McFee is to be congratulated on keeping the balance: he does not give to the Englishman all the virtues: his deep experience leads him to keep an open mind.

His main claim to fame is, however, his determination to write of accidents and incidents. More and more is it evident that we are in for a reaction in fiction. The day of the slipshod, vacillating, introspective herd is over. We are returning very quickly to the man of action and heroic heroes.

XIII

KATHERINE MANSFIELD

BY the death of Katherine Mansfield England loses one of the most sensitive of all her modern writers. She was a pioneer in the art of telling a short story about nothing and creating an unforgettable atmosphere. Many people to-day, C. E. Montague leading them, are demanding a return to the short story of plot and action. With this Miss Mansfield had no part nor lot. She stuck to her own interpretation of life. Her last volume, *The Garden Party*, was typical. She had her husband's trick of " painting-in."

This sort of thing: " Behind them an old sheep-dog, his soaking paws covered with sand, ran along with his nose to the ground, but carelessly, as if thinking of something else. And then in the rocky gateway the shepherd himself appeared. He was a lean, upright old man, in a frieze coat that was covered with a web of tiny drops, velvet trousers tied under the knee, and a wideawake with a folded blue handkerchief round the brim. One hand was crammed into his belt, the other grasped a beautifully smooth yellow stick. And as he walked, taking his time, he kept up a very soft, light whistling, an airy, far-away fluting that sounded mournful and tender." Now this shepherd has nothing to do with the plot. He occurs in a short story where, you would think, there was not much room for digression. Most of us dò not describe the principal characters in our novels with such meticulous care as this. We are too busy hacking away at what to us are the essentials to bother about the externals.

Middleton Murry and Katherine Mansfield by very

careful microscopic analysis of the externals drive by implication far deeper into the essentials than we ever get. They seem to paint for the sake of painting, for the beauty of the scene, and the combined effect suddenly shakes you. You have seen something far behind.

One feels as if Miss Mansfield were being wheeled round a confined space. Every trifle assumes a portentous significance. When Beryl pushed the sugar over to Stanley instead of helping him, we are made to feel that we are on the crater of an active volcano. Soon Stanley goes. "Oh, the relief, the difference it made to have the man out of the house." Healthy people thrive on friction. Not so the Beryls of Miss Mansfield's quiet, ordered brain. The only thing of moment that happens during that lazy day at the bay is late at night when Mrs Kember's husband cajoles Beryl to come out with him as far as the fuchsia bush. No sooner had she got there than she wrenched herself free. "Then why in God's name did you come?" asks the man. The story closes on that note.

There are still people who cavil at stories which do not contain two murders, a divorce, three incredible long arms of coincidence, and a journey from China to Peru. They should take a strong dose of Tchehov. They like every picture to tell a story. Miss Mansfield prefers every story to be a picture. The ordinary man's brain is so addled that he does not willingly pay homage to something new even when it is good. It takes him half a lifetime so see Rubens and Rembrandt. It isn't likely that he will appreciate Manet, Monet, Piccasso, or Gauguin.

"At the Bay" is as nearly perfect a description of a day by the sea as I have ever read. There is colour, there is quiet movement, there are real people. The curtain goes up at dawn and goes down in the dead of night. There is no climax, no fifth act: it is, like Tchehov, a slice of life. It implies everything: it says very little. It is, if you like, a Pharaoh's dream. Miss Mansfield does not insult us by acting as Joseph in the interpretation thereof. It takes even a little time to discover that Stanley's wife is not Beryl, but Linda. We ought to have known that from the fact that he did not say good-bye to her, as a punishment.

There is absolute reality in those children playing, in Lottie's difficulty with stiles and her hopeful, "I'm getting better . . . aren't I ? " No, no; she isn't consumptive—how you magazine-story readers do jump at things!—better at climbing things. The nearest to rebellion is Jonathan, "like an insect that has flown into a room of its own accord," in his city office wanting to get out—nearest that is, after Beryl, who wanted a lover so much that she invited that "cold little devil " from the disgusted Harry Kember.

Better than "At the Bay " is "The Garden Party."

Laura is like her creator—she stops everywhere to wonder at the beauty of things, the friendliness of the workmen putting up the marquee, the "darling little spots " of sun on the inkpot, the lovely lilies. Suddenly we are surprised, horrified. Something has happened. A man has been killed outside the front gate.

"*Not* in the garden ? " interrupted Laura's mother. "Oh, what a fright you gave me ! " she said with relief when she heard the truth. There is all Miss Mansfield in those two sentences, contempt for the whole craziness of life. After the party is over Laura is sent down to the man's cottage with a basket—crumbs of comfort. She sees happiness and beauty in the dead man's face. The inexplicable marvel of life hits her straight in the face. You would scarcely select a meagre plot like this for a story meant to live, would you ? And yet—it is impossible to get this vision of Laura out of one's head.

There are readers who prefer "The Daughters of the Late Colonel," worrying whether to give his top-hat to the porter, worrying about the nurse who "was simply fearful about butter ! "—Nurse Andrews and

her "Lady Tukes" who "had such a dainty little con-
trayvance for the buttah . . . quite a gayme"; Nurse
Andrews, with her laugh "like a spoon tinkling against
a medicine-glass" (how apt and excellent a simile), and
"I hope it's not very bittah marmalayde"; worrying
about the funeral arrangements, "A good one that
will last," as if they were buying a nightgown; worrying whether Cyril ought to have the Colonel's watch—
Cyril who, on his last visit, had to tell his deaf grandfather how fond of meringues his own father was.
Poor, dear, laughable, inconsequent, pathetic old
spinsters! Little mercy do you get from your surgical
creator. Miss Mansfield is not afraid of her scalpel.
She loves the operating theatre. She laughs im-
moderately at the curious viscera she disembowels.
It is all rather horrid, this ruthless dissection, but oh,
how it is clever! What art!

Then there is Mr Dove, escaping from the flower-
snipping dragon of a mother to propose to Anne, taken
to see her pigeons—"the male, bowing and bowing,
and away she runs . . . and that's their whole life,"
laughing away his proposal "it's your check t-tie . . .
we'd be like Mr and Mrs Dove," miserable at his misery.
"Don't pity me, little Anne." The doves "coo" as
he goes. He looks back. "Come back, Mr Dove,"
said Anne. A masterpiece of understatement.

And "The Young Girl," in her blue dress, her blue
eyes, her gold curls, standing on the steps of the Casino,
petulant and bored, not allowed to accompany her
mother inside, taken off to tea by friends, sulking
and rude all the time, taking four cakes after refusing
any, aching to get away by herself, left where she was
found, her dark coat open, her soft young body in
the blue dress like a flower emerging from its dark
bud.

I know no picture of a spoilt darling so complete as
this—and all compressed into ten pages.

Then there is Ma Parker, in service when she was
sixteen, married to a baker, seven of her thirteen
buried, "If it wasn't the 'ospital it was the infirmary,

you might say," a long history of ulcers, consumption, spine trouble, "emigrimation," "going wrong" . . . and then little Lennie, her grandchild, "taking him to the cemetery, even, never gave him a colour ; shake up in the bus never improved his appetite." Even Lennie died, and Ma Parker tries to escape to cry. "There was nowhere." The whole history of generations of charwomen is summed up in her appalling cry : "What have I done ? What have I done ? "

"Marriage à la Mode" is less tragic. William returning to the exquisite freshness of his wife, Isabel, for weekends ; William, sentimental and hungry for her, tired of work, condemned to meet her only among a riotous mob of poets : Dennis with his jejune, heavy "A Lady in Love with a Pine-Apple," "A Lady with a Box of Sardines," "A Lady reading a Letter "; Bill Hunt with his infuriating : "Well, William, and how's London ? " Bill and Dennis, both with enormous appetites, rude, flamboyant, all over the place. "I hardly seem to have seen you," says Isabel, as she sees him off again. He writes to her : "My darling, precious Isabel . . ."—a love letter. She reads it aloud to her congregation : they were almost hysterical. She has eventually the grace to see her vileness. "God forbid, my darling, that I should be a drag on your happiness. . . ." She determines to write. They call to her to go out to bathe. She goes.

There is "Miss Brill" and her fur, sitting by the bandstand watching the lovers, the beautifully dressed boy and girl : "The hero and heroine, of course, just arrived from his father's yacht." Her heart warmed towards them. The girl giggled : "It's her fu-fur which is so funny. It's exactly like a fried whiting." Miss Brill goes home to cry : she even forgets to buy her Sunday treat—a slice of honey-cake at the baker's. Yes; the art is there all right, but Miss Mansfield must have been ill when she wrote "Miss Brill." It is not healthy to dwell on the Miss Brills so lovingly as she does. There is the same low devitalised

note in " The Singing Lesson." Miss Meadows, with
that letter tearing at her heart—" I feel more and more
strongly that our marriage would be a mistake "—
keeping on, keeping on, called away from the appalling
task to receive this telegram: " Pay no attention to
letter must have been mad bought hat-stand to-day.
—Pasil "; returning to tell her class to sing less dole-
fully: " It ought to sound warm, joyful, eager." Oh,
these spinster schoolmistresses and their passionate
aches! How we sigh for the full-blooded lusts of
Somerset Maugham's heroes.

There was the reunion of Janey and her elderly
husband after her long voyage, when she tells him of
the stranger who died " of heart " in her arms the
night before. " Spoilt their evening! Spoilt their
being alone together! They would never be alone
together again." Surely this is where Miss Mansfield
topples over on the farther side. This is the hectic
flush. She is seeing things awry. She is better when
she is merely describing. " Bank Holiday " is better
by far, more full of life, colour and action than any
of the myriad pictures of it. She returns to her pathos
in the picture of old M'Reave, the forgotten father
surrounded by his ideal family. " What had all this
to do with him—this house and Charlotte, the girls
and Harold . . . they were strangers to him. Life
had passed him by. Charlotte was not his wife. His
wife! . . ." His thoughts go back (all Miss Mansfield's
characters think back, never forward—a sure sign of
their lack of health) to a time when a little pale face
was lifted to his and a voice breathed—" Good-bye,
my treasure." She was his wife, that little pale girl
—and all the rest of his life had been a dream.

Miss Mansfield had power all right; she dreamt
dreams, but they were hot-house dreams. She was a
tender, sensitive plant, exotic, meant for the hot-house.
To let her loose in England seemed cruel. We are so
much more fond of the windy heath plants; we prefer
the down orchis to the frail lily, the wild rose to the
garden one.

H

Her art was all her own. She has already had imitators, who only show by their failure how difficult was the medium in which she worked. This is an age rich in short stories, but if C. E. Montague leads the field with his romantic, roistering, intractable and fiery particles, Katherine Mansfield is leading another field which is equally beautiful, in spite of its being static.

XIV

SOMERSET MAUGHAM

FOR some twenty years Mr Somerset Maugham
has been writing novels and plays, hammering
hard on the doors of the critics' studies,
clamouring for a hearing. For a long time they overlooked him. A man of indomitable courage, he has
persevered and gone on from strength to strength until
at last, in *The Moon and Sixpence*, he " rang the bell "
(as the phrase goes) to such purpose that no intelligent
reader could any longer deny him his place among the
really brilliant leaders of modern fiction. There is an
astringency about all his work that is most refreshing.
He has stood his ground always, and refused to pander
to the public taste for the sugary sentimental. He
has remained true to his conception of his art, and he
has won out. After years of struggle as a dramatist
he is now accredited with financial success only second
to that of Barrie. It is salutary to our critical sense
to go back twenty years and see how good he was
long before he was recognised. Take, for instance,
The Merry-Go-Round. The idea of the barrister-
author philandering with the barmaid, marrying her to
save her honour, finding out that by so doing he was
making a hell for two instead of one, has been often
enough exploited, but no one has tackled the theme so
frankly as Maugham. At the end, when Jenny commits
suicide, Basil is at any rate honest : " I made a ghastly
mistake and suffered for it . . . and perhaps it wasn't
all my own fault. . . . For God's sake let us be free.
Let us do this and that because we want to, and because
we must, not because other people think we ought.
And d'you know the worst of the whole thing ? If I'd
acted like a blackguard and let Jenny go to the dogs,

115

I should have remained happy and contented and prosperous, and she, I daresay, wouldn't have died. It's because I tried to do my duty that all this misery came about."

Somerset Maugham is a good author because he never flinches in the face of reality: he is definitely anti-sentimental. "After all," he says to his best friend just after he had seduced Jenny, "if we were all as cool at night as we are in the morning——"

"Life would be a Sunday school," finished his friend.

His mother (herself wanton) denounces his decision to marry the girl in good set terms. "A gentleman doesn't marry a barmaid because he's seduced her—unless he has the soul of a counter-jumper. . . . You're one of those persons who are doomed to mediocrity because you haven't the spirit to go to the devil like a man."

Maugham is like Flaubert in his contemptuous view of humanity. Most of his women have the souls of trollops, most of his men are frankly sensual, loving after feeding, like animals, " as an accompaniment to the process of digestion."

His virtuous characters, like Bella Langton's father, are hard, his worldly characters hypocritical. Once in early days he had a curious lapse into the sentimental. "Even if the beliefs of men are childish and untrue," cries Miss Ley, by far the best character in *The Merry-Go-Round*, "isn't it better to keep them? Surely superstition is a small price to pay for that wonderful support at the last hour, when all else fades to insignificance."

When Reggie Bassett goes off the rocks Miss Ley coolly rounds on his dissolute mother. "A wise mother lets her son go his own way, and shuts her eyes to youthful peccadilloes: but you made all these peccadilloes into deadly sins. . . . Moralists talk a deal of nonsense about the frailty of mankind. When you come to close quarters with vice, it's not really so desperately wicked as all that. . . . All these things are part of human nature, when youth and hot blood are joined together."

Clear-sightedness in Maugham's characters leads them to cruelty. They have no compunction in cutting Gordian knots which may lead to disasters for the weaker party. He is as much a believer in the survival of the fittest as he is in the saving quality of beauty.

Take another of his little-known early works, *The Explorer*. He is quite relentless in hunting Lucy Allerton's lovable but shifty father to prison and death for his weakness. Maugham is almost alone among novelists in facing the utter ruthlessness of life. Just as he refuses to compromise in his art, so does he refuse to allow his characters the false security of a harbour. That is why he is so frequently accused of cynicism and brutality. " Every woman is a Potiphar's wife, though every man isn't a Joseph," is typical of the sort of epigram with which his pages are studded.

" A love for good food is the only thing that remains with man when he grows old," is put into the mouth of an indolent wit ; but we feel that Maugham himself believes it, just as in Alec Mackenzie, the explorer, he paints what he would wish himself to have been, reckless, desperate, the fascination of the unknown ever urging him on to explore the hidden recesses of the material world as well as those of the world of the mind.

In reply to Alec's denunciation of " the greatest imposture of Christian times—the sanctification of labour," he replies : " If I had ten lives I couldn't get through a tithe of what . . . so urgently needs doing."

Strength, simplicity, the greatness of life, beauty— these are the things that Mackenzie and Maugham both worship. It is these things that make them worship Boswell, Homer, Thucydides and Shakespeare, the heart of Africa and the South Seas. Maugham delights in placing his characters not only in dangers but in the most remote places of the earth. They are all, like himself, victims of a wanderlust.

His attitude to life is that of Walker, the fighter :

" I've not had a bad time," he said. " I've loved a

little, and I've worked and played. I've heard some decent music, I've looked at nice pictures, and I've read some thundering fine books. If I can only account for a few more of those damned scoundrels before I die, I shouldn't think I had much to complain of." Abroad he suffers from a nostalgia for the grey, soft mists of England ; at home he suffers from a nostalgia for the wild, riotous, prodigal virgin jungle, the hot sun beating on a blue lagoon. He has something of the bitter scorn of Swift and Samuel Butler for the world's quick changes from idolatry to persecution. " They lick my boots till I loathe them, and then they turn against me like a pack of curs." He might be Coriolanus speaking. Misunderstood, his pride prevents him from explanations. " Take it or leave it, by God, 'tis good," one imagines both the explorer and Maugham saying to a puzzled world. " The British public is sentimental," cries Mackenzie, " they will never understand that in warfare it is necessary sometimes to be inhuman." But these two novels are examples merely of Maugham in his salad days, serving his apprenticeship in a none too tractable medium. His greatness can be gauged from two books : *Of Human Bondage* and *The Moon and Sixpence*—both novels of his maturity.

Of Human Bondage is so good a book that it is impossible (for a long time after reading it) to fall down and worship the young Americans of the Sinclair Lewis type or the intellectual young Englishwoman of the Dorothy Richardson-Romer Wilson type. *Of Human Bondage* is good because it is sincere autobiography—one of the few absolutely sincere documents I have ever read. I would give it, if I could afford copies, to every imaginative boy on leaving school. Let me go through it in detail.

Right from the beginning there is Philip Carey's club-foot, the deformity which made life so hard for him, which warped his character, which made him ultrasensitive, but by reason of which in the end he " acquired that power of introspection which had given him so much delight. Without it he would never have had his keen appreciation of beauty, his passion for art and literature, and his interest in the varied spectacle of life. The ridicule and the contempt which had so often been heaped upon him had turned his mind inward and called forth those flowers which he felt would never lose their fragrance."

Early left an orphan, he had provided for himself (by reading) a refuge from all the distress of life. His schooldays (at King's School, Canterbury, thinly disguised) increased his sensitiveness (one master called him a club-footed blockhead), and made him solitary : he developed a sense of humour and lost his faith in God. He then went to Heidelberg and indulged in much freedom of thought. It was here that he met the feckless Hayward, who gave him a sense of taste, and Weeks, who helped him to put off the faith of his childhood, like a cloak that he no longer needed. He began to yearn for experience, especially with women, and to see things for himself. When he got home again he drifted into a liaison with the elderly Miss Wilkinson.

There are few things more grim than the picture of Philip steeling his heart to take what this grotesque, unattractive woman had to offer. " She had taken off her skirt and blouse, and was standing in her petticoat. . . . She wore a camisole of white calico with short arms. . . . Philip's heart sank as he stared at her . . . but it was too late now. He closed the door behind him and locked it."

He was lucky to escape even to that appalling London office of Herbert Carter & Co. and his lodgings in Barnes : for ten loathsome months he learnt how to fail as an accountant and (under Hayward's guidance) went to study painting in Paris. It was here that he met the slatternly Fanny Price, unhealthy, unwashed and starving, who hanged herself when she found that neither her pictures nor herself were marketable commodities in a ruthless world. The picture which Maugham draws of these artists, all desiring to have mistresses, all indulging in endless discussions on art, is excellent. Cronshaw, the poet, in particular, stands out, yearning " for the love of chamber-maids and the conversation of bishops," preaching his gospel of pleasure, finding the meaning of life in a Persian carpet. It is in Paris that Philip hears that creed of the artist: " An artist would let his mother go to the workhouse," let his wife and children starve, sacrifice everything for the sake of getting on to canvas with paint the emotion which the world gave him.

It was from Foinet, the master, that he learnt the importance of money. " There is nothing so degrading as the constant anxiety about one's means of livelihood. I have nothing but contempt for the people who despise money. . . . Money is like a sixth sense without which you cannot make a complete use of the other five. Without an adequate income half the possibilities of life are shut off. . . . You will hear people say that poverty is the best spur to the artist. They do not know how mean it makes you. It exposes you to endless humiliation ; it cuts your wings ; it eats into your soul like a cancer. It is not wealth one asks for, but just enough to preserve one's dignity, to work un-hampered, to be generous, frank and independent. I pity with all my heart the artist, whether he writes or paints, who is entirely dependent for subsistence upon his art." He goes back to Blackstable, a failure as an artist, after two years of jollity, two years of learning to look at hands, at houses and trees against the sky— years of discovery that shadows are not black but coloured . . . that sort of thing.

So he now makes his third fresh start, this time to learn something about medicine, armed with a deeper philosophy of life, determined to be swayed by no prejudices, to follow his inclinations " with due regard to the policeman round the corner," and to find out man's relation to the world he lives in, man's relation with the men among whom he lives, and man's relation to himself. He delighted in the robust common sense of Thomas Hobbes : his mind was concrete. Almost immediately he got entangled with Mildred, another unattractive girl, with narrow hips and the chest of a boy. Only her face and her teeth passed muster. She worked in a tea-shop. He did not think her pretty; he hated the thinness of her; she was common and unhealthy; she showed no pleasure in his company, and yet he was hungry for her; his want of her became a poison, permeating his whole system. She gave him no encouragement; she only went out with him because he was "a gentleman in every sense of the word "; he even offered to marry her, but she preferred to go off with Emil (already married, with three children), so Philip is left with his unslaked thirst and his passion to travel.

It was during these medical student days that he met Norah Nesbit, with the pleasant, ugly face, who lived on writing penny novelettes. In spite of the fact that he did not love her, he made her his mistrsss and companion, and had some measure of satisfaction until Mildred (deserted by Emil) came back. This meant breaking off with Norah and looking after Mildred until her baby was born. Then (as much in love with her as ever) he gives her up to his friend, Griffiths, who, of course, deserts her. He had the luck to meet a forty-eight-year-old journalist, Thorpe Athelny, who lived with his wife and family (which included Sally) on three pounds a week, earned as press agent to a linendraper, and gave Philip a zest for El Greco, that painter of the soul, and for the beauty of Spain.

He again runs across Mildred (now a harlot) and provides for her a home with him, in spite of the fact that his love for her was now finally killed. They have a row; she makes havoc of his furniture and leaves him. Philip loses the little money he has left on a gamble on the Stock Exchange and sinks to starvation. He is rescued by Athelny, who makes him live with him and finds him a job as shopwalker at six shillings a week. Once more he finds Mildred, now a victim to venereal disease, and passes his final examination at the hospital.

He accepts a locum tenens post in Dorsetshire, which leads to the offer of a partnership, which he refuses on the ground that he wants to travel. He goes back to Athelny and immediately seduces the amiable, buxom, rosy-cheeked Sally. He did not love her, but he had conceived a great affection for her ; he admired her magnificent healthiness. When she came to let him know that she was going to have a child he was torn between his life's ambition to get away and travel to Spain and the South Seas and his duty to her. " I'm so damned weak," he said despairingly. He screws himself to offer to marry her, when she tells him that it was a false alarm, and suddenly he discovers that all his desires to wander were as nothing compared with the desire of his heart. " Always his course had been swayed by what he thought he should do and never by what he wanted with his whole soul to do." He had failed to see that the simplest pattern, that in which a man was born, worked, married, had children and died, was likewise the most perfect—so he discovered the meaning of the pattern on the Persian carpet at last. " Amor omnia vincit "—was that it ?

Of Human Bondage is of great length : six hundred and fifty pages, closely packed, and not one of them could be spared. Maugham, like Philip Carey, is one of the few persons who gain a different standpoint from every experience that they undergo. His sensitiveness enables him to recoil more than most of us do from ugliness, and respond more than most of us do to beauty. To fail and fail again, ever to have courage to climb once more, to be interested in every type he meets, and to meet as many types as possible, to put his beliefs to the proof, to discard, prune, re-embellish all the time ruthlessly—these are the qualities that made Philip a man and Maugham an artist. He sees with a holy compassion the long procession of unfortunates, deformed in body and warped in mind, ill in the spirit, craving for sweetness and light; he sees the goodness in the bad, but is not sentimental enough or cowardly enough to shut his eyes to the power of evil.

He will not pretend that things or people are attractive when they are not. He is probably the least of a hypocrite, as he is one of the finest in spirit, among modern authors.

By comparison with, shall we say, Hugh Walpole's *Fortitude*, *Of Human Bondage* stands out as immeasurably superior to most of even the best work in this kind of our time. It is a human document of incalculable value to all men who wish to leave the world richer for their experiences. It is a model of what the autobiography in fiction ought to be. *The Moon and Sixpence* is the model of what every biography in fiction ought to be. It is a masterpiece of brevity. It extenuates nothing. It is as close to genius as the work of the painter Gauguin whose story it tells. It has the added virtue of giving us an insight into Maugham's own life. We see now why he takes refuge in cynicism. He is of all living writers the most sensitive, the most easily perturbed by the ruthlessness of the world. Having discarded the useful cloak of sentimentalism which we, more blunted and coarse than he is, keep on in all weathers, he stands shivering in the cold, burnt up in the heat. He is like a medieval saint or a modern Brahmin: he likes to submit himself to as many buffetings as possible: he suffers incredibly in stripping off the lendings of illusion—and we gain through his suffering. Through his illness we arrive at a book which is the healthiest I have ever read.

"God damn my wife," writes Charles Strickland. "She is an excellent woman. I wish she was in hell."

That is so healthy that we can scarcely credit it of an artist.

It is not insignificant that this rude robustiousness is a late growth in a man who at the time when he was forty was a colourless, commonplace stockbroker with two pleasant children and a hospitable wife.

His sole peculiarity was physical: he was a big-boned, muscular man.

When he suddenly cut adrift from the pleasant backwater of family life and ran away to Paris it was taken for granted that he must have done so for the sake of some woman. The narrator of the story— let us call him Maugham—goes out to effect a reconcilia- tion and finds him untidy, ill-kempt, perfectly happy, brutally unconcerned about his family, determined to paint. Never a talker at the best of times, he has difficulty in conveying to Maugham his passion for painting. He has no difficulty in being rude. His most commonly reiterated remarks are " Go to Hell ! " and " You blasted fool ! " He had the directness of the fanatic and the ferocity of the apostle. His wife, on learning of his passion, hopes that he will rot with some loathsome disease (he does). If he had left her for a woman she would have taken him back, but the injury to her pride on discovering that he merely left her to pursue art was so deadly an insult that she could never forgive him.

Five years passed, and Maugham met Strickland through the agency of a quixotic painter whose work was as bad as his taste was good. This man, Stroeve, was the first to recognise Strickland's genius. He brought Maugham into touch with him again. Five years of struggling had increased his strength, added to his brusquerie and made him cadaverous. Maugham found him sensual and yet indifferent to sensual things, selling no pictures, making no attempt to sell any, indifferent to fame, striving to free himself of the meshes of the body. As Maugham sees him, he walks with his head among the stars, with his feet in the mud. He falls desperately ill and after great difficulty is discovered at death's door and taken home by Stroeve, against the wishes of Stroeve's wife, who hates and fears him. When he recovers he turns Stroeve out of his own flat and robs him of his wife. Incapable of love himself he had, at any rate, the capacity to call it up in others. When Stroeve's wife had served his purpose (she was one of his best models) he leaves her to poison herself with oxalic acid without compunction. It distresses Maugham to think of the contradictoriness of Nature. Here was Stroeve, with the passion of

Romeo in the body of Sir Toby Belch, only capable of inspiring contempt in his wife, for whom he would have gone (and did go) through hell, losing her to a man who watched her go to her death on his account with complete indifference. Maugham is so sensitive that he is driven to dwell on the burning of her vocal cords with the acid, on the wetness of her pillow. " She's too weak to use a handkerchief, and the tears just run down her face." It was this sort of thing that makes him confess to a sudden wrench of the heart-strings. Poor Maugham ! so anxious to avoid the sentimental he is lacerated almost beyond endurance by the needless cruelty of the world. He is like Swift with his " Only a woman's hair." Stroeve is able to bear his own loss better than Maugham bears the death of this girl who was nothing to him. Stroeve, the prosperous bagman, has resilience ; he can come and come and come again. Maugham is brittle ; his is the sort of sensitiveness that breaks under sudden stress.

Stroeve finds Strickland's picture of his nude wife— refrains from destroying it because he realises the greatness of art : he goes back to Amsterdam with the picture to forget. Maugham meanwhile is driven to wonder how he can continue to take interest in so callous a creature as Strickland. He defends himself by suggesting that Shakespeare devised Iago with a gusto which he never felt when he imagined Desdemona. It is left to Strickland to exclaim the woman's point of view : " A woman can forgive a man for the harm he does her, but she can never forgive him for the sacrifices he makes on her account." His own point of view is explained in this passage : " I know lust; that's normal and healthy. Love is a disease. Women are the instruments of my pleasure. I have no patience with their claim to be helpmates, partners, companions. . . . The soul of man wanders through the uttermost regions of the universe, and she (woman) seeks to imprison it in the circle of her account-book. . . . Life has no value. Blanche Stroeve didn't commit suicide because I left her, but because she was a foolish

and unbalanced woman. . . . She was an entirely
unimportant person."

This is, as Strickland says, a very healthy point of
view, but the sentimental Maugham must needs dwell
on the " cruellest thing of all," the fact that, indeed,
Blanche's death made no great difference.   Strickland
at last shows Maugham his pictures—thirty of them,
the work of six years.   He was taken aback by what
seemed to him the clumsiness of technique, the crudity
of the colours.   Stroeve had realised that here was a
manifestation of a revolution in art ; to Maugham there
was merely ugliness and a striving to be liberated from
a strong power.

Strickland goes to the South Sea Islands, and
Maugham never sees him again.   He begins to realise
that his relations with his wife and Blanche were quite
insignificant episodes in the man's life.   He begins
to see at last that his real life consisted of dreams and
of tremendously hard work.   The sexual appetite was
unimportant but irksome : in spite of his cruelty, his
selfishness, his brutality and sensuality he was a great
idealist.   Artistic creation was the only thing that
mattered to him.   He never compromised.   He was
willing to sacrifice not only himself—many can do that
—but others.   He had a vision.   " He was great and
odious. . . ."   Fifteen years later Maugham went out
to Tahiti : Strickland had then been dead nine years.
He sought and found many who had known the painter
in his last days.   There was Captain Nichols, who told
him of Strickland's fight with Tough Bill at Marseilles
and his escape as a stoker on an Australian boat.
There was the French Jew, Cohen, who had lent
Strickland (then a beachcomber) two hundred francs,
which he repaid with a picture, which Cohen afterwards
sold for thirty thousand francs.   There was Tiaré
Johnson, the proprietress of the Hôtel de la Fleur,
who gave the seventeen-year-old native girl, Ata
(" never promiscuous like some—a captain or a first
mate, yes, but she's never been touched by a native ")
to Strickland to live with for a month to see how he

liked her. For three years Strickland lived with Ata in a lonely bungalow, fishing, bathing, painting, reading, happy. " The place where he lived had the beauty of the Garden of Eden . . . a corner hidden away from all the world, with the blue sky overhead and the rich, luxuriant trees, fragrant and cool. . . . He was an extraordinary figure, with his red beard and matted hair, and his great hairy chest. . . . He had gone native with a vengeance. . . . Here there was never a sound, and the air was scented with the white flowers of the night." Here Strickland was held with a passion to create beauty, haunted by a divine nostalgia, a ruthless demon. Here Dr Contras found him stricken with leprosy, deserted by all except Ata and her babies, painting the walls of the house. Three more years went by, and the doctor was privileged to make a last visit—to see the dreadful, mutilated, ghastly object which had been Strickland dead on the floor, and on the walls tremendous, sensual, passionate revelations in colour of things which it is unholy for men to know. Ata tells the doctor that he had been blind for a year, uncomplaining, courageous, serene and undisturbed. He had ordered her to burn the house when he died.

" He had made a world and saw that it was good. Then, in pride and contempt, he destroyed it." His boy, " very like his father in appearance," worked on one of the lagoon schooners. In the end Maugham returns to tell Strickland's wife in London what he had found out about her husband.

He finds on her walls coloured reproductions of several of his pictures, one a version of the Holy Family in which the Virgin and the Christ were Ata and her first son.

I have heard this novel called " terrible," usually by the people who ask me what the title means.

I see nothing of the terrible in it. It is the simple story of a man who set out to do something and did it. The " terrible " story has yet to be written : the story of the man who set out to do something and failed to do it. Had Strickland not risen superior to the forces set against him—his wife, security, comfort, financial prosperity, domesticity, Blanche, Maugham, conventional codes—there might have been cause for terror. As it is, we can only thank God that he responded to the call of Beauty, and left the world the richer for his sacrifice.

The question is, Would you rather have Gauguin's pictures or be without them ? So much for the moral. But with regard to the artistry of the biographer ? It is hard to keep one's enthusiasm for that within decent bounds. The dialogue is terse, crisp, nakedly sincere, devoid of all trappings of wit and humour. The effect is heightened by a rigid economy of phrase, and the masterly way in which the artist keeps his eye always on the object.

Here is no tragedy : tragedy tells of the fall of great men. This tells of the rise of a great man. Here is no tragedy : tragedy lies in the fact of a man effecting worthless sacrifices when a pseudo-artist sacrifices his mother, his wife and child to no purpose, merely to satisfy a convention. Shelley sacrificed Harriet, Samuel Butler sacrificed his father, because they had to. There was no tragedy there.

Maugham ought to be one of the most formative influences of the present day. There is certainly no one who could exert such a healthy restraint on the young writer who fears to face the truth. Maugham, like Adam, is strong enough to be naked and unashamed.

XV

JOHN MIDDLETON MURRY

I DO not propose to spend time discussing Murry's first novel, *Still Life*. It seemed to me when it came out to be derived wholly from the Russian. I remember very little about it. I have no desire to reread it. It was prolix, introspective, clever, modern, and perhaps (I don't know) autobiographical.

The Things We Are is a very different piece of work. It has beauty, it is wholly sincere, it will live, it is short, it moves swiftly and yet it probes the depths. It expresses what nearly every good modern novel expresses —divine discontent.

It is hard to say how interest in characters is aroused. My passion is for the energetic man who rides roughshod over every convention. Duncan Havelock Boston, known to his mother as Havy, disinclined to rub shoulders with the world, is not at all the sort of man I expected to rouse my enthusiasm. Left alone with £2000, he lived on about £2 a week, willing himself to do hateful things. He was frigid and precise in his secretarial duties and " became an adept at compiling useless statistics and drawing up impeccable reports " daily from ten o'clock till six. He did this for four years, and seemed prepared to go on doing it for forty. In the evenings he wandered in a sharp and jagged world " irremediably alien." He read to lose himself and found that he could only lose himself in the real. He met an enthusiastic journalist called Bettington, in the rain : he lent him an umbrella : friendship was cemented.

" I've been working in London ten years now and I've never had an umbrella lent me by a total stranger before," says Bettington.

Bettington talks. He finds life interesting and exciting. "It used to be quite certain that you were rather wicked if you ran away with somebody else's wife . . . you felt very uneasy. . . . Now you still feel quite uneasy—for quite different reasons. Chiefly because there's nothing to feel uneasy about." Bettington is very much a man of loose ends. Boston is very much the reverse. He suddenly escapes from life by the simple expedient of walking to Hampstead and getting into a tram bound for Barnet. A seventeen-year-old waitress in a tea-shop, freckled of face, fuzzy-haired, with tilted nose, smiles at him, and offers to show him the road out into the country. They walk without talking, without making love: she cries at parting : he kisses her hand : they separate for ever. He goes on into the night and finds accommodation at a clean, small inn with casement windows opening on to a moon-lit garden. He has the luck to find in his hostess, Mrs Williams, a mothering, gossiping soul who puts him entirely at his ease. He spent his first day walking into St Albans, to wire his resignation of his post and an invitation to Bettington to join him. Bettington arrives while he is playing cards in the parlour with the innkeeper and his wife, and is joined the next day by Felicia, the girl in whose company he was on the night of the umbrella episode. Boston spends the week they stay with him swayed between loving pity and resentful hatred for this pair who seem unable to grasp their happiness with each other. On the last day Boston and Felicia go for a walk together and discover that they have both of them more in common than either of them has with Bettington—that they are in love with each other. When she goes he describes himself to her in a letter as a "discriminating blood-sucker." He writes to Bettington to implore him not to marry Felicia. Bettington recognises (he is a little more blunt than his friend) that Boston is a sick man and Felicia a sick woman. They are sick with want of each other. He, on the other hand, is "ordained to be solitary

and find his strength in solitude." He bicycles out to
Boston and catches him at breakfast. He tells him
that he must marry Felicia. He also gets rid of a bit
of useful philosophy: " The truth I've had to discover
is that, instead of being what we are, if we aren't
something better, we're nothing at all. . . . Either
you get better or you get worse, finer or grosser. You
have to choose. If you don't choose, you've chosen
more finally than ever. It doesn't sound very much,
I know, and yet it's all I've got to show for ten years
of my life." Boston congratulates himself upon the
fact that he is getting simpler. He is able at last to
explain himself, to show Bettington how he tried to
surrender himself, how he hated Felicia and Bettington
for disturbing him : he had to struggle to lose his life
before he could save it. He found out the paralysing
truth that other people were not to be used. Felicia
chased after Boston too, not on a bicycle, but in a
car, with her friend Miss Considine, who thought that
she would like to marry Bettington. She wanted the
chance of ruffling his hair. She told him so. We leave
Boston telling Felicia that she is " extraordinarily
lovely."

The Things We Are is a refreshing, disconcerting
book. It holds one in thrall. It is all in a minor
key: it is still . . . we should hear a pin drop, but
Mr Middleton Murry is careful to see that no pins shall
drop.

It is too intellectual to be robust. We are inclined
to think that the characters talk too much and act too
little. That is because they are so dreadfully concerned with their motives. They are like a dog over
a bone with each memory they indulge in, each phrase
that springs to their lips, each sight they see. Everything in life has an appalling significance. Unforgettable, for instance, is the quiet walk of Boston with the
tea-girl out of Barnet. It is beautiful, inexpressibly
beautiful, and remains in the mind when all the blare
and shouting of more full-blooded, hectic novels is
forgotten.

It is significant that when a Murry hero wants to escape from life he does not think of Samoa or Russia : he takes a tram to Barnet.

To get outside oneself and adopt a detached attitude —that is one of life's first lessons. Then only do we begin to see the things we are—then only do we begin to live.

XVI

J. C. SNAITH

THE fact that I have just been reading *The Van Roon*, a sprightly enough description of a fight for a valuable picture between delightful heroine and villainous uncle, reminds me that Mr Snaith once wrote a novel that was not merely entertaining.

In *The Sailor* (supposed by some to be the life story of Masefield) he built to last, not merely to make money. With some novelists—Conrad is an example —it is safe to say that if you like one you will like them all; with others, Mr Snaith especially, the name of the author is no criterion of the excellence of the book. The wise man on finishing *The Sailor* will not rush out and buy all the rest of Mr Snaith's work: he will turn back to the beginning and read the book again. It is queer to think that this is a really great book. Masefield or no Masefield, there never can have been a boy like 'Enry 'Arper, born in the gutter, illiterate, highly strung, sensitive, who made good before the mast, developed into a first-class professional goal-keeper, ultimately to become a brilliant novelist. Again, there is a quite understandable dislike on the part of the public for novels in which the heroes are themselves novelists. It only goes to prove that plots matter not at all; it is the method that counts. Everything that happens to the Sailor is so vividly portrayed that we question none of the incredible things that happen to him. We suffer with him as Auntie hounds him down the foggy lane, whip in hand, threatening to do him in at every step . . . we are still suffering with him when in his simplicity he is hoodwinked by the harlot into marriage. In other words, 'Enry convinces us, even if his experiences pass all the bounds of credulity. Mr Snaith has inherited a quite Dickensian knowledge of the habits, manners and speech of the working classes. He recognises their courage, their kindliness and their humour. Like his own Sailor, he is sharp as a needle, uncommonly shrewd and observant, and as much at home on the *Margaret Carey* as he is at Blackhampton. He gives his hero the priceless gift of the power to keep on keeping on, and his reward is great. Even while he is in the depths he is given moments of exaltation : he may grow white with fright when ordered to go aloft, but he also glows with intoxication at the majesty and beauty of the universe. There was plenty of terror and stupefaction in the gales that swept over the sea and over the souls of his seniors, but there was also a time of calm when Nature and mankind were harbingers of peace. There were ecstatic moments when the gates of heaven opened and he saw orange, crimson, gold, purple and every other imaginable colour dancing before his eyes.

He had to fall among sharks before he plumbed the high and awful mystery of life, but these experiences were necessary to bring about those sea-changes in him that were to make him. The craven strain had to be burnt out of him before he could rise on the ashes of his dead self. And always at the right moment there was the helping hand. First Klondyke, the old Etonian, with his " stick to the reading and writing, old friend," before he could do either ; then " Ginger " Jukes helping him to get a place in the Blackhampton Rovers team ; then Edward Ambrose, the kindly editor of *Brown's Magazine* (extraordinarily like Reginald Smith of *Cornhill*), who nursed him into fame ; and lastly Klondyke's sister Mary, who draws him up to herself and finally rescues him from the tide that might so easily have overwhelmed him. Yes, the sailor had luck, but he also had " guts," as Klondyke saw, to endure those six years on the *Margaret Carey*, fearful of the elements all the time. Those years had made him lean and hard-muscled, given him eyes—not eyes to penetrate the evil of the land sharks, but eyes to seize upon the beauties of the material world. There is no description of professional Association football comparable with Mr Snaith's account of Sailor's connection with the Blackhampton Rovers.

Mr Augustus Higginbottom, chairman of the club, stands for all the Olympians of the " Soccer " world I have ever seen. His expansive fur coat, his superb contour, his spats, his red face, the flower in his button-hole, the large cigar with the band round it stuck in the side of his mouth, his " 'Arper—who the 'ell's 'Arper ? Ginger's no class. Moves like a height-year-old with the staggers," his six satellites craning to catch his ukase . . . how well I know him. Mr Snaith has a gift for nailing down the essentials in the briefest possible space. " Sailor's " prodigiously speedy climb to fame with his equally speedy fall in that wonderfully described Cup-tie against Duckingfield Britannia is perhaps the most convincing part of the book. We all know a good deal about football . . . it would be so easy to pick holes if Mr Snaith went wrong, but he doesn't. A whole army of referees swims into our ken as we read of that " cock-sparrow in knickerbockers," a hundred different audiences become merged into one, as we read of the sudden change from unreasoning idolatry to devilish hatred that comes over them as they realise that Sailor has " sold the match."

Then follow the days at Bowdon (why not Rowton ?) House—sixpence a night, nightgowns a penny—where he meets Mr Esme Horrobin, formerly Fellow and Tutor of Gamaliel College, Oxford, translating the *Satyricon* of Petronius Arbiter after an exhausting life of " bear-leading the aristocracy." Again in time of need comes the helping hand. It was this sybarite who put him in touch with Mr Rudge, bookseller of the Charing Cross Road, for ever employed in taking notes for his forty-volume " History of the World." For forty-two years Mr Rudge had been filling tin trunks with notes, coded and docketed, and as yet only the first sentence of the first volume, " In the beginning, says

Holy Writ, was the Word," had been evolved. Even that pregnant sentence had yet to be put on paper. It was while in the employ of Mr Rudge that Sailor came upon *The Adventures of George Gregory: A Tale of the High Seas*. "Without being aware of it he had found his kingdom. Here were atmosphere and colour, space and light."

Here was a reward for those laborious days of learning to spell and read. . . . As Mr Snaith says: "One thing leads to another." *The Adventures of George Gregory* led 'Enry 'Arper to go one better. *The Adventures of Dick Smith on the High Seas*, by Henry Harper, was written, sent to Edward Ambrose, Ambrose sent for Harper, *Dick Smith* was revised and earned for its author £300 for the serial rights, Cora Dobbs collared both the money and the author, and Sailor suffered yet another sea-change. *Dick Smith* appeared and was hailed as a second *Robinson Crusoe*, and Henry was lost in the grip of a passion, not for Cora, but for knowledge. He becomes "lionised" by literary coteries, meets and makes a tremendous impression on Mary Pridmore, the sister of Klondyke. He discovers his wife's true nature and (as an antidote) Milton. "It simply takes my head off," he says of the latter. "I almost want to shout and sing. It's another new world to me." So was Mary, the "daughter of the gods, tall, slender, virile, an aureole of purest poetry upon her brows." But to escape from Cora he had to take to the sea again . . . this time accompanied by Milton, the Bible, Shakespeare, *Don Quixote*, Boswell, Homer and a Greek lexicon. "This royal company did much to hold the trolls at bay." Luckily Cora died of drink . . . and in the end he attained his heart's desire as well as the fulfilment of his worldly ambitions.

The Sailor is a great novel, after the school of Fielding, picaresque, adventurous, full-blooded, a novel of action, in which a man is shown in the making. It is certainly Mr Snaith's high-water mark.

XVII

HUGH WALPOLE

HUGH WALPOLE once wrote a novel, *Mr Perrin and Mr Traill*, that went close to being great, and one " romance " (as he called it), *Fortitude*, which bears rereading. At first he was praised too highly. He met with success rather too easily. Then he became the official interpreter of England to America, as H. L. Mencken has become the " producer," preface-writer, interpreter, trumpeter of young America to England. The young writers are all very angry with Walpole. They say that he is too smug ; they attribute his success, if it was a success, in America to the fact that his father is a Bishop. They accuse him of being a snob. Perhaps a snob is a man who hasn't the decency to be ashamed of having a father who has to be called " my Lord." I have only seen him once. He looked far too happy and prosperous to be a good author. But that is nothing to go by.

Gilbert Cannan is undoubtedly a good author, and he is the happiest man by far that I have ever met. No man has a right to be happy as Gilbert Cannan is happy. His happiness is of the sort that makes me really angry. He is physically strong, he likes oysters and the Derby . . . and yet he thinks, thinks quite clearly. He is so simple-minded that I have the very greatest difficulty in understanding a word he says. On the other hand, I feel that I should understand Walpole always. We are both parsons' sons ; we have both been schoolmasters. I envy him his command of English. I don't at all envy him his pomposity. He reminds me extraordinarily of his own Adam Brandon, Archdeacon of Polchester. He wouldn't be

pleased.   Let us look a little more closely at Brandon
and the book which tells his life history.   I am inclined
to rate *The Cathedral* very high.   I have found every
book of Walpole's readable : all his characters interest
me, but *Mr Perrin and Mr Traill* haunts me.   It is the
best Public School story ever written.   It is written
from the only possible angle, that of the schoolmaster.
The Cathedral is a fierce indictment of a passing age,
just as *The Duchess of Wrexe* was an exposition of the
last kick of an effete aristocracy.

   " It's the Cathedral," said the shadowy iconoclast
who is at the bottom of all the trouble at Polchester—
" It's the Cathedral that I fear. . . . It has a spirit of
its own, a life, a force that all the past years and all the
worship that it has had have given it. . . . It has
become a god demanding his own rites and wor-
shippers. . . . It uses men for its own purposes, and
not for Christ. . . . It almost hates Christ.   It is so
beautiful, so lovely, so haughty, so jealous."

   Brandon is one of its products, superb in carriage,
in dignity, in his magnificent recognition of the value
of ceremony.   He was a power in Polchester . . . and
he was made to suffer incredible things because of it.
The cloud on his horizon was Ronder, a new Canon,
who saw him first at the unfortunate moment when
the elephant had trampled his hat in the dust.   But
there were clouds in his own family.   There was Falk,
his son, sent down from Oxford, who ran away to marry
the local publican's daughter.   There was his wife, who
hated him and eventually ran away with one of the
city vicars.   There was the drunken artist, Davray,
who hated Brandon's presumption. . . . But most of
all there was Ronder, loving intrigue, his only passion,
discovering in Brandon a stupid, autocratic, retro-
gressive, good-natured child.   It was Ronder who became Brandon's thorn in the flesh.   It began simply.
Brandon had had things all his own way till Ronder
came.   Then Ronder reversed his decision about the
school roller — a little thing, but ominous.   Ronder
was clever and subtle, but everything went well for his

plans without his having to rouse himself very much. There were the whisperings about the Brandon *ménage*, whisperings about Falk and Annie Hogg, whisperings about Mrs Brandon and Morris, whisperings about Brandon's determination that Forsyth should be given the Pybus St Anthony living, rather than the revolutionary Wistons. For some time Brandon was in happy ignorance of these things. Then his wife suddenly refused to attend Early Service. Then he became obsessed with the idea that Ronder was obstructing him; subconsciously he sensed the truth that Ronder, who really liked him, was set on destroying him. It is very like Perrin and Traill over again, this. I myself have seen in elder colleagues when I was a schoolmaster what Ronder saw in Brandon, fine fellows, but stupid, blind, conceited, but in spite of all that, a fineness that would never be mine. With just a slight turn of the screw things might have gone so very differently. Mrs Brandon would have gone with her son if only he had sympathised with her instead of his father, but Falk was too much concerned with his own affairs to bother overmuch about his lonely mother. He had formed a strange relationship with the independent, reserved, proud, honest Annie. " I'll marry you if you want me," she had said, " or I'll live with you without marrying, or I'll live without you and never see you again. . . . I'd rather be hurt than be dependent." Falk goes to Ronder and takes his advice : he goes—and marries the girl. That is Brandon's first blow. Davray meets him and taunts him with it. " Your patronage and pomposity and conceit . . . we're sick of you . . . we're going to get rid of you. . . . This is the first step. Your son's gone with a whore to London, and all the town's laughing at you." Falk's defalcation determines his mother. She cannot bear the loneliness any longer— so she gives herself to Morris. Brandon has the misfortune to meet Ronder at a lunch with the Bishop. They drive away together afterwards and Ronder mentions Wistons' name as candidate for Pybus. On the instant the choleric Archdeacon is ablaze. He shows his hand and quarrels violently with the Canon. It is all exactly like Perrin and Traill. He even gets down from the wagonette and refuses to go on with his enemy.

The story becomes known—Brandon becomes the laughing-stock of the community. His action drives Ronder at last into a remorseless, implacable anger. Immediately a busybody comes to him with an intercepted letter from Mrs Brandon to Morris beginning "Dearest." He sends her to Brandon, whose wife confesses her guilt and her hatred of him. "I've hated you for years . . . because of your conceit and pride. Because you've never thought of me. Because I've always been a piece of furniture to you. . . . Because you've been so pleased with yourself, and well-satisfied and stupid . . . never seeing anything, never knowing anything and always—so satisfied. . . . I'm glad! I'm glad! I'm glad." Poor Brandon gets it properly in the neck all round. He is set upon by Davray and Annie's father. His wife deserts him. "Now, at last, perhaps, you will realise that loneliness is worse than any other hell." Only his daughter Joan is left. It's like *A Bill of Divorcement*. He is being driven out of his mind. His head and heart both "conk out." Within six months of Ronder's arrival he is driven to bay, putting up his last struggle, to get Forsyth into the living of Pybus. He fails and dies. There is exactly the same combination of malign forces against him that defeated Mr Perrin.

There is a tale of De la Motte Fouqué quoted in *The Cathedral* which exactly sums up life as Walpole interprets it. A young traveller is trying to reach a certain castle. His journey is easy until he reaches a small wood through which he must pass. In this wood more sinister than the obstacles are its inhabitants, evil, malign, foul and bestial, who devote their lives to the destruction of travellers. In this wood the traveller feels as though the world has changed, that his weapons are no longer of any avail. "He has in the heart of that wood many perilous adventures, but worst of them all, when he is almost at the end of his strength, is the sudden conviction that he has himself changed, and is himself become one of the foul, gibbering, half-visioned monsters by whom he is surrounded."

Mr Walpole has one unique gift: no one can paint the growth of petty hatreds as he paints them. There was something of this power evident in *Prelude to Adventure*, more of it in *Mr Perrin and Mr Traill*, and most successfully is it seen in *The Cathedral*, which we now find to be not his latest, but his first novel. I thought I was right. Walpole matured very early. Success has done him no good.

XVIII

VICTORIA SACKVILLE-WEST

MISS SACKVILLE-WEST has already shown in her poetry and her first novel, *Heritage*, how deep and true is her passion for beauty, especially the beauty of the English country-side. She has interpreted the peculiar splendour of the Kentish weald admirably. In *The Dragon in Shallow Waters* she gave us terror, purgings through pity . . . but of all her work I think the most characteristic, the most memorable is her short story (not so very short, one hundred and twenty pages), *The Heir: A Love Story.* It is one of the world's perfect love stories . . . the growth of love in a man for a house.

Mr Peregrine Chase, the sandy, weakly, freckled insurance manager of Wolverhampton with the washy blue eyes, had been called from his work to attend the funeral of his aunt, Phyllida Chase, Lord of the Manor of Blackboys in Kent, and see (as the sole heir) solicitors about the selling of a property that had been in his family for five hundred years, but was now mortgaged up to the last shilling. The house was a perfect specimen of Elizabethan, but as it contained no bathrooms, no electric light, no garage, no central heating, the lawyers were doubtful whether it would fetch more than twenty-five thousand. Of course the furniture, tapestries and pictures would bring in another twenty thousand, which would clear off the mortgage. All that Chase would get out of it when the whole place had gone would be an income of a few hundreds.

Chase was a cheerless hard worker who lived in lodgings, had neither loved nor married, was old-maidish and anæmic . . . but the house that he had inherited woke him up. Its façade of old, plum-coloured bricks,

142

the inverted V of the two gables, the creamy stucco of the little colonnade, the green stillness of the moat, its quiet grandeur and dignity lying in the hollow at the bottom of the ridge, the thirty or forty peacocks sitting all the way up the low stone wall —these things began to soften him. Then inside there was the grey-green tapestry, the polished boards, the friendly greyhound, to give him the sense that he was not the interloper he seemed to himself to be. Wolverhampton becomes more and more a forgotten dream. Here he is the squire, the descendant of twenty generations. No one in Wolverhampton knew so much as his Christian name. He enjoyed his new sense of solitude, companioned only by the greyhound. He began to wander about the estate, to make friends with the farmers and cottagers, his tenants. They all took to him. He fed the peacocks with crumbs. They seemed to take to him too. "Folks about here do say the peacocks'll die off when Blackboys goes from Chase's hands." So ran the legend. In the place of stagnation he recognised stability . . . the lands, the farms, the rickyards, the sown, the fallow, taught him wisdom. He turns away visitors with "orders to view." Instead of going back to Wolverhampton he remained for hours "gazing in a silly beatitude at the large patches of sunlight that lay on the grass." When the inventory men came he chafed. The dealers with their cigars, paunches, check waistcoats, signet-rings, insolent plump hands, shiny lips and small eyes infuriated him. He went back to Wolverhampton. A rich Brazilian with immaculate son and daughter came to see the house. Visitors came and left bottles and bits of paper about the grounds. At length came the day of the sale. Chase was not there. Four lots were knocked down when Chase arrived, haggard and ill. He watched one of his tenants trying to buy in the cottage where he had lived for twenty-five years. The pain of watching his property go maddened him. To see the house up for sale was like seeing one's mistress in a slave market.

He madly resented this interference with his property.
At last (too quickly) came Lot 16—the manor-house,
the pleasure-grounds of eight acres, and one hundred and twenty-five acres of parkland adjoining.
An American joined issue with the Brazilian when the
bidding rose to twenty-five thousand guineas, but
retired gracefully at thirty thousand. The house was
on the point of being knocked down to the Brazilian
when Chase at last came to his senses and began to
fight " to shield from rape the thing he loved." They
could not defeat him. Bidding in these outrageous
sums that need never be paid over, he was possessed
of an inexhaustible fortune. . . . There was nothing
criminal or even illegal in his buying in his own house
if he wanted to.

The sale was brought to an end. Chase was left
leaning against a column of the porch thinking that
thus must married lovers feel when after the confusion
of their wedding they are at length left alone together.
He was poor, but he could work, he would manage :
" his poverty would not be bitter, it would be sweet.
Blackboys ! Wolverhampton ! What was Wolverhampton beside Blackboys ? What was that drudgery
beside this beauty, this pride, this Quixotism ? "

There is an amazing sense of quiet satisfaction to
be got out of this story. We are made to feel that
it really is one of the world's great love stories.

Miss Sackville-West's prose is a clarion call to slack
Englishmen to look to the rock whence they were hewn
and to make some effort to stem the foreign invasion.
The old squirearchy are being displaced by commercial
plutocrats who know nothing of, and care nothing for,
the beauty of the English country-side. She strives to
make us realise the heritage that is ours in such places
as Knole before they are dismantled and changed.

XIX

E. H. YOUNG

DURING the last twelve years there have been four novels from Miss Young: *A Corn of Wheat, Yonder, Moor Fires,* and now *The Bridge Dividing.* It is quite time that those who love the quiet and the beautiful realised the extraordinary charm of Miss Young's work.

There is surprising quality in the opening paragraph of her latest novel:

" On the high land overlooking the distant channel and the hills beyond it, the spring day, set in azure, was laced with gold and green. Gorse bushes flaunted their colour, larch-trees hung out their tassels, and celandines starred the bright green grass in an air which seemed palpably blue. . . . Far away, the channel might have been a still, blue lake, the hills more soft blue veils and, like a giant reservoir, the deeper blue of the sky promised unlimited supplies."

In this setting a sulky, handsome horseman, Francis Scales, remonstrates with the girl, Rose Mallett, who cannot return his love. Rose is the young step-sister of two elderly unmarried daughters (Sophia and Caroline) of a raffish (dead) general. The three women live together in easy circumstances and are joined by their raffish (also dead) brother's daughter, Henrietta, who is left destitute. Francis in pique at Rose's refusal of him goes away and reappears with a wife who takes a terrible toss while hunting and becomes crippled. Rose finds when it is too late that she loves Francis, a fact which his wife of course discovers and continually harps on. Rose has more restraint than Francis, and is prepared to go on loving him indefinitely, when the young Henrietta complicates matters by falling in love with him, fully realising that she was thereby robbing her aunt. When Francis kisses her, Henrietta cruelly communicates the fact to Rose, who immediately releases Francis from his bond. She succeeds in making him believe that she too has changed. " There was a time," said Francis angrily, " when you went white like paper when we met, and your eyes went black. Now I might be a sheep in a field."

In spite of the fact that she is fond of an unfortunate lover called Charles Batty, Henrietta is willing enough to run away with Francis when he suggests it. Two things prevent the girl from consummating her folly: Francis does not turn up; Charles, at the instigation of Rose, does. Also at the instigation of Rose, Charles has the sense to tell Henrietta that she is the best and most beautiful woman in the world. In the end, of course, the path is left clear for Francis to marry Rose, and Henrietta marries Charles. The plot matters scarcely at all. What does matter is the atmosphere of beauty that breathes through the pages. There are practically no incidents. The death of the elderly Miss Caroline after the ball, and Miss Sophia after the garden-party, the hunting accident, a few stealthy meetings between Francis and Rose, Francis and Henrietta . . . things like that, nothing more. But there is extraordinary verisimilitude in the dialogue. Here are Henrietta and Charles at the end of the book, Charles devoted, tempting her with houses, rings, fidelity:

" Suddenly she leaned towards him and put her head on his knee. His hand fell on her hair. ' This doesn't mean anything,' she murmured; ' but I was just thinking. You're tempting me again. First with the ring because it was so pretty, and now with a house.'

" ' How else am I to get you ? ' he cried out. ' And you know you were feeling lonely. That's why I came.'

" ' You thought it was your chance ? '

" ' Yes,' he said. ' I don't know the ordinary things, but I know the others.'

" ' I wonder how,' she said, and he answered with

the one word, ' Love,' in a voice so deep and solemn that she laughed. . . .

" ' The Malletts don't marry,' Henrietta said. ' There's something in us that can't be satisfied. It was the same with my father, only it took him the other way.'

" ' I didn't know he was married more than once. Nobody tells me things.'

" ' Charles dear, you're very stupid. He was only married once in a church.'

" ' Oh, I see.'

" ' And if I did marry, I should be like him.' She turned to him and put her face close to his. ' Unfaithful,' she pronounced clearly.

" ' Oh, well, Henrietta, you would still be you."

" She stepped backwards, shocked. ' Charles, wouldn't you mind ? '

" ' Not so much,' he said stolidly, ' as doing without you altogether.'

" ' And the other day you said you need never do that because '—she tapped his waistcoat—' because I'm here.'

" He showed a face she had never seen before. ' You seem to think I'm not made of flesh and blood,' he cried. ' You're wanton, Henrietta, simply wanton !' and he rushed out of the room.

" She heard the front door bang : she saw his hat and stick lying where he had put them : she smiled at them politely and then, sinking to the floor beside the fender, she let out a little moan of despair and delight. The fire chuckled and chattered and she leaned forward, her face near the bars. ' Stop talking for a minute ! I want to tell you something. There's nobody else to tell. Listen ! I'm in love with him now.' She nodded her head. ' Yes, with him. I know it's ridiculous, but it's true. . . . I'm in love with him. Oh dear !' ' "

Just as in these few sentences Henrietta lives for us clear-cut, human, intricate, altogether woman, so elsewhere in the characters of the blunt Caroline, the tender Sophia, the mysteriously silent Rose we get subtle delineations of extraordinary clarity. Miss E. H. Young reminds me of Jane Austen with the sting left out. She has the same acute vision; she takes the same sorts of people; she wisely narrows her field, and within her limits she excels all her competitors because she does not allow her brain to override her heart. She realises the beauty that lies behind everything: she can even bring her heroine to see the joke that lies in the attainment of things that one has longed for when the longing has passed: there is no bitterness in her. She is among the optimists for whom the word "frustration" has no meaning. Valuing love as highly as anyone, she faces the fact that it is brittle. Miss Young never obtrudes: she is the most reticent of all modern writers, but when all the banging of drums dies down and the heady work of most novelists is forgotten we find ourselves back in Radstowe quietly watching and loving the family of Malletts.

PART II

SOME MODERN CRITICS

DEAN INGE
MIDDLETON MURRY
WALTER RALEIGH
LYTTON STRACHEY

I

DEAN INGE

" THE most able intellect of our time." That is the commonest description of this successor of John Donne. For my part, I know no whetstone on which to sharpen the thinking instruments of the young comparable with *Outspoken Essays*.

There is no braver, no more honest man living than Dean Inge, but how the lazy clergy of his Church must hate him!

When he sets out to tell us what his credo is we know that he will have arrived at it from first principles, hard thinking and a refusal to accept comfortable words which mean nothing. He labels himself as a Christian Platonist, and as he knows more about Christianity and about Platonism than any of his colleagues we may allow his description to stand.

At the beginning he warns us that " we cannot make a religion for others, and we ought not to let others make a religion for us." No wonder he has little use for the Roman Catholics. " Our own religion is what life has taught us." That explains why " religion " with most of us is a mewling, puking child . . . life teaches us practically nothing. It takes most of us most of our time to rid ourselves of " spectral half-beliefs, conventional acceptances and the mere will to believe."

" The important question," says the Dean, " is not whether God exists, but what we mean when we speak of God. . . . The average man . . . appeals to a kindly governor of the world . . . such as men themselves are, such will God appear to be." He fights strongly against the dualism that science gives facts without values and religion values without facts, and

151

more strongly still against the still prevalent superstition that we are on the way to perfection. "There is not, and cannot be, any progress in the universe as a whole, and there is no probability that the human race will either reach perfection or find the laws of nature much more conformable to its desires than they are now. Any philosophy which postulates either any kind of progress in the universe as a whole . . . is demonstrably moonshine. . . . Our species has probably half-a-million years in which to try every possible and impossible experiment in social and economic reform. . . . When we look at the moon we may say with tolerable assurance, ' That is what our home will look like at no incalculably distant date.' To throw our ideals into the future is the death of all sane philosophy and science."

That is plain speaking of a kind very rare to meet in a priest, salutary, sharp, a wholesome corrective to the sloppy thinking that passes for philosophy in the pulpit and on the platform. We are for once facing facts.

> " Though earth and man were gone,
>   And suns and universes cease to be,
>   And Thou wert left alone,
>   Every existence would exist in Thee."

So sang Emily Brontë . . . and, as the Dean says, such "mystical experience" is the "bedrock of religious faith." There have been saints who have come near to the felt presence of God, but it is given to few to be saintly. "The pearl of great price is not so easily found. But do we know of any who have sought after the knowledge of God as diligently as other men seek after wealth and honour, and have come away empty-handed ? "

There is nothing to get worried about in accepting the quite unmistakable evidence that the universe is slowly running down like a clock. "If the universe is running down in time, it must have been wound up in time, and whatever unknown power wound

it up once may presumably be able to wind it up
again."

The Dean believes in three Absolute Values : Truth,
Goodness, Beauty. " There are many things in the
world more divine than man. Anthropolatry is the
enemy . . . true philosophy is theocentric. The
world is a hymn sung by the creative Logos to the glory
of God the Father. . . . We are justified in believing
that the world as God sees it is far more beautiful and
harmonious than the world as we see it."

It is splendidly ironical that the Dean who has been
labelled " gloomy " should be the priest who said : " I
have never understood why it should be considered
derogatory to the Creator to suppose that He has a
sense of humour. . . . The world is full of absurdities
which to a Superior Being may afford infinite merriment."

He makes no attempt to solve the problem of evil,
but what he says on the subject is illuminating. " The
unsolved mystery of evil is not so much the prevalence
of suffering as the apparently reckless waste and destruction of the higher values." But he allows that
this apparent waste is analogous to the wastefulness
of nature in the creation and destruction of lower
values. " It is the lavishness of a Creator who draws
from inexhaustible stores."

" The beauty of the world," he says in another place,
" is the strongest evidence we have of the goodness and
benevolence of the Creator."

But it is on the subject of immortality and survival
that the Dean puts in some very necessary clarifying,
if not scorching, vituperation.

" A working class audience in particular listens with
marked impatience to addresses upon human immortality. The working man is apt to think that the
preacher is trying to put him off with cheques drawn
upon the bank of heaven, the solvency of which he
greatly doubts, in order to persuade him not to claim
what he conceives to be his rights here and now. . . .
Our revolutionists think that heaven and hell . . .

bolster up social injustice. . . . These people as a class
(well-intentioned people who call themselves Christians)
. . . have hopes in Christ, but in this life only.
Christianity for them is mainly an instrument of social
reform."

Belief in a future life is by no means always a religious
belief. Very definite is the Dean's condemnation of
those who imagine that the desire for a future life to
compensate one for a miserable present has anything
to do with religion. "If a man seeks in the good life
anything apart from itself, it is not the good life that
he is seeking."

The old ideas of reward and punishment are long
a-dying, but the Dean has done some honest work to
finish them off.

Our main duty, the Dean would have us believe, is
to posterity. Salvation lies in birth control. "Either
rational selection must take the place of the natural
selection which the modern state will not allow to act,
or we shall deteriorate as surely as a miscellaneous
crowd of dogs allowed to rear puppies from promiscuous
matings."

So far as the cultured are concerned, he is, of course,
preaching to the converted. It is only the poorest
among the working classes who have unlimited families,
and they only through ignorance, not through mistaken ideas about religion. Unrestricted propagation
leads to poverty, unemployment, wars of extermina-
tion, physical, moral and intellectual degeneration . . .
and any sane man looking over the sides of a bus
in the London streets to-day must agree. There are
far too many people alive who do not pull their weight
in the civic boat. If a man does not take the trouble
to produce there is no reason why the world should
trouble to keep him in the boat.

So we get the Dean's confession of faith; he hates
Labour; he admires only the aristocracy of intellect;
he has little patience with Christianity as at present
preached and practised. "The worst enemies of
Christianity are Christians. A religion will never be

destroyed by worldliness, sensuality, or malicious
wickedness." The Church has very little influence,
but is in no danger of being submerged. "Nothing
could destroy the Christian churches except the complete decay and submergence of the white race, a most
improbable contingency." The Yellow Peril to the
Dean is solely an economic peril—the Japanese and the
Chinese can cut us out in low wages all the time.

In his latest volume Dean Inge includes five most
valuable lectures on the history of the State, Visible
and Invisible. He is no happier about civil government
on earth than he is about our attitude to the government of our souls. "A good government," he says,
"remains the greatest of human blessings, and no
nation has ever enjoyed it."

His first lecture is an attack on Theocracies, which
"make the people believe that the priests hold the keys
of heaven and hell," which "keep education in their own
hands, and endeavour to press the ductile minds of
children into the mould which they desire them to keep
through life. The miserable results of this policy,
which the Roman Catholic Church would establish
everywhere if it could, are apparent in Poland, in
Canada, and above all in Ireland. . . . The machinery
of Theocracy generates a violent revulsion against
every kind of religion."

His second lecture deals with the Greek City state:
"The whole structure of ancient civilisation depended
on the City as the unit." This lecture gives the Dean
his chance to extol Plato and to denounce democracy.
"Under a democracy every citizen thinks that he is
qualified to govern the country and the result is utter
inefficiency." Political power is always abused by the
ruling class to plunder . . . but if this power is in the
hands of the few it is less dangerous than when it is in
the hands of the mob, who vote themselves doles and
pensions and exhaust the whole of a nation's resources.

Plato's remedy for this was to put political and
economic power into the hands of two different sets of
men. The governing class were to be heavily penalised

by being deprived of everything that most men value; they were to be held in honour, but to have no property, no family. " The union of political power with economic temptation has been the source of innumerable acts of injustice, and has been one of the greatest obstacles to human happiness."

" To put," says the Dean, " the power in the hands of the most unselfish class is at any rate an experiment well worth trying." In Plato's mind the only remedy for selfishness and ignorance is education and therefore pay more attention to nurture than nature.

The medieval ideal was dominated by the three ideas of Hebrew theocracy, Greek philosophy and Roman imperialism. " The two main features of modern history are the development of nationalities and the growth of individual freedom," and so we get to the God-State " which has brought civilisation to the brink of ruin."

" To establish a republic in a country where there are gentry, *you cannot succeed unless you kill them all*," said Machiavelli, indicating the policy followed by the Bolsheviks of our own age.

It is useful to be reminded that Nationalism is a wholly nineteenth-century product and has been condemned by Lord Acton as a theory " more absurd and more criminal than that of Socialism." The Dean thinks that there is a possibility that we are on the threshold of an epoch " in which other associations, either wider than the nation, like the Catholic Church, or Labour, or narrower than the nation, like the groups which it is proposed to form into trade guilds, may claim and receive the same immoral and unquestioning devotion which when given to the State has brought such hideous calamities upon the world." . . . " To worship the State," he says in another place, " is to worship a demon who has not even the redeeming quality of being intelligent."

" The great issue before the world is not between monarchy and democracy, but between nationalism and internationalism. . . . The question before the

world is whether the principle of nationality has been
so discredited by the war that it is going to be abandoned
and a universal civil war of classes put in its place. . . .
The God-State has gone with the Kaiser into banish-
ment : the question is whether we are to have States at
all in future. . . . I am not favourably impressed with
internationalism as I have met with it. . . . The two
international organisations which confront each other
are ultramontane Catholicism . . . and international
Socialism, which is frankly based on a predatory class
war."

"If I were asked," he says at the end of these
lectures, " to state in one word the cause of the failure
of our civilisation, I should answer 'Secularism.'
There must surely be some very deep ground for the
universal discontent and malaise which have overtaken
Western civilisation. There is but little happiness
and content anywhere, and the reason is that we have
lost faith in the values which should be the motive
force of social life. Capitalism is in danger, not so
much from the envious attacks of the unpropertied as
from the decay of that Puritan asceticism which was
its creator. . . . The working man . . . has too often
no pride and no conscience in his work. He works in
the spirit of a slave, grudgingly and bitterly, and then
ascribes his unhappiness to the conditions of his
employment. He is becoming well educated : but he
twists everything round, even religion, to his alleged
economic grievances. . . . Industrialism drags on,
because the alternative is starvation. . . . Civilisation
presents the spectacle of a mighty tree which is dying
at the roots."

It is not surprising in the light of this to find the Dean
more than sceptical about the idea of progress.

"The Greeks prided themselves on being the degenerate descendants of gods, we on being the very
creditable descendants of monkeys . . . the Church
has never encouraged the belief that this world is
steadily improving . . . the survival of the fittest
does not mean that the most virtuous, or the most

useful, or the most beautiful, or even the most complex, survive . . . of progress . . . there cannot be a trace. Nor can there be any doubt about the fate of our own planet. Man and all his achievements will one day be obliterated like a child's sand castle when the next tide comes in."

" The living dreadnoughts of the Saurian age have left us their bones, but no progeny. But the microbes, one of which had the honour of killing Alexander the Great at the age of thirty-two, and so changing the whole course of history, survive and flourish. . . . Civilisation is a disease which is almost invariably fatal, unless its course is checked in time. The Hindus and Chinese, after advancing to a certain point, were content to mark time : and they survive. But the Greeks and Romans are gone : and aristocracies everywhere die out. Do we not see to-day the complex organisation of the ecclesiastic and college don succumbing before the simple squeezing and sucking apparatus of the profiteers and trade unionist ? If so-called civilised nations show any protracted vitality, it is because they are only civilised at the top. Ancient civilisations were destroyed by imported barbarians ; we breed our own. It is also an unproved assumption that the domination of the planet by our own species is a desirable thing, which must give satisfaction to its Creator. We have devastated the loveliness of the world : we have exterminated several species more beautiful and less vicious than ourselves . . . if it is progress to turn the fields and woods of Essex into East and West Ham, we may be thankful that progress is a sporadic and transient phenomenon in history. . . . There has been no physical progress in our species for many thousands of years. . . . Mentally . . . the men of the Old Stone Age . . . had as large brains as ours." Progressive degeneration the Dean does see.

" The European talks of progress," said Disraeli, " because by the aid of a few scientific discoveries he has established a society which has mistaken comfort for civilisation."

"We must cut down our hopes for our nation," concludes the Dean, "for Europe, and for humanity at large, to a very modest and humble aspiration. We have no millenniums to look forward to; but neither need we fear any protracted or widespread retrogression."

In his lecture on "The Victorian Age" the Dean describes it as the latter half of the most wonderful century in human history. Remarkable for scientific advance it was (in the Dean's eyes) equally remarkable for magnificent types of faces, for the production of literature which "flourishes best when it is half a trade and half an art." "I have no doubt that the Elizabethan and the Victorian ages will appear to the historian of the near future as the twin peaks in which English civilisation culminated."

He joins Ruskin in his abuse of machinery, the influence of which is bad "because it destroys variety and individuality." He quotes Dr Freeman's indictment with approval that it destroys industry, degrades and vulgarises man, "endows the inferior man with political power which he employs to the common disadvantage . . . and by its reactions on the activities of war constitutes an agent for the wholesale physical destruction of man and his works—the extinction of human culture."

The remedy? The elimination of the unfit . . . sterilisation . . . voluntary segregation of the fit. Standardised commodities have standardised our minds: we are the slaves of our machines. The dilemma of civilisation is that civilised man in enslaving the forces of Nature has become less of a man than he was before.

" Our working classes need more than ever some other guidance than that of the politician and journalist: neither of these will lead them to see beyond the horizon of class interest, or enable them to look upon the nation as an ever-changing organisation," says Professor Karl Pearson. To-day money is poured out on the education of those who show themselves unfit to be educated. The State takes upon itself the burden of providing for the defectives that are born : it ought to have right to insist that the number of these shall not be " wantonly increased." Eugenics, eugenics, eugenics is the Dean's cry.

Outspoken Essays are clarion notes to the young. The intelligent youth of to-day, sick of shams, may well find in this fearless philosopher not so much a solution of his difficulties as a sane facing of them. The Dean never burkes an issue, never runs away. Truth, Goodness, Beauty . . . there yet live these three absolute values of the kingdom of the State Invisible. Pride, sensuality and selfishness are the three enemies that cut the soul off from its true and happy life in the eternal world. Surely that is clear-cut enough. That is the Dean's creed, and it is one which does not insult our intelligence.

Not until we search for the Kingdom of God for its own sake are we likely to find it : not until we search for a right government on earth in an equally disinterested manner are we likely to secure terrestrial happiness. The Dean is an optimist. He really believes that there are disinterested people.

For those who want their thinking done for them in even simpler language I would recommend Harold Begbie's (I suppose " A Gentleman with a Duster " *is* Harold Begbie) *Seven Ages*, in which he gives an epitome of the philosophy of Socrates, Aristotle, Christ, Augustine, Erasmus, Cromwell and John Wesley as a counterblast to the loose materialism of our own day. *Seven Ages* and *Outspoken Essays* are complementary.

II

MIDDLETON MURRY

COUNTRIES OF THE MIND are essays of maturity. Middleton Murry has played himself in and got set early in the game. He at any rate is not going to get out for a " blob." He is, although he deals in the main with the spirit of disillusion, a cheerful critic. He realises that criticism for money entails mutilation of opinions, theories and ideals, but " compulsion," he says, " has produced far more good literary work of every kind than the unembarrassed pursuit of an artistic ideal has ever done." Certainly if these subjects were forced on him we can only express delight at the result. As four of them celebrate centenaries it is likely. A good habit, these hundredth birthdays and deathdays.

He states his own position as a critic in a critical credo at the end of the book : " ' The stability of truth ' —Johnson's phrase—is what the critic stands or falls by, including his skill in communicating his truth. He obeys certain laws. He has to convey the whole effect of the work he is criticising, and for this purpose to examine a perfectly characteristic passage." (How well he has himself succeeded in obeying his laws is seen in his essay on Doughty.)

Incidentally a careful reading of the critic ought, I am sure, to be a reliable guide to the critic's own personality, just as he reveals the personalities of others.

At any rate I feel that I know Middleton Murry himself after reading his interpretations of the spirits of other men. In the first place, he has penetrated the perfect happiness of human love. You have only to see the cleverness with which he presents the gracious silence of the exquisitely delicate Virgilia, "Shake-speare's neglected heroine," and the equal cleverness with which he shows that Shakespeare's attitude to love can only be understood when we measure the sonnets by the plays and not the plays by the sonnets, as Frank Harris does, to realise that.

So far as love of women is concerned, Murry is on the side of the angels. Then there is the academic side of him. Nobody has interpreted Robert Burton so well as Murry interprets him. It is an entirely new picture, this of a scholar hankering after another life, this fine, magnanimous spirit chafing at the waste not only of his own life, but of all that humanity and education might accomplish. He is a disappointed idealist, professing a cynicism which he does not in his heart of hearts really believe. He rages against his own futility: eager to see the wonders of the world, he dares only to undertake journeys at second hand, in an age more adventurous than any. "He played for safety"—the most appalling epitaph, surely, that could be inscribed on any man's tombstone. His tragedy is the greater in so far as his mind is a practical and sane one. He is against terrorism in religion, against the torture of convention. Hopelessly at odds with the world, he retires into his hermitage and it is not easy to disintegrate the real man, "wise, tender, romantic, sensitive and charitable," that sits in the centre of his self-imposed labyrinth.

So far Murry. It is exquisite criticism, true, novel, enlightening and honest. This is that interpretation of the spirit that we look for too often in vain in criticism. He penetrates to the heart of William Collins in a phrase: "He was prevented from feeling by the impatience of his intense desire to feel." Once only, in the *Ode to Evening*, did he receive a deep emotion which he could recollect in tranquillity with perfect success. Collins may be grouped with Flaubert as exhibiting the dangers that pursue the man haunted by a sense of style. It is inevitable that Murry should write about John Clare. The rediscovery of this

singer who adored the English country-side much as
W. H. Davies adores it is significant.   This is an age
in which sensitive men have had to keep their eyes
fixed lovingly on Nature to escape the terrors of
the industrial revolution, the war, the end of all
faith. . . . There are six lines of Clare which sum
many a modern's longing :

" I long for scenes where man has never trod ;
  A place where woman never smiled nor wept ;
  There to abide with my Creator, God,
  And sleep as I in childhood sweetly slept ;
  Untroubling and untroubled where I lie :
  The grass below—above the vaulted sky."

There is the same longing to escape in de la Mare,
the realisation that the " dream we live by is more real
than the reality we ignore."   Murry shows us a de la
Mare running to Arabia, Tartary, Alulvan, Thule, from
this " life haunted by death, beauty by decay."

" To recognise that a dream is a dream, yet to refuse
to put it away, this is the vital act of comprehension
which animates the enduring part of the poetry of
the present age."   Though we throw away all else,
we may still believe in beauty . . . beauty that is
transient . . . but perhaps all the more precious for
that.

" Look thy last on all things lovely every hour"—
a wonderful motto for life.

To see Murry at his best turn to his treatment of
Doughty. He builds up with precision and economy
of phrase a splendid picture of the indomitable courage
of the man who wandered unfriended for two years
among nomad tribesmen, hammering out a language
fit to interpret the harshness of Arabia.   For ten years
Doughty forged his material with a " hard ascetic
purity" that stands out in every line of his book,
obeying his own laws.   Murry selects a long passage
for quotation which has only to be read aloud to any
imaginative person to alter his whole outlook on life.

Well may Murry be led to the tongue-tied whisper: "Arabia Deserta is incomparable." One can only hand on the phrase.

Murry dwells rather at length on the metallic solidity, the absolute immobility of Baudelaire's verse. Detesting the world, his way of escape lay on the sea. In revolt like the rest of us against "industrial progress," he was miserably affected by a strange paralysis of the will. Murry puts him among the great poets of a decadence, certainly not himself a decadent. He is like Amiel, Dostoievsky, Nietzsche, Hardy and Stendhal, God-seekers or Stoics . . . out to discover a morality.

"The strength of a truly great writer," says Murry, "endures either because he builds upon the foundations of a morality which he accepts, or because he is animated by the intense desire to discover one. The greatest writers [he is quoting Tchehov] have always had axes to grind." Murry is kind to Baudelaire, unkind to Flaubert, who "was a good deal of a Philistine," who showed no traces of development, who was deficient in the range of his sensibility and the robustness of his creative imagination, whose work never ceased to smell of the lamp, who came as near to genius as a man can by taking pains, but is still one of the minor heroes of letters. Luckily for himself Murry admits that Flaubert's correspondence shows him as one of the most lovable of writers. It is as well, for the recent publication of the George Sand–Gustave Flaubert Letters in English has made a great number of people who accepted Flaubert as a master of style and nothing else revise their opinion of the man's personality.

Countries of the Mind ends with an estimate of Stendhal which should be read in conjunction with Lytton Strachey's *Henri Beyle*, written six years earlier. Murry of course stresses the paradox in the man who recalled Racine, yet was so much the idolater of Shakespeare, whose style suggested the influence of Voltaire, whereas the real influence was Rousseau.

Murry sees in Stendhal a tragic realist, a naïve

amateurishness, a miniature, desiccated Shakespeare. "Beyle is," he says, "perhaps, the smallest of great men ; but he is also one of the most compact." You have only, I say, to compare Murry's estimate of Stendhal with that of Lytton Strachey to realise the fundamental difference between the critic who is also a graphic historian and the critic who is fundamentally literary. Murry is mathematical in his criticisms ; he is always classifying into schools—Flaubert, greatest of minors, Stendhal, least of the great. Is it better to be head of the Lower VIth, or bottom of the Upper VIth ? Murry is a most conscientious craftsman, never sacrificing truth to the *mot juste* : he is in love with goodness. He has very little of the historian, very much of the moralist, and some of the technician in his criticism. He avoids the heavy pontifical utterances adopted by the leaders of successful coteries, just as much as he avoids the cheap platitudinising of the critic who merely claps his authors on the back with a " jolly good, old man, jolly good ! "

III

WALTER RALEIGH

I WAS walking up the "High" from the Examination schools on a hot day in June 1907 when I saw looming out of the middle distance the thin, tall, shaking figure of the Professor of English Literature. I had met him some two or three times at dinner. He was an enthusiastic follower of all University sport and had welcomed me as a runner. On this occasion he bore down on me. There was no way of escape.

"Why so lugubrious?" was his greeting.

"The lists," I answered. "I've just come from Schools. I only got a 'Third' in 'Mods.'" I was woefully dejected.

He laughed. "You athletes have more important things than work to think about."

"I don't feel like going on thinking mathematically," I said.

"You want a complete change of school," he said. "Give Mathematics a rest."

"And take 'Greats' or History? I know none."

"Why not English?"

It was my turn to laugh.

"There can be few undergraduates who have read as little as I have," I replied.

"Great oarsmen frequently come from non-rowing schools," he said. "Come up and lunch with me at Ferry Hinksey to-morrow and I will give you a list of books to read during the 'Long.'"

I was astonished.

"Do you really mean that I may tackle a Final Honour school without any grounding?" I asked.

"I mean that you are the sort of zealot we want to

166

go out later into the world as missionary. There are only a dozen or so men who take English. If you put the same enthusiasm into Literature as you put into running you needn't fear about the result. Classes aren't everything. I want you to enjoy life."

For two years under the direct tutelage of Walter Raleigh I enjoyed life. For two years I attended lectures which were as inspired as my Mathematical lectures had been uninspired. In 1909 I took another "Third," but this time I was not dejected. Raleigh had sown in me the seeds of a life passion. And now Raleigh is dead. It is impossible to visualise an Oxford without him. His personality dominated the University. He stood for all that one would wish to be. He was the least of a pedant, the least of a bookish man, among all the dons I met.[1] As a witty conversationalist he outshone them all. As a critic he is known to the outside world as the author of a brilliant study of Milton, Wordsworth, Shakespeare, Stevenson and Doctor Johnson, the author of a youthful pyrotechnic display on *Style*, and a useful handbook on the history of the Novel.

It is perhaps just possible to convey some slight impression of the sort of man he was from an examination of his criticism.

For, as he himself says in *Milton* : " In this association with great spirits which we call reading we receive but what we give, and take away only what we are fit to carry . . . in the end it is the critic, not the author, who is judged."

Even in his little essay on *Style*, which he himself regarded as stilted and juvenile, there are gleams of the man, traces of his scorn of convention and the safeguards of artificiality, his hatred of " those idle, jocular classes to whom all art is a bugbear and a puzzle," his loathing of the " inanity " that " dogs the footsteps of the classic tradition." We should expect a descendant of the great Sir Walter, who, incidentally, resembled him in feature as he did in his love of

---

[1] Surely *Laughter From a Cloud* is evidence of that.

romantic adventure, to chastise the lovers of the immutable. " This is the error of the classical creed," he says, " to imagine that in a fleeting world, where the quickest eye can never see the same thing twice . . . language alone should be capable of fixity and finality . . . words must change to live, and a word once fixed becomes useless for the purposes of art."

He is merciless in his treatment of " the stubborn reluctance of writers . . . to repeat a word or phrase." One remembers in this connection Sir Arthur Quiller-Couch's similar attitude : " In literature as in life he makes himself felt who not only calls a spade a spade, but has the pluck to double spades and re-double."

Raleigh says : " A kind of interdict . . . lies on a once used word . . . if he be called on to marshal his ideas on the question whether oysters breed typhoid, he will acquit himself voluminously, with only one allusion (it is a point of pride) to the oyster by name. . . . Question, hypothesis, lamentation and platitude dance their allotted round and fill the ordained space, while Ignorance masquerades in the garb of criticism, and Folly proffers her ancient epilogue of chastened hope. When all is said, nothing is said."

He has little that is good to say of the public taste. " The British public is not seen at its best when it is enjoying a holiday in a foreign country, nor when it is making excursions into the realm of imaginative literature. . . . Many readers bring the worst of themselves to a novel : they want lazy relaxation, or support for their nonsense, or escape from their creditors, or a free field for emotions that they dare not indulge in life."

Consequently we are made to realise that insincerity is the deepest vice; " All self-expression is a challenge thrown down to the world, to be taken up by whoso will."

This is the kind of forthright sentence that rings as " true Raleigh " even in his salad days : " Knowledge has two uses ; it may be frankly communicated for the benefit of others, or it may minister matter to thought."

And again this: "To keep language in immediate touch with reality, to lade it with action and passion, to utter it hot from the heart of determination, is to exhibit it in the plenitude of power." And, to make an end, this: "Plagiarism is a crime only where writing is a trade . . . the words were once Shakespeare's; if only you can feel them as he did, they are yours now no less than his. The best quotations, the best translations, the best thefts, are all equally new and original works."

It is in the concluding paragraph of this by no means unilluminating essay that we get a foretaste of what Raleigh's mission in life is to be. "The main business of criticism, after all," he says, "is not to legislate, nor to classify, but to raise the dead."

It is our business now to see how far he was successful in raising the dead Shakespeare, Milton and Wordsworth.

It is easy enough to realise the attraction that Shakespeare would have for a man who possessed so many points in common with him. It is less easy to realise why he chose to exert his tremendous power on two poets in some respects alien to him.

Again, like Sir Arthur Quiller-Couch, Sir Walter Raleigh was most at home with the earthy.

"I return to knock in at the old tavern with the cosy red blinds," says "Q" at the end of his lecture on the seventeenth-century poets, "where I may meet Don Quixote, Sancho Panza, Douglas and Percy, Mr Pickwick and Sam Weller, Romeo and the Three Musketeers—above all, Falstaff, with Mistress Quickly to serve me. I want the personal—Shakespeare, Johnson, Goldsmith, Lamb, among men: of women I need to worship no Saint Teresa, but Miranda the maid, Imogen the wife."

Not thus baldly and explicitly does Sir Walter Raleigh give himself away.

"The indispensable preliminary," says Sir Walter, "for judging and enjoying Shakespeare is not knowledge of his history, not even knowledge of his works, but knowledge of his theme, a wide acquaintance with

human life and human passion as they are reflected in
a sensitive and independent mind." I have met no
man who possessed this indispensable preliminary in
so marked a degree as Sir Walter. "This is," he says
in another place, "indeed the everlasting difficulty of
Shakespeare criticism, that the critics are so much
more moral than Shakespeare himself, and so much
less experienced." Raleigh's talent, like Shakespeare's,
"consisted in sympathy with human nature in all its
shapes, degrees, depressions and elevations."

Shakespeare condemns no one, high or low: he
certainly pays no homage to the ascetic ideal, and one
cannot imagine either Shakespeare or Raleigh voluntarily "chanting faint hymns to the cold fruitless
moon."

Just as Raleigh sweeps away any idea of there being
a moral attached to the tragedies, so he sweeps aside
the antiquaries and the commentators. To get near
to the heart of Shakespeare he recommends (following
Dr Johnson's advice) the rapid, alert reading of the
plays. The picture that he draws of the man Shakespeare is that of a seeker after happiness, lovable and
humble. "Children, we feel sure, did not stop their
talk when he came near them, but continued, in the
happy assurance that it was only Master Shakespeare.
The tradition of geniality clings to his name like a faded
perfume. Everyone was more himself for being in
the company of Shakespeare." We get an impression
of a lover of clear, decisive action.

"I am convinced more and more," wrote Keats,
"every day, that fine writing is next to fine doing,
the top thing in the world." How cordially would
Shakespeare have agreed with that. It follows from
this that the finest things of all have never been
written: they have been done; instead of thoughts
they have been actions . . . and the finest things
said in Elizabethan days were nearly not said at all
. . . it was the merest chance that they were not
translated into deeds. The greatest poem that Sir
Philip Sidney wrote was his life, the *magnum opus* of

Sir Thomas More was his life, but Shakespeare is kept back among the writers because of the wide, restless, curious searchings of his intelligence and imagination. " The central drama of his mind is the tragedy of the life of imagination." To see this mind at work is the aim of the critic. And the first thing which strikes us is his mastery over language—his profound knowledge of the human heart. How he acquired these two fundamental gifts is made clear in this passage : " Shakespeare lived in an age of glitter and pageantry, of squalor and wickedness, of the lust of the eye and the pride of life—an age of prodigality, adventure, bravery and excess. . . . The plays give abundant evidence of his knowledge of the town. Tavern-life counted for much in that day . . . he does not fear to expose the purest of his heroines to the breath of this (darker side of the life of the town) infection . . . in nothing is he more himself than in the little care that he takes to provide shelter for the most delicate characters of English fiction." And yet—" the simple pieties of life were at all times dearest to him." " His ultimate sympathies are with human frailty, human simplicity, human unreason," whether in the books which he ransacked for stories, or in the men he met. Ever and always he was at the mercy of beauty. " What the love of power was to Marlowe, the love of beauty was to him."

It was this love of beauty which gave to the Sonnets their magic music and their intensity of feeling. Raleigh is in no doubt whatever about the personal nature of these Sonnets. " All who love poetry love it because in poetry the profoundest interests of life are spoken of directly, nakedly and sincerely . . . poetry is a touchstone for insincerity : if anyone does not feel that which he desires to express, he may make a passable oration ; he will never make a great poem."

In his plays we are shown the unfailing care that Shakespeare bestowed on the externals, the importance of his opening scenes, the trouble he took to get hold always of a dramatic story, the limitations of his frame, the amazing way in which Shakespeare followed his characters "into those dim recesses of personality where the hunted soul stands at bay, and proclaims itself, naked as it is, for a greater thing than law or opinion," his discovery of each point of Christian morality through anguish of thought and sympathy, so that his " words are a revelation, and the gospel is born anew." Most of all are we shown the pure spirit of delight that accompanies the great figures of his comedy, men cast in the Falstaff mould . . . for it is with the Falstaffs that Shakespeare and Raleigh find themselves most at ease.

It is, as I said, curious to find one whose sympathies lay with the frequenters of taverns tackling Milton and Wordsworth. In fact Sir Walter allows at once that Milton's "lack of humour has alienated the interest of thousands. . . . Almost all men are less humorous than Shakespeare : but most men are more humorous than Milton." But almost at once we are drawn into the net to realise that Milton is big enough to be able to do without this human salt. The rare nobility and simplicity of this passionate, egotistical politician poet are enough. Love was not his, his guiding star was not Christianity, he knew human nature only in the gross, but he was a patriot and a warrior, with a vocabulary so rich, a melody so subtle, a scheme so audacious, a wealth of imagery so vast, and a scholarship so profound, that our reverence and admiration know no bounds.

Unlike his Adam and Eve, we are only too glad to escape from an Eden in which there are " no villages and farms, no smell of hay, no sheaves of corn, no cottages, no roads, and no trace of . . . the thin blue scarf of smoke rising from a wayside encampment . . . we cannot settle down in the midst of this ' enormous bliss ' ; we wander through the place, open-mouthed with wonder, like country visitors admiring the Crown jewels, and then—we long to be at home. . . . The introduction, in *Paradise Lost*, of a real human child . . . would be like the bringing of a spark of fire into a powder magazine. None of these edifying speeches could be made in the presence of such an auditor, or such a critic. The whole system would be blown into fragments."

So with Milton's God: "Milton, in short, has hardened the heart of the God that hardened Pharaoh's heart, and has narrowed his love and his power."

So with Milton's Satan: "We are left to conceive of Satan as of a lover of beauty reluctantly compelled to shatter it in the pursuit of his high political aims."

"Of our two grandparents Eve is the better drawn and the more human. Milton did not intend that it should be so, but he could not help it. . . . Eve is generous and loving . . . it is easy to understand how tired Eve might well become . . . of Adam's carefully maintained superiority." The reason for the successful delineation of Eve is that Milton was "extraordinarily susceptible to the attractions of feminine beauty and grace."

Not only was Milton original in the matter of his poem: he was original in its form. He learned his blank verse from the dramatists; "he tightened its joints, stiffened its texture, and one by one gave up almost all the licences that the dramatists had used . . . he continually varies the stresses in the line, their number, their weight, and their incidence . . . his chief study . . . is to vary the word in relation to the foot, and the sentence in relation to the line. . . . He chooses his every word. You cannot guess the adjective from the substantive, nor the end of the phrase from its beginning . . . it is this quality of Milton's verse that makes the exercise of reading it aloud a delight and a trial. Every word is of value . . . to drop one out, or to slur it over, is to take a stone from one arch . . . the packed line introduced by Milton is of a greater density and conciseness than anything to be found in English literature before it." And yet the success of *Paradise Lost* was not only immediate and startling; it was permanent.

"Milton," concludes Raleigh, "built an altar in the

name of the Lord, and he made a great trench about
the altar, and he put the wood in order, and loaded
the altar with rich exotic offerings, cassia and nard,
odorous gums and balm, and fruit burnished with
golden rind.   But the fire from Heaven descended on
the hastily piled altars of the sons of Belial, and left
Milton's gorgeous altar cold. . . . I have tried to
understand Milton ; and have already praised him as
well as I know how, with no stinted admiration, I trust,
and certainly with no merely superstitious reverence."

But—we feel—Raleigh is glad to escape from the
Garden of Eden to Eastcheap . . . and again it is the
critic, not the author, who is judged.

And so lastly we come to his treatment of Wordsworth.   Here we are taken by the hand and adjured
to read Wordsworth's poetry " as he would have
wished it to be read, and to find in it what he attempted
to express. . . . All poetry begins from the beginning.
. . . Criticism must do the same : it must follow the
poet, if he gives any token of being worth the following, step by step, re-creating his experiences, hanging
on his words . . . believing in him and living with
him."   " The history of his first thirty years is all that
need be studied " . . . " The Prelude " enough by
way of biography.   " While he spoke only of what
he saw, his speech was like the speech of one in a
dream, musical, rapt, solemn, uncouth sometimes and
stammering, but always intense, convinced, and
absorbed in the novelty and wonder of his vision."
Raleigh would always have us bear in mind the part
that memory plays in Wordsworth's mind.   " Poetry,"
according to his famous definition, "takes its origin
in emotion recollected in tranquillity ; the emotion is
contemplated till . . . the tranquillity gradually disappears, and an emotion . . . is gradually produced."

" A large part," says Sir Walter, " of his poetry is
taken up with these resuscitated feelings—all memories,
then, had either an inherent or a potential value for
Wordsworth ; and ' The Prelude ' is one long exercise
of memory . . . a poet . . . is to be had for the

making; and the secret of the making, if ever it should be divined, would be found . . . exactly at that point where the free and vigorous life of sense and thought in any young creature is . . . arrested, surprised, checked, challenged and turned in and back upon itself. Then for the first time the soul makes an inventory of its wealth, and discovers that it has great possessions."

"It is not easy," says the critic later, "to match this case of a great poet who pays scant respect to the formal aspects of his craft, and who distrusts his own boyhood because it delighted in melody and choice diction and gorgeous phrasing. Wordsworth . . . was a pure spiritualist in poetry and disliked poetic ritual."

We are shown the violent, impulsive and passionate disposition of the poet in his youth, his avid delight in the French Revolution, his refuge in the political philosophy of Godwin, the insecurity of that refuge and the slow process by which he ultimately won his way out to poetry. It was his sister who restored to him the life of the senses as an escape from "the dark tyranny of a life of abstract thought." Hereafter he is all mystic, distrustful of all rational processes. "His unflinching determination to see things as they are, without ornament and without sophistication, produced the great poems," poems which, as he himself said, "are to be considered as experiments," experiments, as everyone knows, as much in form as in matter. It is worth noting, however, that so far as his poetic diction goes "he hardly ever observes his own rules, and the poems in which he most nearly observes them are often among his best. . . . While passion holds him, while he is moved or exalted, his language keeps its naked intensity."

This same naked intensity can be seen in his beliefs. "The happiness that is to be pitied is blind happiness, which nourishes itself on its own false fancies. The happiness that is to be coveted is the happiness of fearless vision, 'and frequent sights of what is to be borne.' And it is by the daylight of truth, not by 'the light that never was on sea or land,' that the poet desires to look upon the things of earth. He is strong enough to bear it, and can face a lifelong grief without flinching. . . . The greatness of Wordsworth's best work derives from this calm and almost terrible strength. . . . The drama that he tried to transfer to the poets' small stage was played from beginning to end in silence ; it rested with him to translate it into words, and hence, in his view, poetry, the poetry of words and metre, was always a secondary thing.''

Over and over again Sir Walter calls on us to notice how large a part happiness plays in Wordsworth's life. ''His heart leaps up when he beholds a rainbow in the sky. The daffodils, dancing in the breeze, fill him with the spirit of gaiety, and live in his mind and heart, a joyful memory . . . it is the mark of all mystics that they make the intellect feed the emotions, not the emotions the intellect . . . his joy in trivial things seemed a trivial joy, which it was not.''

Happiness is one quality on which the critic insists, another is martial ardour. '' Had [Wordsworth] followed his early leanings and taken the army for his calling, he would have been an incomparable soldier.''

Again, we are warned against looking for a second sense in Wordsworth. '' This poet is a true visionary, and deals not in allegories or dreams. . . . Vision is his greatest gift.'' And so he makes an end in these words :

'' Something of the freshness of emotion that went to the first making of the poem, something of the excitement, the glee, the passion, must be shared by the intending critic, if he is to understand what the poet meant, he must feel as the poet felt. In this attempt to follow Wordsworth we have watched him making his way along the precipitous edge which is the boundary of thought. We have seen him, in his effort to grapple with the mystery of the common things of life, trying all new ways—breaking with literary tradition, with social usage, with language itself, lest they should encumber his further progress.

He attained to a clearer and truer view of life than is granted to most poets, and he paid the price of this great happiness in a great and incurable solitude of spirit . . . he pressed onward to a point where speech fails and drops into silence, where thought is baffled, and turns back upon its own footsteps. But it is a good discipline to follow that intense and fervid spirit, as far as may be, to the heights that denied him access. . . . Sanity holds hard by the fact, and knows that to turn away from it is to play the recreant. Here was a poet who faced the fact, and against whom the fact did not prevail. To know him is to learn courage ; to walk with him is to feel the visitings of a larger, purer air, and the peace of an unfathomable sky."

In the light of these extracts it is perhaps easier to see why a critic who had so much of all-pervading humanity and toleration and kindliness and humour of Shakespeare should have devoted so much of his time to such different men as Milton and Wordsworth. Professor Sir Walter Raleigh was no ascetic, but in his criticism of these austere and noble spirits he divulges his own nobility. Milton and Wordsworth were happy warriors, and so was Walter Raleigh. But to see Raleigh most at home we must read his *Six Essays on Johnson*, which is in many ways a revolutionary book. His estimate of Boswell is wise: " His character was destitute of all the vices, and all the virtues, which are popularly, and in the main rightly, attributed to the Scottish people . . . he had simplicity, candour, fervour, a warmly affectionate nature, a quick intelligence, and a passion for telling all that he knew. These are qualities which make for good literature."

Having appraised the work of Boswell, Raleigh puts in a plea for Johnson the writer. He even dares to call *The Rambler* " that splendid repository of wisdom and truth." We need reminding that Johnson is a writer, that he cared passionately for truth and nothing for novelty. " Among all his discourses on human life he utters hardly a single precept which had not been brought home to him by living experience."

M

What he has to say of poverty merits a hearing when we realise that he was miserably poor for thirty years. He was tortured by bouts of indolence, and on that subject too he moves us by his sincerity. He is at his best on the graver topics, and yet on the lighter he is more subtle, curious and profound than Addison. This on Bashfulness for instance :

"No man is much regarded by the rest of the world . . . while we see multitudes passing before us, of whom, perhaps, not one appears to deserve our notice, or excite our sympathy, we should remember that we likewise are lost in the throng."

Raleigh draws attention to the unexpectedness of Johnson's repartee, as in the touch of surprise that we get in his comparison of a ship to a gaol. He emphasises Johnson's dislike of sentiment, gesticulation and demonstrative emotion, his fever of agitation in reading, his writing in the white heat of imagination, his growing to power culminating with *The Lives of the Poets*, written when he was nearly seventy, "a book of wisdom and experience, a treatise on the conduct of life, a commentary on human destiny."

Raleigh finds the judgments contained therein, "on the whole, wonderfully fair." But in the end of all he cannot resist the inevitable conclusion that Johnson is greater than his works. "He thought of himself as a man, not an author : and of literature as a means, not as an end in itself."

"Books," said Dr Johnson, "without the knowledge of life are useless ; for what should books teach but the art of living ? "

"Johnson was an author almost by accident : it is the man who is dear to us, the man with all his dogmatic prejudices, his stoical courage, his profound melancholy, his hatred of sentimental palliatives, his fits of narrowness, his tenderness to all human frailty. If he has had less reputation than he deserves as a writer it is because he has overshadowed his own fame."

In the essay on *Johnson without Boswell* we get an admirable corrective to many superstitions. We

have, for instance, taken it for granted that Johnson
was always in fear of death. Raleigh neatly corrects
this: "It was not death that he feared: it was
Boswell on death . . . grim fancies on death were
natural to him: tittle-tattle about it he could not
bear." Boswell had no more thought deeply about
death than Mrs Thrale had thought about poverty;
consequently Dr Johnson rebukes them both fiercely
when they touch on these topics.

Then there is the Macaulay superstition, the grotesque
caricature of the man " tearing his meat like a tiger,
and swallowing his tea in oceans." Yet . . .

"I look upon myself," said the Doctor to Boswell,
" as a very polite man"; and to Mrs Thrale: " You
may observe that I am well-bred to a degree of needless
scrupulosity." We get too from Boswell a distorted
view of Johnson's dislike of the Scots. " Johnson's
invectives against Scotland," said Bishop Percy, " were
more in pleasantry and sport than real or malignant."
It was Dr Johnson who said: " There are more gentlemen
in Scotland than there are shoes " . . . " a people,"
comments Raleigh, " that is poor and proud could
deserve no finer compliment."

There are Mrs Thrale's memories of the Doctor at
Streatham joining in the children's games, riding to
hounds for fifty miles without being tired or amused.
"I have now learned," he said, " by hunting, to
perceive that it is no diversion at all, nor ever takes
a man out of himself for a moment: the dogs have
less sagacity than I could have prevailed on myself
to suppose; and the gentlemen often call to me
not to ride over them. It is very strange, and very
melancholy, that the paucity of human pleasures
should persuade us ever to call hunting one of them."

It was Fanny Burney who said: " Dr Johnson has
more fun, and comical humour, and love of nonsense
about him, than almost anybody I ever saw."

Boswell stresses too much his solemn side.

All the other biographers make a point of his playfulness, and his delightful fancy of the kind seen in his

description of the habit of bustle as " getting on horse-back in a ship."

Boswell only knew Johnson in his period of established pre-eminence: he didn't see him as Mrs Thrale saw him, " in the everyday round of domestic life "; as Goldsmith saw him, as an equal and a brother; as Fanny Burney saw him, playful, gentle, nonsensical; as Savage knew him, young and proud. Boswell, says Raleigh, has distanced the others not because he was a fool, as Macaulay thinks, " but because he loved Johnson better than they did."

There is an excellent attempt to overthrow Macaulay's statement that " it would be difficult to name a more slovenly, a more worthless, edition of any great classic " than Johnson's edition of Shake-speare, a statement which, says Raleigh, has nothing but emphasis to commend it.

" Johnson's work on Shakespeare," says Raleigh, " has not been superseded. He has been neglected and depreciated ever since the nineteenth century brought in the new æsthetic and philosophical criticism."

Raleigh taunts the romantic critics with insincerity : " Those who approach the study of Shakespeare under the sober and vigorous guidance of Johnson will meet with fewer exciting adventures, but they will not see less of the subject."

But in his own time he created enemies. " The head and front of Johnson's offending was that he wrote and spoke of Shakespeare as one man may fitly speak of another."

" The reader who desires to have Johnson to himself for an hour, with no interpreter, cannot do better than turn to the notes on Shakespeare. They are written informally and fluently : they are packed full of observation and wisdom ; and their only fault is that they are all too few."

Before tackling Johnson's *Lives of the Poets* Raleigh gives us an admirable summary of what had been done in the world of literary biography before Johnson's day. By far the most entertaining of the earlier gossips was John Aubrey, who had a wonderful eye for the picturesque. It is to him we owe that picture of Hobbes at ninety, lying in bed singing to strengthen his lungs; of Suckling depressed through gambling losses, dressed in glorious apparel to exalt his spirits; of Prynne with his pot of ale every three hours and quilt cap three inches over his eyes to serve him as an umbrella, and of the humorous Kettell of Garsington, the Oxford don who cut off undergraduates' hair when it displeased him.

But Johnson's engagement "to write little Lives and little Prefaces, to a little edition of *The English Poets*" was a quite new thing. It was a philosophy of letters. "I wrote them," he said, "in my usual way, dilatorily and hastily, unwilling to work, and working with vigour and haste."

Raleigh finds them in every way admirable, showing Johnson's vigour of judgment as a critic of life and letters at its zenith. "To get rid of the affectations, conventions and extravagances of literature: to make it speak to the heart on themes of universal human interest: to wed poetry with life—these were Johnson's aims." The best of the lives is, of course, that on Savage, written thirty-five years earlier. "For delicacy and power it is one of the few great lives in English. It is an apology for the poetic temperament, the truest and most humane apology that has ever been written."

It takes a great man to write of great men nobly. Raleigh wrote of the greatest English men of letters in such a way as to make them seem nobler than ever. It was the stamp of his own greatness.

IV

LYTTON STRACHEY

EVERYONE realises how big a debt all future biographers owe to Lytton Strachey: he has revolutionised the art. This is not to say that he has eclipsed Boswell. What it does mean is (what I have heard no one suggest, but is surely the obvious) that Boswell relied on conversation and letters, which was fitting for an age that excelled in both. We excel in neither. We haven't time for good talk: we haven't time to write a letter. Therefore the modern biographer must start from first principles. He has to make his subject interesting. Lytton Strachey not only made Queen Victoria interesting; he made her live just when she was in danger of becoming a myth. So with Arnold, Manning, Florence Nightingale and Gordon. All the five of them would prefer to see our sloppy, inaccurate, vague, sentimentalised oleographs of them swept into the fire, and these clear-cut portraits (wart and all) put up in their place. The Victorians were eminent all right: it is only we who failed to realise their eminence till Lytton Strachey and Dean Inge came (in widely differing ways) to their rescue.

What is less well known is that Lytton Strachey is infinitely the finest English critic alive of French literature. In *Books and Characters* he proves himself not only a good critic of the French, but an unexpectedly appreciative critic of several English writers. His attempt to arouse a proper interest in Beddoes may well prove to be the most important contribution to contemporary criticism. No intelligent reader could read his essay on *The Last Elizabethan* without going out and buying *Death's Jest Book* to read for himself.

182

For let there be no mistake about it : when Lytton Strachey wrote the following sentence he was speaking the literal truth :—" This extraordinary poet has not only never received the recognition which is his due, but has failed almost entirely to receive any recognition whatever." By the time this book appears let us hope Lytton Strachey's attempt to reinstate Beddoes will have succeeded. Sooner or later this amazing man will come into his own. His greatest misfortune certainly was, as Strachey says, to be born at the beginning of the nineteenth, and not at the end of the sixteenth, century. Among his fellows, Marston and Ford, he stands high ; as marking the transition from Shelley to Browning he stands nowhere.

The queer thing is that he has escaped notice in spite of the fact that his life was extremely eccentric and adventurous. One would have thought that many people would have been driven to read his work if they knew the facts of his life. Maria Edgeworth was his aunt. His father was a famous Clifton doctor, lecturer in Chemistry to Oxford University until he was kicked out at the time of the French Revolution for his political opinions. Sir Humphry Davy, his pupil, said that "he had talents which would have exalted him to the pinnacle of philosophical eminence, if they had been applied with discretion." Like father, like son ; the father was no less independent than the poet son. Doctor Beddoes was in the habit of ordering cows to be conveyed into his patients' bedrooms that they might inhale the animals' breath. . . . T. L. Beddoes was educated at Charterhouse, and there delighted in Elizabethan drama : he wrote a novel after the style of Fielding while still at school. In 1820 he entered Pembroke College, Oxford, and published some narrative verses remarkable only for the fact that they are all about death. *The Bride's Tragedy* appeared in 1822, and contains detached passages of great beauty. The critics liked it. Barry Cornwall praised it in the *Edinburgh*, and became not only friendly with Beddoes, but the means of Beddoes meeting Kelsall, his closest and dearest friend.

The poet went in 1825 to study medicine at the University of Göttingen, and there devoted himself to writing *Death's Jest Book*, and becoming more and more engrossed in medicine. Suddenly he turned from both his passions and threw in his lot with the revolutionaries. He was turned out of Würzburg by the King of Bavaria. He was present in Zurich when six thousand peasants—half unarmed, half armed with dung forks, scythes and poles—came into the town and overturned the government. He is to be seen, a strange, solitary figure, with tangled hair and meerschaum pipe, wandering mysteriously all over Germany and Switzerland—back in England once or twice, growing more and more eccentric. He set out one night to burn Drury Lane Theatre down with a lighted five-pound note. In 1847 he was living in Frankfort with a nineteen-year-old baker called Degen, who was so dear to him that when they quarrelled Beddoes cut his leg with a razor. the leg had to be amputated: Degen went back to him. On the 26th January 1849 he poisoned himself. On his breast was found a pencil note: "My dear Philips, I am food for what I am good for—worms. . . . I ought to have been among other things a good poet."

Among other things, as Strachey makes us realise, he was.

In one of his letters Beddoes says: "Say what you will, I am convinced the man who is to awaken the drama must be a bold, trampling fellow—no creeper into worm holes—no reviver even—however good."

That exactly describes Beddoes—"a bold, trampling fellow," a true Elizabethan, one with Marlowe in his intoxicating delight in language.

> "Let me make
> A staircase of the frightened breasts of men,
> And climb into a lonely happiness."

This is the authentic note :

> " When she moves, you see,
> Like water from a crystal overfilled,
> Fresh beauty tremble out of her and lave
> Her fair sides to the ground."

Again in this " you can almost hear the kisses," as
Strachey says :

> " What shall I do ?   I speak all wrong,
> And lose a soul-full of delicious thought
> By talking.   Hush !   Let's drink each other up
> By silent eyes.   Who lives, but thou and I,
> My heavenly wife ? . . .
> I'll watch thee thus, till I can tell a second
> By thy cheek's change."

And by way of contrast " one can almost hear the
gnashing of the teeth " in this :

> " There lies no grain of sand between
> My loved and my detested !   Wing thee hence,
> Or thou dost stand to-morrow on a cobweb
> Spun o'er the well of clotted Acheron,
> Whose hydrophobic entrails stream with fire !
> And may this intervening earth be snow,
> And my step burn like the mid coal of Aetna,
> Plunging me, through it all, into the core,
> Where in their graves the dead are shut like seeds,
> If I do not——   O, but he is my son ! "

Is this enough by way of extract to send you hustling
along to the Muses Library to buy Beddoes for yourself ?   It certainly ought to be.
When you read two lines of this sort,

> " Death hath his dimples everywhere ;
> Love only on the cheek, which is to me most fair,"

you must realise that you are among the gods.

Songs beginning:

> " Lady, was it fair of thee
>   To seem so passing fair to me ? "

Dying men saying:

>   " I begin to hear
> Strange but sweet sounds, and the loud rocky dashing
> Of waves, where time into Eternity
> Falls over ruined worlds."

Lovers crying:

> " For thy rare sake I could have been a man
> One storey under God."

Dirges so exquisite as that which begins:

> " If thou wilt ease thine heart
>   Of love and all its smart,
>   Then sleep, dear, sleep. . . ."

—these things, I say, ought to be enough to whet your appetite. Beddoes' mind, says Strachey, " was like one of those Gothic cathedrals of which he was so fond— mysterious within, and filled with a light at once richer and less real than the light of day ; on the outside prim and towering . . . embellished, both inside and out, with grinning gargoyles."

" He was a man whom it would have been a rare delight to know." Of course he was : that is true of all his peers, the Elizabethans : he is just one with them in imagination, robustness, coarseness, courage and delicacy.

Books and Characters would outlive every other book of contemporary literary criticism on the merits of the Beddoes essay alone.

But there is more, much more, even about English writers. There is excellent stuff on Blake's mysticism, the conception of which, as Strachey says, was expressed once and for all in the lines:

> " And throughout all Eternity
> I forgive you, you forgive me.
> As our dear Redeemer said:
> ' This the Wine and this the Bread.' "

Blake, says Strachey, was an intellectual drunkard. His poems are more like the works of Heaven than the works of man. They have, besides, the two most obvious characteristics of Nature—" loveliness and power."

There is a splendid chapter on the style of Sir Thomas Browne. " Anyone who is jarred by the expression ' prodigal blazes ' had better immediately shut up Sir Thomas Browne." He quotes with all the joy of a lover of the ornate the phrases, " to subsist in bones and be but pyramidally extant," " sad and sepulchral pitchers which have no joyful voices," " predicament of chimeras " . . . these, he says, " singly deserve whole hours of delicious gustation, whole days of absorbed and exquisite worship. It is pleasant to start out for a long walk with such a splendid phrase upon one's lips as : ' According to the ordainer of order and mystical mathematics of the city of Heaven,' to go for miles and miles with the marvellous syllables still rich upon the inward ear, and to return home with them in triumph."

" Who," he asks, " but the most expert of artists could have produced this perfect sentence : ' Nor will the sweetest delight of gardens afford much comfort in sleep ; wherein the dullness of that sense shakes hands with delectable odours, and though in the bed of Cleopatra, can hardly with any delight raise up the ghost of a rose ' ? . . . One could read him floating down the Euphrates, or past the shores of Arabia, and it would be pleasant to open the *Vulgar Errors* in Constantinople, or get by heart a chapter of the *Christian Morals* between the paws of a sphinx."

If we have to read him in England, Oxford (Strachcy is a Cambridge man) is the place.

There is a merciless chapter on Shakespeare's final period, showing that the critics are all wrong in talking of the dramatist's " serene self-possession " in his last plays. The very contrary is the fact. Half bored to death he may have been, half enchanted by visions of beauty and loveliness, but serene ? no ; benign ? no ; pastoral ? no ; on the heights ? no.

" You taught me language, and my profit on't
    Is, I know how to curse."

It might be Job addressing God.

" The south fog rot him," says Cloten to Imogen. It is worth while rereading the last plays in the light of this criticism. There is, too, a delightful short paper on *The Lives of the Poets*. " Johnson's æsthetic judgments," he says, " are almost invariably subtle, or solid, or bold ; they have always some good quality to recommend them—except one : they are never right. . . . He has managed to be wrong so cleverly that nobody minds. . . . Johnson never inquired what poets were trying to do : he merely aimed at discovering whether what they had done complied with the canons of poetry. . . ."

" But other defects, besides lack of sympathy," he says in another place, " mar *The Lives of the Poets*. . . . Johnson had no ear, and he had no imagination."

Once we allow these things the book becomes more than ever delightful. We go to it to see what Dr Johnson thought—"it is not for the sake of the exercise that we set out, but for the sake of the view."

Having thus refreshed our memory and given us new reasons for going back to old writers at home, he darts across the Channel and puts in a glorious plea for Racine. " To have grown familiar with the voice of Racine, to have realised once and for all its intensity, its beauty and its depth, is to have learnt a new happiness, to have discovered something exquisite and splendid, to have enlarged the glorious boundaries of art." Strachey allows, of course, that " his object was to depict the tragic interaction of a small group of persons at the culminating height of its intensity." There is restraint, clarity, refinement and precision in Racine which we dislike : we hate coldness and uniformity: we want to tingle with eagerness and bravado. " It is as if we had become so accustomed to looking at boxes . . . that the sight of an exquisite minuet produced no effect on us."

" Racine's triumph is precisely this—that he brings about, by what are apparently the simplest means, effects which other poets must strain every nerve to produce."

Racine suppresses detail, dislikes emphasis and imagery. Above all he wrote for the stage—and it is by the effect of hearing and seeing his plays on the stage that he should be judged.

After Racine, Madame du Deffand, whose letters to Horace Walpole created such a sensation. Here we have Strachey in biographical vein, building up an unforgettable picture of a Paris drawing-room in the eighteenth century. " For a fortnight she had been the Regent's mistress ; and a fortnight, in those days, was a considerable time."

Strachey talks at length of the manners and customs of this aristocracy which required in its votaries the absolute submission that reigns in religious orders : personal passion was not allowed : love never : flirtation disguised as love, yes. Politics were tolerated as a game. The scepticism of that generation was the most uncompromising that the world has known —it simply ignored. Profound levity, antipathy to enthusiasm and innate scepticism—these three were the controlling virtues of the age in which Madame du Deffand ruled. At fifty-seven she went totally blind ; she rose at five in the evening ; at six she began her reception ; at nine came the great moment of the day —supper. She had an income of £1400 a year and half of it went on food. The grand business of the night was conversation. "In the circle that, after an eight hours' sitting, broke up reluctantly at two or three every morning to meet again that same evening at six, talk continually flowed . . . brilliant, charming, easy-flowing, gay and rapid, never profound, never intimate, never thrilling ; but also never emphatic, never affected, never languishing and never dull."

She wrote constantly to Voltaire letters of marked common sense and precision: "The vocabulary is very small, but every word is the right one."

To Voltaire she showed her brilliant exterior, to Horace Walpole she reveals her soul : "Bitterness, discontent, pessimism, cynicism, boredom, regret, despair " peep out from every page. Walpole was a blasé bachelor of fifty when Madame du Deffand at seventy conceived a violent passion for him. Walpole behaved badly. By far the greater part of the book is taken up with Voltaire. First there is Voltaire in conflict with the aristocracy in France, driven over to England, being jeered at in some London street as a French dog, jumping on a milestone and turning their jeers to applause with his " Brave Englishmen ! Am I not sufficiently unhappy in not having been born among you ? "

The outstanding feature of this essay is the eulogy of the book that Voltaire wrote as the result of his English visit. *Lettres Philosophiques* contains but little on the institutions and manners of England, but compressed within its two hundred pages is " the whole philosophy of Voltaire." He touches on everything— the theory of gravitation, inoculation, immortality, the satires of Lord Rochester—" and every touch tells. It is the spirit of humanism carried to its furthest, its quintessential point. . . . The matters treated of are so many and so vast, they are disposed of and dismissed so swiftly, so easily, so unemphatically, that one begins to wonder whether, after all, anything of real significance can have been expressed." We need not wonder. Strachey brings out very clearly the singular contradiction in Voltaire : the revolutionary intellect combined with the timid Toryism of his æsthetic taste. On Newton he is " succinct, lucid, persuasive and bold " ; to Shakespeare's genius he is " utterly blind." In France, at any rate, once the letters were condemned to be burned, Voltaire's success was assured. Toleration, free inquiry, enlightened curiosity spread everywhere. Voltaire had learned these things in England, but he dealt his blows with a reckless audacity, a fierce, uncompromising passion, completely foreign to the English temperament.

" He had no time for the nice discriminations of an elaborate philosophy, and no desire for the careful balance of the judicial mind : his creed was simple and explicit, and it also possessed the supreme merit of brevity. ' Écrasez l'infâme ! ' was enough for him."

There is a chapter on Voltaire's tragedies, remembered now mainly for his work as a precursor of the Revolution ; to his own age he was as much a poet as a reformer. His plays were performed to crowded houses, plays in which " heroines go mad in epigrams and villains commit murders in inversions. Amid the hurly-burly of artificiality, it was all his cleverness could do to keep its head to the wind ; and he was only able to remain afloat at all by throwing overboard his humour. The classical tradition has to answer for many sins : perhaps its most infamous achievement was that it prevented Molière from being a great tragedian. But there can be no doubt that its most astonishing one was to have taken—if only for some scattered moments—the sense of the ridiculous from Voltaire."

The most interesting of the Voltaire papers is, however, that dealing with his relations with Frederick the Great. Here Lytton Strachey falls back into his biographical vein : richly picturesque, he makes us laugh, not altogether without a spice of malice, at the two men, one of whom made modern France, the other, modern Germany.

Voltaire was forty-two and very famous when he first received a letter from the twenty-four-year-old heir-apparent to one of the secondary European monarchies. "It was a correspondence between a master and a pupil." Frederick had developed a passion for French poetry. Four years later the "prince philosophe qui rendra les hommes heureux" (Voltaire's phrase for him) plunged Europe into war and made Prussia a great military power. Voltaire went to Berlin, but had to leave Madame du Chatelet behind him : he went back to her. She died, was succeeded by Madame de Pompadour, and he went back to Berlin in 1750 as Court Chamberlain at £800 a year. Frederick recognised that Voltaire was a scoundrel, but a scoundrel of genius, who could help the Emperor to become a French poet. Frederick imagined that he had only to crack his whip to keep this monkey in order —but the monkey turned out to be a devil. Voltaire was fifty-six and " his life's work was still before him." He was entirely without feeling for Frederick ; he went to Berlin for his own purposes, although " at times, in this Berlin adventure, he seems to resemble some great buzzing fly, shooting suddenly into a room through an open window and dashing frantically from side to side ; when all at once, as suddenly, he swoops away and out through another window which opens in quite a different direction towards wide and flowery fields ; so that perhaps the reckless creature knew where he was going after all."

There was, of course, explosion after explosion.

" When two confirmed egotists decide, for purely selfish reasons, to set up house together, everyone knows what will happen."

" When one has sucked the orange, one throws away the skin," said Frederick about Voltaire.

" Does the man expect me to go on washing his dirty linen for ever ? " said Voltaire of Frederick.

Frederick's Court was full of second-rate men : Göllnitz, who " had unfortunately been obliged to change his religion six times "; Chasot, the retired military man, with too many debts, and Darget, the good-natured secretary, with too many love affairs ; la Mettrie, the doctor, exiled from France for atheism

and bad manners, who died after a too heavy supper
of pheasant pie, calling on " Jésus ! Marie ! " and
finishing with an oath.

But it was Maupertius, the President of the Academy
of Sciences, who really roused Voltaire's anger. He
played into Voltaire's hands by being singularly foolish over the discovery of an important mathematical
law, the principle of least action, which he took to be
his own, and when faced with the fact that Leibnitz
had expressed the law more accurately and earlier, he
not only denied the fact, but pronounced the mathe-
matician, Koenig, who had brought the fact to his
notice, to be a forger. Though Maupertius was the
close friend of Frederick, Voltaire published a statement, " deadly in its bald simplicity, its studied
coldness, its concentrated force, of Koenig's case
against Maupertius."

The King was furious. Voltaire was out to do as
much damage as he could. " Shut up all day in the
strange little room . . . with its yellow walls thickly
embossed with the highly coloured shapes of fruits,
flowers and birds, the indefatigable old man worked
away at his histories, his tragedies, his *Pucelle* and
his enormous correspondence." He was very ill, upon
the brink of death ; the worse he grew the more
furiously he worked. . . . Maupertius wrote a dull
book of reveries. Voltaire swooped on to it and
produced the famous *Diatribe du Docteur Akakia*,
" still fresh with a fiendish gaiety after a hundred
and fifty years . . . there is a bubbling, sparkling
fountain of effervescent raillery . . . the raillery of a
demon with a grudge." When Frederick read it he
laughed till the tears ran down his cheeks and ordered
it to be destroyed. Little did he know Voltaire. In
a month all Germany was swarming with *Akakias*.
" Votre effronterie m'étonne " wrote Frederick furiously. In 1753 the two men parted for ever, and
Voltaire was at last free, free to shape his own
destiny by the Lake of Geneva. " There the fires,
which had lain smouldering so long in the pro-

N

fundities of his spirit, flared up, and flamed over
Europe."

Twenty years passed and Frederick was still submitting verses to Voltaire, recognising at last the
greatness of his master.

There is a chapter of literary criticism on Henri
Beyle, that "too-French French writer," which should
be compared with Middleton Murry's chapter on
Stendhal. It is illuminating to see two such widely
different temperaments at work on the same model.
Strachey succeeds in making the Frenchman romantic,
adventurous, laughable, interesting. We see the man
behind the work, the delightful man who in old age
registered his successful love affairs upon his braces.
"Beyle occupies a position in France analogous to
that of Shelley in England. Shelley is not a national
hero, not because he lacked the distinctive qualities
of an Englishman, but for the opposite reason—
because he possessed so many of them in an extreme
degree." So Beyle possesses the French characteristics
in too undiluted and intense a form. He was eccentric,
adored Italy, scorned convention, was devoted to
literature, and "there had never been a moment when
he was not in love." "His novels are full of passages
which read like nothing so much as extraordinarily
able summaries of some enormous original narrative
which has been lost . . . perhaps the best test of a
man's intelligence is his capacity for making a summary.
Beyle knew this."

"In his blood there was a virus which had never
tingled in the veins of Voltaire. It was the virus of
modern life—that new sensibility, that new passion-
ateness" which we associate with the name of
Rousseau. "If Beyle was a prophet of anything, he
was a prophet of that spirit of revolt in modern thought
which first reached a complete expression in the pages
of Nietzsche." He scorned the Christian virtues, he
loved power, he was aristocratic in outlook, repudiating
both the herd and the herd's morality.

In his essay on Lady Hester Stanhope he carries on

his peculiar method of biography — Manning's hat, Beyle's braces, Lady Hester's nose. Lady Hester's was a nose of wild ambitions, of pride grown fantastical, a nose that scorned the earth, shooting off, one fancies, towards some eternally eccentric heaven. After three hectic years with Pitt her uncle, a reckless love affair with Lord Granville Leveson Gower, attachments to Canning and Sir John Moore, marriage with Hill, she left England for ever, accompanied by her English maid, Mrs Fry, and her private doctor, Dr Meryon. She was conveyed in battleships, lodged with ambassadors, wrecked off the island of Rhodes, "the turning-point of her career," because she was forced to don a pair of Turkish trousers ; " a dress she never abandoned. She wore a turban of cashmere, a brocaded waistcoat, a priceless pelisse, and a vast pair of purple velvet pantaloons embroidered all over in gold." She had a triumphal procession from Cairo to Damascus, into which city she rode unveiled at midday. " The population were thunderstruck : but at last their amazement gave way to enthusiasm, and the incredible lady was hailed everywhere as Queen."

She then plunged into the desert to Palmyra, which she reached in 1813 : " it was the apogee of Lady Hester's life." She was received everywhere as a royal, almost as a supernatural, personage. At Laodicea she caught the plague. On her recovery she rented an empty monastery on the slopes of Mount Lebanon, and until her death twenty-three years afterwards she lived on that mountain. Her house was right on the top of a bare hill : she paid £20 a year rent . . . the ignorant and superstitious populations around her feared and loved her : she plunged into divination and astrology : her expenses were big ; she ran into debt and was swindled by her servants : she took to her bed by day and sat up all night talking to her doctor, " talk that scaled the heavens and ransacked the earth . . . stories of Pitt and George III. . . . mimicries of the Duchess of Devonshire—mingled . . . with doctrines of Fate and planetary influence, and

speculations on the Arabian origin of the Scottish
clans."

Three dozen hungry cats ranged through the rooms.
Arab war-mace in hand, Lady Hester rampaged
among her dependents. Her health broken, alone
except for her vile servants, crushed by debts, she
lived for nearly a year after her doctor left her, and
when she died her servants possessed themselves of
every movable object in the house.

Books and Characters is an amazing book; but it
reveals to us the personality of its author. It is
worth noticing precisely who the characters are that
he delights to trace: eccentrics all, romantics all,
revolutionaries all, stylists, adventurers.

The way he handles his material, the witty, subtle,
detached manner in which he writes, the perfectly
balanced sentence, the unforgettable *mot juste* . . .
all mark Strachey out as a master of his subject, a
master of English prose style. It is impossible to
imagine him failing to be interesting on any topic;
a man of immense reading, he always picks out some
gorgeous tit-bit, some coloured thread to excite and
astonish us. But in the end of all I love Strachey
because he makes me love others. I should never have
bothered about Beddoes if I had not read *The Last
Elizabethan*. I owe him that . . . and I owe him all
the little that I know about the French.

PART III

SOME
MODERN AUTOBIOGRAPHERS

MICHAEL FAIRLESS
EDMUND GOSSE
ARTHUR MACHEN

MICHAEL FAIRLESS

THE ROADMENDER has now been out for twenty years. It has run into forty-eight editions; over a quarter of a million copies have been sold. I read it when it first appeared. My belief in God was then profound. I read it again last week as the result of a pilgrimage to her grave. I know Steyning well. I had not before taken the trouble to diverge from the beaten track to Ashurst. I found a tiny church, surrounded by trees, a pleasant country house adjoining the churchyard. I wandered round the graveyard and found a plain wooden cross on which was inscribed the words, " Lo ! How I loved thee," and under them "Margaret Fairless Dowson, aged thirty-three, August 24, 1901." Next door to her grave was a plain white stone slab on which was inscribed a name far more romantic : "Hardress O'Grady Standish, Fifth Viscount Guillemore." I had never heard either surname before. Mr Lewis Hind calls Michael Fairless—Margaret Fairless Barber. I don't know if there is a mystery, but why none of the usual " beloved wife of" or " beloved daughter of " ? . . . I wandered up a path strewn with ripe blackberries, crossed the main road, and tried to trace the path from the authoress's grave to her house at Mock Bridge Farm. I was turned back twice by farmers and once by water. She has not so many pilgrims to her shrine as Ann Hathaway, I gather. After some difficulty with the dirty waters of the Adur and more with hedges I arrived on the London road and saw the white house that had once been her home. It was not, as I expected, quiet. Within a stone's-throw was an inn—The Bull. Disgorged motor

char-à-banc excursionists were raucously peevish. Why
had they chosen this spot on a September Sunday
afternoon ? The ways of the tourist are indeed strange.
Not one, I dare bet, had ever heard of Michael Fairless.
What else was there to see save her home ? Sher-
manbury Park ? Perhaps. I rather think it was the
convenient mileage—an afternoon's circular trip round
the weald of Sussex—the sort of thing that I was glad
to escape. Let me get back to the stone-breaker sitting
"by the roadside on a stretch of grass under a high
hedge of saplings and a tangle of traveller's joy, wood-
bine, sweetbriar and late roses." This lady of simple
faith is of the brotherhood of the epicurean Hazlitt
and Stevenson. She must needs lie with her face in
the grass and toy with the snake who can bring sleep
and a forgetting without mauling and tearing. She
dwells lovingly on the virtues of the ice-cold well from
which she fills her huge earthenware pan ; even her
bucket must be moss-grown. She tramps five miles
to worship her God in the little church at the foot of
the grey-green downs, and then climbs to stand on the
summit, hatless, the wind blowing through her hair,
the salt smacking her cheeks. The hours pass, and
she lies in her niche under the stunted hawthorn
"watching the to and fro of the sea, and Æolus
shepherding his white sheep across the blue." Later,
when the sun has died and the stars have risen out of
a veil of purple cloud, she goes home across the miles
of sleeping fields to her little attic, ice-cold well, and
wrinkled, kindly, deaf housekeeper. Epicurean roadmender ! Are there any delights comparable in life
with these ? She annexes no less a man than Wagner
to accompany the breaking of her stones ; tramps of
the tribe of Ishmael join her noonday meal ; the dis-
gruntled drive her to lament the decay of individual
effort and plead for a race of intelligent mechanics.
"Stone-breaking should be allotted to minor poets or
vagrant children of Nature like myself." The Stone-
breaker is at any rate privileged to see rare things, the
Brotherhood of the Poor, the passing on life's way of

merry wedded couples, or sad procession of funeral cortège. Sadness follows a comparison between the old ways when the herd led his flock and to-day when he drives them.

The ear that is sensitive to catch the music of Bayreuth in the leap and lick of the fiery tongues in the wood fire is not likely to let pass the inexpressible beauty of "the unused day." Like a true daughter of the soil, she would have her day begin and end at five. Comes autumn and the Roadmender leaves her great and wonderful work where she has learned the truths of three great paradoxes : "The blessing of a curse, the voice of silence and the companionship of solitude."

In the second part of the book she is a roadmender no longer, but lying "where the shadow is bright with kindly faces and gentle hands." This lover of the fields and woods with her pantheistic craving for tree and sky has to exchange "the loneliness of the moorland" for "the warmth and companionship of London's swift-beating heart." She lives in a world of sight and sound : she hears the traffic but sees no road — only the silent river of her heart "with its tale of wonder and years, and the white beat of sea-gulls' wings in strong inquiring flight." She watches the nightly progress of the lamplighter as he comes to open "the great yellow eyes that wake the dark," rain with its "strong caressing fingers," wet sparrows, dumb Chrysostoms, "perpetual signs of the remembering mercies of God." "Necessity," she says later, "can set me helpless on my back, but she cannot keep me there ; nor can four walls limit my vision." Not for her the mystics' creed of separating themselves from creation. "The Greeks knew better when they flung Ariadne's crown among the stars, and wrote Demeter's grief on a barren earth, and Persephone's joy in the fruitful field. For the earth is gathered up in man . . . the universe is full of miracle and mystery : the darkness and silence are set for a sign we dare not despise."

And lastly, "At the White Gate," a great joy comes

to her. She is restored to the lean grey Downs, the
lap of Mother Earth. " As I write I am lying on a
green carpet, powdered yellow and white with the
sun's own flowers ; overhead a great sycamore where
the bees toil and sing ; and sighing shimmering poplars
golden-grey against the blue. The day of Persephone
has dawned for me." The early scythe song is more
jocund than the sound of traffic, the fragrance of the
warm air sweeter than the smells of London. " Ay,"
as Old Dodden said, " 'tis better to stay by the land
. . . till time comes to lie under it." Her garden is an
epitome of peace : she has come home to die among
her own people. " Verily I think that the sap of grass
and trees must run in my veins, so steady is their
pull upon my heart-strings. London claimed all my
philosophy, but the country . . . asks of me only the
warm receptivity of a child in its mother's arms. . . .
I feel not so much desire for the beauty to come, as
a great longing to open my eyes a little wider during
the time which remains to me. . . . I have lost my
voracious appetite for books ; their language is less
plain than scent and song and the wind in the trees,
and for me the clue to the next world lies in the wisdom
of earth rather than in the learning of men. . . . There
is a place waiting for me under the firs in the quiet
churchyard. . . . I am most gladly in debt to all the
world : and to Earth, my mother, for her great beauty
. . . surely a man need not sigh for greater loveliness
until he has read something more of this living letter."

" It is not the worship of beauty we need," she says,
" so much as the beauty of holiness." The Ten Com-
mandments have less truth than the believing cry :
" Come from thy white cliffs, O Pan ! "

" The marigolds with their orange suns, the lilies'
white flame, the corncockle's blue crown, the honey-
suckle's horn of fragrance "—will not these things give
place after death to an even finer feast of opening
eyes ?

" Revelation is always measured by capacity."

So her last plea is for vision : " Let us see visions,

visions of colour and light, of green fields and broad rivers, of palaces laid with fair colours, and gardens where a place is found for rosemary and rue."

Who, everyone asked, was this courageous, holy invalid who claimed England with her swelling breasts and wind-swept, salt-strewn hair for her mother, Scotland, which "gave me my name," for father, Germany for her real Fatherland, this perfect stylist, this exquisite lover of Nature, this devotee of the Greek mythology, versed in all tongues, Latin and Italian, Greek and German, this strange girl who pretended to be a man, who found it "ideal to live on the charity of her fellow-men"? I suppose at this time of day everyone knows. What matters is that she has left an imperishable pæan of gratitude to this English earth. This rich Sussex is the richer for her pen. *The Roadmender* is a golden book. It seems to me to matter very little who the Roadmender was : it matters only that she was a splendid interpreter of material beauties. I do not think she would bear gladly the foolish easy acceptance of the comfortable way of a number of her followers.

II

EDMUND GOSSE

HAZLITT'S idea of always rereading an old book whenever a new one appeared might with advantage be followed to-day. I have just read Mr J. St Loe Strachey's autobiography, *The Adventure of Living*. Its direct result was to send me back to reread Gosse's *Father and Son*. I have just read Mr Geoffrey Dennis's brilliant novel, *Mary Lee*, with its merciless record of the influence of a Plymouth Brethren upbringing on a sensitive girl: I turned back to reread that courageous passage in Gosse where he finally flings the gauntlet down: "I have surely the right to protest against the untruth (would that I could apply to it any other word!) that evangelical religion, or any religion in a violent form, is a wholesome or valuable or desirable adjunct to human life. It divides heart from heart. It sets up a vain chimerical ideal, in the barren pursuit of which all the tender, indulgent affections, all the genial play of life, all the exquisite pleasures and soft resignations of the body, all that enlarges and calms the soul, are exchanged for what is harsh and void and negative. It encourages a stern and ignorant spirit of condemnation; it throws altogether out of gear the healthy movement of the conscience; it invents virtues which are sterile and cruel; it invents sins which are no sins at all, but which darken the heaven of innocent joy with futile clouds of remorse. There is something horrible . . . in the fanaticism that can do nothing with this pathetic and fugitive existence of ours but treat it as if it were the uncomfortable ante-chamber to a palace which no one has explored, and of the plan of which we know absolutely nothing."

It all seems so long ago, but even to-day there must be country vicarages where devotees of *The Spectator* will rub their eyes once or twice in amazement when they read their beloved editor's quotation from Lord Halifax on the subject of belief: "I believe as much as I can: and God Almighty will, I am sure, pardon me if I have not the digestion of an ostrich."

Whenever I read a modern book on the evils of repressions and complexes I turn back to *Father and Son*. It is a topsy-turvy world: we only appreciate the sweetness of things in so far as that sweetness is a forbidden thing. Would Gosse have developed into the ardent man of letters that he now is had his literary path been made smooth and his love of poetry fostered by cultured and easy-going parents?

Read any diary, memoirs, or life—and you will come back to Gosse to see how this sort of thing ought to be done.

"This book," he says, "is nothing if it is not a genuine slice of life." It is not sentimental, it is not "falsified by self-admiration and self-pity." He makes no attempt to make his rigid parent out to be an ogre: "There was an extraordinary mixture of comedy and tragedy in the situation which is here described . . . even if the comedy was superficial and the tragedy essential."

There, in little, is the beau-ideal. How few writers have been able to carry it out! Self-consciousness, a mistaken sense of loyalty, fear of what people will say —these things have militated against the honest self-expression that we have a right to demand of artists. Samuel Butler and Edmund Gosse are almost alone in their scrupulous truthfulness. The whole of Gosse's early years were passed in learning to keep some spark of individuality alive. His father was thirty-eight, his mother forty-two when they married: they were always as poor as they were saintly. "Neither knew nor cared about any manifestation of current literature . . . pleasure was found nowhere but in the Word of

God, and to the endless discussion of the Scriptures each hurried when the day's work was over." The elder Gosse's one mundane interest was zoology.

On the day that Edmund was born his father records in his diary : " E. delivered of a son. Received green swallow from Jamaica." It does not follow, says Gosse quaintly, from this that his father was as much interested in the bird as in the boy. " What the wording exemplifies is my father's extreme punctilio. The green swallow arrived later in the day than the son, and the earlier visitor was therefore recorded first."

Owing to their poverty, for three years after their marriage the boy's parents never left London for a day, never ate a meal away from home, but were, in spite of the physical unwholesomeness of such a life, completely contented. Owing to his father inheriting a small sum of money and becoming a prey to acute nervous dyspepsia, they then took nearly a year's holiday in Devonshire, returning to a life of comparative fame and less isolation, a life of " perfect purity, perfect intrepidity, perfect abnegation." At the age of four young Gosse learned to read—fiction was, however, rigidly excluded. There were no fairies, no pirates to beguile the child's imagination : voyages of discovery formed his most secular entertainment : a passion for geography, engendered by poring over maps, became his most ardent pursuit. " I cannot recollect a time when I did not understand that I was going to be a minister of the Gospel." Yet in spite of the fact that he had no story-books, no young companions, no outdoor amusements, he was neither discontented nor fretful : his parents were often unexpectedly cheerful, gay and playful : occasionally there was corporal chastisement, occasional terrors by night; always there was the Bible; and when he was seven his mother's death, followed by the necessity of his father to give lectures all over the country to avoid starvation. The boy was thrown into companionship with his father, and they became fast friends, until the advent of Miss Marks, " a mixture of Mrs Pipchin and Miss Sally

Brass," who became his governess, but was foiled in
her attempt to become his stepmother. On his eighth
birthday they moved to Devonshire from the ugliness
of Islington, and a new element entered into his life:
"It was the sea, always the sea, and nothing but the
sea . . . no other form of natural scenery . . . had
any effect upon me at all."

He accompanied his father on his natural history
expeditions, and enjoyed long cosy talks together
with him over the fire. "Our favourite subject was
murders." Yet his health (always bad) did not
improve. "The dampness of the house was terrible
. . . under my bed-clothes at night I shook like a
jelly, unable to sleep for cold, though I was heaped with
coverings." His father, torn between his devotion
to geology and his belief in Biblical inspiration,
clung to the ancient tradition and turned his back
on Darwin and his other fellow-scientists for ever,
confining his attention thenceforward to the "Saints"
in the village, a quite surprising number of whom
suffered from consumption: yet he was still "most
easy, most happy, most human" when he was tramping over his hunting ground on the beach acquir-
ing biological specimens, compiling his *History of the
British Sea-Anemones and Corals*, still a standard
classic. It was at this period of the boy's life that
he first met Charles Kingsley and Sheridan Knowles
(who first introduced him to Shakespeare). Strangely
enough it was due to his father that he woke first to
the amazing beauty which existed in the sound of verses.
"Formosam resonare doces Amaryllida silvas" was
the line that his father chanted to him from Virgil,
"most evangelical of the classics"—and ever afterwards, "as I hung over the tidal pools at the edge of
the sea, all my inner being used to ring out with the
sound. . . . Formosam resonare doces Amaryllida
silvas."

He regards this early training in zoology as a
valuable aid to concentration, definition and accuracy
of vision. It taught him the virtue of never flagging

when interest began to decline. At the age of ten he was publicly baptized " as an adult," and people travelled from Exeter, Dartmouth and Totnes to witness so extraordinary a ceremony.

"I cannot recall anything but an intellectual surrender : there was never joy in the act of resignation . . . through thick and thin I clung to a hard nut of individuality." His mind was far away on the emerald and amethyst islands set on the Caribbean Sea : " the reading and rereading of *Tom Cringle's Log* did more than anything else to give fortitude to my individuality . . . my soul was shut up like Fatima in a tower . . . the daring chapters of Michael Scott's picturesque romance of the tropics " provided him with a telescope and a window.

Then came his father's second marriage to Miss Brightwen, the sympathetic Quaker whose alliance with the boy provided him with a lodge in his garden of cucumbers. She opened the windows of his bedroom and allowed some air to penetrate the windows of his soul. He owed much to her. It was through her that he became " instantly and gloriously enslaved " to *Pickwick* and to Blair's *Grave*; it was through her that he went to a boarding-school, which, however, he left " unbrightened and unrefreshed by commerce with a single friend." He never revealed the fact that all the religion he imbibed there was a dreary, unintelligible exercise in mumbo-jumbo. Boys do not reveal this sort of thing about their schools.

It was at this time that he found Coleridge; and in the reading of *Hero and Leander* was "lifted to a heaven of passion and music." For his excursions into Marlowe he was denounced by his father in unmeasured terms for bringing into the house " so abominable a book." He was told that if anyone found him with such a book in his possession he would be immediately set down as a profligate. He was captivated by Keats and *The Golden Treasury*; repelled at first by *Queen Mab* and Wordsworth; wrote a tragedy on Shakespearean lines on an evangelistic subject, and

parodied *Prometheus Unbound*. He made one last
attempt to strive after holiness. He implored God
to take him to Paradise: his fervent prayer was
unanswered. "The Lord has not come, the Lord will
never come," he muttered, and the "artificial edifice
of extravagant faith began to totter and to crumble."
The boy went to London, pursued by a postal in-
quisition, snatching delight from Carlyle and Ruskin,
more and more growing to dislike the Bible, but "I
was docile, I was plausible, I was anything but com-
bative ; if my father could have persuaded himself to
let me alone . . . all would have been well. . . . What
a charming companion, what a delightful parent, what
a courteous and engaging friend my father would
have been . . . if it had not been for this stringent
piety which ruined it all." His father accuses him of
" insidious infidelity."

Either the boy must cease to think for himself or
his individuality be instantly confirmed, and the
necessity of religious independence emphasised. "As
respectfully as he could, without parade or remon-
strance, he took a human being's privilege to fashion
his inner life for himself."

Among an ocean of biographies it is good to come
back again and again to this amazingly frank confession
and see what are the qualities that raise it so far above
the rest.

Its most striking quality is, of course, its absolute
sincerity. Mr Gosse is at pains to portray real people ;
nothing is set down in malice, there is no gross adula-
tion, no petty spite. He accentuates the fact that
his father was no fanatical monomaniac : he dwells
lovingly on his interest in water-colour paintings, his
assiduous study of botany, his fame as a man of science,
his playfulness, the time when the carpenter said of
him, "He can zing a zong, zo well's another, though
he be a minister." The tragedy is intensified by all
this. Had the boy hated his Calvinistic parent it
wouldn't have mattered half so much. It is the
Calvinist behind the man, squeezing out all the innate

o

sweetness and light that were in him, that drives us to fury. It is like watching a man possessed of an evil spirit. We pity the father far more than the son. The child was strong enough to break the shackles. The man's tragedy was that the shackles enmeshed him ever more and more.

To Samuel Butler's and Edmund Gosse's revolt against parental despotism do we owe our present-day liberty of the conscience. They are much more than literary artists. They are, with Cromwell, fathers of English freedom, liberators of the soul of youth from the mumbo-jumbo of orthodoxy.

III

ARTHUR MACHEN

ONE of the secrets of Hazlitt's irresistible appeal
to us is his habit of writing in this vein: "It
was in January 1798 that I rose one morning
before daylight, to walk ten miles in the mud, and
went to hear this celebrated person [Coleridge] preach."
" . . . It was on the 10th of April, 1798, that I sat
down to a volume of *The New Eloïse*, at the inn at
Llangollen, over a bottle of sherry and a cold chicken."
We are at our best when we are most simple. This
bald statement of the time, and the place, the climatic
conditions, and the food we ate and the wine we drank
when we first came under the influence of a great man
or a great book is of eternal interest.

So Arthur Machen in his autobiography, *Far-Off
Things*, dwells lovingly not only on his first acquaintance with the books that formed his taste, but also on
the conditions under which he came into contact with
them.

"I shall always esteem it as the greatest piece of
fortune that has fallen to me, that I was born in that
noble, fallen Caerleon-on-Usk, in the heart of Gwent.
. . . The older I grow the more firmly am I convinced
that anything which I may have accomplished in
literature is due to the fact that when my eyes were
first opened in earliest childhood they had before them
the vision of an enchanted land."

The only child of a country parson set down in a
remote and romantic country, how could he develop
otherwise than as a creative artist ? Think of that
lucky, impressionable boy, distracted neither by parents
harassed by business nor by games, alone with the
Celtic Usk, " grey and silvery and luminous, winding

211

in mystic esses, and the dense forest bending down
to it, and the grey stone bridge crossing it." Little
wonder that the child's imagination was stirred with
the wonder and awe and mystery of that strange land.
" Give me a child till he is seven," said some educa-
tionist, " and you can do what you will with him after
that." " Give a child loneliness on the moors," say
I, " and you have given him a vision which will
last him through life." " With unlimited leisure for
mooning and loafing and roaming and wandering from
lane to lane, from wood to wood," the young Machen
found out all the wisdom he wanted for one lifetime
before he was eighteen. " Solitude and woods and
deep lanes and wonder ; these were the chief elements
of my life . . . and the run of a thoroughly ill-selected
library." What could youth want more ? More
books ! He saw and bought and instantly loved De
Quincey's *Confessions of an English Opium Eater*,
at Pontypool Road station. He never takes up De
Quincey in later years without thinking " of the dismal
platform at Pontypool Road, and the mountains all
about me as I stood and waited for my father and the
trap, and read the first pages of the magic book."
Then there was the visit to Llanfrechfa Rectory, at
the age of seven or eight, and the discovery there of
the fat, dumpy little book, *The Ingenious Gentleman,
Don Quixote de la Mancha*, " and those are words that
will thrill a lettered man as the opening notes of certain
fugues of Bach will thrill a musician."

Then there was *The Arabian Nights*, bought at
Hereford station, and the mighty romances of Sir
Walter Scott read in the drawing-room at Llanddewi.
"I can see myself now curled up in all odd corners of
the rectory reading *Waverley, Ivanhoe, Rob Roy, Guy
Mannering, Old Mortality*, and the rest of them, curled
up and entranced so that I was deaf, and gave no
answer when they called to me, and had to be roused
to life—which meant tea—with a loud and repeated
summons. . . . I took Sir Walter to my heart with
great joy, and roamed enraptured through his library

of adventures and marvels as I roamed through the lanes and hollows. . . . They are vital literature, they are of the heart of true romance. What is vital literature, what is true romance ? . . . vital literature is something as remote as you can possibly imagine from the short stories of the late Guy de Maupassant."

And occasionally the outside world made itself heard in these fastnesses of wild Wales.

"I remember how the news of the fall of Khartoum came to the rectory. I had been spending the evening with some friends across a few miles of midnight and black copse, and ragged field and wild and broken and wandering brook land, and I remember that not a star was to be seen as I came home, wondering all the while if I ever should find my way. One of my friends had been in Newport that day, and had seen a paper, and so when I got back at last, and found my father smoking his pipe by the fire, I announced the news in a tag of Apocalyptic Greek : 'Khartoum he polis he megale peptoke, peptoke ' : Khartoum the mighty city has fallen, has fallen ; and sometimes I wonder now in these days, when I am nearer to the heart of news-papers, whether our work in Fleet Street, with its anxious, flurried yell over the telephone, its tic-tac of tapes, its slither and rattle and clatter of linotypes, its frantic haste of men, its final roar and thunder of machinery, ever gets itself delivered at last on a midnight hillside so queerly as the tragic news of Khartoum was delivered in the ' parlour ' of Llanddewi Rectory."

Yes, certainly the boy who had the imaginative faculty so developed was destined for literature all right. But great writing only comes after great tribulation, and at the age of eighteen he went down into the deep waters. "My father and I set out one fine morning for Paddington " : his first " habitat was in the High Street of a southern suburb," his second in Turnham Green, his third, Notting Hill Gate. Then came his " cataclysmic " discovery of *Songs before Sunrise*, bought at Denny's at a time when he was trying to pass the preliminary examination of

the Royal College of Surgeons: he began to write
poetry, "stumbling and struggling and blundering
like a man lost in a dense thicket on a dark night."
    "If the clear-voiced rulers of the everlasting choir
are to suffer so and agonise, what of miserable little
Welshmen stammering and stuttering by the Wandle,
in the obscure rectory amongst the hills, in waste
places by Shepherd's Bush, in gloomy Great Russell
Street, where the ghosts of dead, disappointed authors
go singing to and fro?" Thirty years were to pass
before he became a journalist; but he strove for a
footing, and went on reading Boswell, *The Earthly
Paradise* and Herrick. He was working for a living on one pound a week for a firm of publishers in
Chandos Street, "a peg of no particular shape in a
perfectly round hole, feeling very miserable indeed,"
while three cheerful young colleagues of his "took
albums out of tissue paper and put them back into
tissue paper all day long." "I hated it all . . . I
took no interest . . . saw no reason why it should be
done at all. . . . I looked about me and . . . got a
little teaching of small children at twenty-five shillings
a week." These were days when he lived in a tiny
garret, "ten feet by five," with no fireplace, days of
strong green tea, of an improvised bookshelf made
between the rungs of a step-ladder, days when his
midday meal consisted of a large captain's biscuit and
a glass of beer, days of rambling into old taverns, days
when he discovered Kensal Green: "it added new
terror to death. I think I came upon Kensal Green
again and again: it was like the Malay, an enemy for
months . . . my horror at the sight of Kensal Green
was due to this, that . . . I had never seen a cemetery
before. Well I knew the old graveyards of Gwent,
solemn amongst the swelling hills, peaceful in the
shadow of very ancient yews. . . . These places of
the dead were solemn with old religion." Another
horror was Harlesden, "this sudden and violent
irruption of red brick in the midst of a green field."
Just as he was struck dumb as a child with "the awe

and solemnity and mystery of the valley of the Usk, and the house called Bartholly, hanging solitary between the deep forest and the winding esses of the river," so did the sensitive adolescent shrink in later years from the horror of Harlesden and heathenry of Kensal Green.

So he takes us with him in 1883 " tramping, loafing, strolling along interminable streets and roads lying to the north-west and the west of London, a shabby, sorry figure : and always alone." Only the Strand comforted him : " To be in the Strand was like drinking punch and reading Dickens. One felt it was such a warm-hearted, hospitable street, if one only had a little money." And always there was that little room in Clarendon Road, where night after night he went on reading—Homer, Disraeli, Pepys, " with ravishment," Burton's *Anatomy of Melancholy*—" a great refuge, this last, a world of literature in itself " —Carlyle's *Sartor Resartus*—" I think a good many young men of this age would be all the better for a Carlyle course. . . . I know not any man of these days that is worthy to dust Carlyle's hat, or to clean his pipe for him." " So I read and meditated night after night, and I am amazed at the utter loneliness of it all, when I contrast this life of mine with the beginnings of other men of letters. . . . I, all alone in my little room, friendless, desolate ; conscious to my very heart of my stuttering awkwardness whenever I thought of attempting the great speech of literature . . . and so having enough sense . . . to know that I could not write a serious treatise concerning the high doctrines that entranced me. I wrote a grave burlesque of what I loved." (He is talking of his book, *The Anatomy of Tobacco*.) " But if I could only have written the real book—that is, the dreamed, intended book—and not the actual book ! Then, I promise you, you should have had high fantasies . . . you should have had an English Rabelais." Perhaps now that he has given us *The Secret Glory* he is content.

For eighteen months he went on teaching : then his pupils " mysteriously disappeared," and he, " being destitute, returned to Gwent."

" For many days I was in a sort of swoon of delight. . . . It was bliss to stroll gently in that delicious air, to watch the mists vanishing from the mountain-side in the morning, to see again the old white farms between Twym Barlwm and Mynydd Maen gleaming in the sunlight. . . . I came back to Gwent as to Avalon : there to heal me of my grievous wounds."

Then his book appeared, and he was commissioned to translate three or four French texts of the *Heptameron*, " . . . and so I did, for the sum of twenty pounds sterling. I wrote every night when the house was still, and every day I carried the roll of copy down the lane to meet the postman on his way to Caerleon-on-Usk."

So thirty years afterwards, at a literary dinner, while he is being complimented on this translation, his mind reverts to his boyhood. " . . . I saw myself, a lad of twenty-one . . . strolling along this solitary lane on a daily errand. . . . I would hear him [the postman] coming from far away, for he blew a horn as he walked. . . . The postman would put the parcel in his bag, cross the road, and go striding off into the dim country beyond, finding his way in a track that no townsman could see, by field and wood and marshy places, crossing the Canthner brook by a narrow plank, coming out somewhere on the Llanfrechfa road, and so entering at last Caerleon-on-Usk, the little, silent, deserted village that was once the golden Isca of the Roman legions, that is golden for ever and immortal in the romances of King Arthur and the Graal and the Round Table."

You will wonder, perhaps, why I have quoted so freely from this magic autobiography of an artist's early years. It was for two reasons : one was to convince you of his extraordinary affinity with his beloved De Quincey, the other to lend point to a judgment of his own about the Celtic spirit.

" It is quite true," he says, " that the Celt—the

Welsh Celt, at any rate—has directly contributed
very little to great literature . . . yet there is in
Celtdom a certain literary feeling which does not exist
in Anglo-Saxondom. . . . It perceives the music of
words and the relation of that music to the world. I
was taking a lesson in Welsh pronunciation some time
ago, and uttered the phrase, ' yn oes oesodd '—from
ages to ages. ' That is right,' said my Welsh friend,
' speak it so that it makes a sound like the wind about
the mountains ' and . . . I would say that the spirit
of that sentence is very near to the heart of true
literature."

And so is Mr Arthur Machen in *Far-Off Things* very
near himself to the heart of true literature, owing to
his wonderful luck in being born an only child, a Celt,
the son of a country rector, in a land of wonder and
mystery, and having endured the abomination of
desolation—penury, desolation and hateful toil in the
grim City of Adventure.

In *Things Near and Far* he continues the story of
those days of cataloguing books on the occult in
Catherine Street, of the time when he was captured by
" a malignant tribe of anthropoid apes " and tortured
by them into writing for money. Once he actually
inherited a small fortune. He spent it in travel.
Once he underwent a sea-change : an ecstatic, incom-
municable glow possessed him, changing his whole life.
At thirty-nine he became an actor. Always he finds
wonder, mystery, awe and the sense of a new world in
unlikely places, in Barnsbury and Brentford, King's
Cross Station and the Gray's Inn Road. He speaks of
being a beggar in his sixtieth year, but fame is at last
coming his way. Peter Whiffle describes him as the
most wonderful man writing English to-day. His first
editions are fetching high prices. People are beginning
to collect his work.

PART IV

SOME MODERN POETS

G. K. CHESTERTON
THOMAS HARDY
A. E. HOUSMAN

I

G. K. CHESTERTON

MR CHESTERTON dedicates his latest volume of poems, *The Ballad of St Barbara*, to the memory of his brother, and it is a book worthy of that brave spirit. The longest poem is that which gives its title to the book. St Barbara, he tells us, is the patron saint of artillery, and of those in danger of sudden death : the poem deals with the war.

But in this selection at any rate the poet is at his happiest when he is at his most ironic. The " Elegy in a Country Churchyard " is typical :

> " The men that worked for England
> They have their graves at home :
> And bees and birds of England
> About the cross can roam.
> But they that fought for England,
> Following a falling star,
> Alas, alas, for England,
> They have their graves afar.
> And they that rule in England,
> In stately conclave met,
> Alas, alas, for England,
> They have no graves as yet."

He still shouts to the skies his wonder at the mystery of common things :

> " If sunset clouds could grow on trees
> It would but match the may in flower :
> And skies be underneath the seas
> No topsy-turvier than a shower . . .
> Though all other wonder dies
> I wonder at not wondering."

221

He re-sings an old song on the Embankment in stormy weather which rouses us to re-discover England :

" I saw great Cobbett riding,
The horseman of the shires :
And his face was red with judgment
And a light of Luddite fires :
And south to Sussex and the sea the lights leapt up
    for liberty,
The trumpet of the yeomanry, the hammer of the
    squires :
For bars of iron rust away, rust away, rust away,
Rend before the hammer and the horseman riding in,
Crying that all men at the last, and at the worst and
    at the last,
Have found the place where England ends and
    England can begin."

He takes the old delirious delight in high-sounding words :

" Our souls shall be Leviathans
In purple seas of wine
When drunkenness is dead with death,
And drink is all divine :
Learning in those immortal vats
What mortal vineyards mean :
For only in heaven we shall know
How happy we have been."

It has not been for want of G. K. C.'s telling us if we have failed to realise our happiness.   He sometimes shouts too loudly—as if he were afraid that he would lose his happiness if he kept silent and had no need to write his " blameless blasphemies of praise," his " nightmares of delight."

And yet do we not hate ourselves when we in crabbed age call upon the child to desist from singing because it harasses us ?

" When all my days are ending
And I have no song to sing,

I think I shall not be too old
To stare at everything :
As I stared once at a nursery door
Or a tall tree and a swing."

It is as well that he should go on making us realise
the terror in the tree and the shine in the stones :

" Men grow too old for love, my love,
Men grow too old for wine,
But I shall not grow too old to see
Unearthly daylight shine,
Changing my chamber's dust to snow
Till I doubt if it be mine.
Behold, the crowning mercies melt,
The first surprises stay ;
And in my dross is dropped a gift
For which I dare not pray :
That a man grow used to grief and joy
But not to night and day."

Night, clouds, the ground " too solid to be true,"
" incredible " rafters, " strange crawling carpets of
the grass," " wide windows of the sky "—these are
the things to which he can never grow accustomed :

" Still I am stung and startled
By the first drop of rain."

And these are the things that he keeps eternally fresh
for us. He sounds a loud pæan of praise for the four
guilds—of the Glass Stainers who

" . . . have woven and spun
In scarlet or in golden green
The gay coats of the sun,"

—the Bridge Builders—" who fashion the road that
can fly," the Stone Masons—" who have graven the
mountain of God with hands . . . being great with a
mirth too gross for pride," and " the Bell Ringers,"
" God's most deafening demagogues "—drawing the

cords that can draw the people. He sings six wildly satiric songs of Education which give us quick flashes into the heart of the man.   Here is " History " :

> " O Warwick woods are green, are green,
>   But Warwick trees can fall :
>   And Birmingham grew so big, so big,
>   And Stratford stayed so small.
>   Till the hooter howled to the morning lark
>   That sang to the morning star :
>   And we all became, in freedom's name,
>   The fortunate chaps we are.

Chorus

> The fortunate chaps, felicitous chaps,
>   The fairy-like chaps we are.

> The people they left the land, the land,
>   But they went on working hard :
>   And the village green that had got mislaid
>   Turned up in the squire's back-yard :
>   But twenty men of us all got work
>   On a bit of his motor car ;
>   And we all became, with the world's acclaim,
>   The marvellous mugs we are :

Chorus

> The marvellous mugs, miraculous mugs,
>   The mystical mugs we are."

In " Geography " we learn that :

> " The earth is a place on which England is found,
>   And you find it however you twirl the globe round :
>   For the spots are all red and the rest is all grey,
>   And that is the meaning of Empire Day. . . .

> Our principal imports come far as Cape Horn ;
>   For necessities, cocoa : for luxuries, corn ;
>   Thus Brahmins are born for the rice-field, and thus,
>   The gods made the Greeks to grow currants for us :

Of earth's other tributes are plenty to choose,
Tobacco and petrol and jazzing and Jews ;
The jazzing will pass, but the Jews they will stay ;
And that is the meaning of Empire Day. . . .

. . . Lancashire merchants whenever they like
Can water the beer of a man in Klondike
Or poison the meat of a man in Bombay ;
And that is the meaning of Empire Day. . . .

. . . The Day of the Empire from Canada came
With Morden and Borden and Beaverbrook's fame
And saintly seraphical souls such as they :
And that is the meaning of Empire Day."

He takes the A. S. M. Hutchinson attitude to the business mother who can't look after her own children :

" For Mother is dancing up forty-eight floors,
For love of the Leeds International Stores,
And the flame of that faith might perhaps have
        grown cold,
With a care of a baby of seven weeks old.
For mother is happy in greasing a wheel
For somebody else, who is cornering steel."

In " Citizenship " we find what are the important elements in Civics :

" He knew not at the age of three
    What Lord St Leger next will be
    Or what he was before :
A Primrose in the social swim
A Mr Primrose is to him,
    And he is nothing more.
But soon, about the age of ten,
He finds he is a Citizen,
    And knows his way about :
Can pause within, or just beyond,
The line 'twixt Mond and Demi-Mond,
    'Twixt Getting On—or Out."

P

But the poems that remain in the memory after we close the book are the colourful poems, the loud blasting shout of the modern Robin Hood:

" His horse hoofs go before you,
    Far beyond your bursting tyres:
    And time is bridged behind him
    And our sons are with our sires.
    A trailing meteor on the Down he rides above the
        rotting town,
    The Horseman of Apocalypse, the Rider of the Shires.
    For London Bridge is broken down, broken down,
        broken down:
    Blow the horn of Huntingdon from Scotland to the
        sea—
    . . . Only a flash of thunder-light, a flying dream of
        thunder-light,
    Had shown under the shattered sky a people that
        were free."

When he sings like that we could listen to him for ever. There is all too little riotous expression of thanksgiving in life. Chesterton does much to urge us to bellow as he bellows, if less melodiously. Noise is a good thing, as the Psalmist said.

II

THOMAS HARDY

IT is well worth dwelling for a moment upon the startling fact that by far the finest achievement in poetry produced in 1922 was the appearance of Hardy's *Late Lyrics and Earlier*. The only possible runner-up was A. E. Housman's *Last Poems*. Hardy was then eighty-two and Housman sixty-three— and only a little time ago we were taught that any poetry written over the age of thirty was calculated to ruin the reputation of any poet. It is also noteworthy that Hardy and Housman take an almost identical view of life.

" But take it," sings Housman, " if the smack is sour,
 The better for the embittered hour."

" If way to the Better there be," sings Hardy,
" It exacts a full look at the Worst."

They are both courageous and simple-minded men, who use very much the same language. They both recognise the real function of poetry to be " the application of ideas to life."

Hardy is perhaps more concerned to keep poetry alive than Housman the scholar is.

"Whether owing," says Hardy in his Apology to his latest volume, "to the barbarising of taste in the younger minds by the dark madness of the late war, the unabashed cultivation of selfishness in all classes, the plethoric growth of knowledge simultaneously with the stunting of wisdom, ' a degrading thirst after outrageous stimulation,' or from any other cause, we seem threatened with a new Dark Age . . . men's minds appear to be moving backwards rather than on."

227

Somewhat surprisingly he continues: "What other purely English establishment than the Church, of sufficient dignity and footing, and with such strength of old association, such architectural spell, is left in this country to keep the shreds of morality together ? " He "forlornly hopes" that we may have drawn back *pour mieux sauter.* So far as his own Muse is concerned, he has certainly jumped forward. His own epitaph is very finely conceived and brilliantly sums up his attitude :

" I never cared for life : life cared for me,
    And hence I owed it some fidelity.
    It now says, ' Cease : at length thou hast learnt to grind
    Sufficient toll for an unwilling mind,
    And I dismiss thee—not without regard
    That thou didst ask me no ill-advised reward,
    Nor sought in me much more than thou couldst find.' "

I rather fancy that this volume will come as a surprise to those who think of Hardy in terms of *Tess, The Last Lamp at Tooting Common, Jude,* and the poem about the dog who buried his bones in his mistress' grave. The very first poem sounds a note of pure lyrical enjoyment which is quite foreign to the popular conception of Hardy :

" This is the weather the cuckoo likes,
    And so do I ;
    When showers betumble the chestnut spikes,
    And nestlings fly :
    And the little brown nightingale bills his best,
    And I sit outside at ' The Travellers' Rest,'
    And maids come forth sprig-muslin drest,
    And citizens dream of the south and west,
    And so do I."

" Faintheart in a Railway Train " strikes a light note of an unaccustomed type :

" At nine in the morning there passed a church,
    At ten there passed me by the sea,

At twelve a town of smoke and smirch,
At two a forest of oak and birch,
And then on a platform, she :
A radiant stranger, who saw not me.
I queried, ' Get out to her do I dare ? '
But I kept my seat in search of a plea,
And the wheels moved on.   O could it but be
That I had alighted there.''

In "Going and Staying" we get the true, steady
facing of things that so endears him to us :

" The moving sun-shapes on the spray,
The sparkles where the brook was flowing,
Pink faces, plightings, moonlit May,
These were the things we wished could stay ;
    But they were going.

Seasons of blankness as of snow,
The silent bleed of a world decaying,
The moan of multitudes in woe,
These were the things we wished would go :
    But they were staying.

Then we looked closelier at Time,
And saw his ghostly arms revolving
To sweep off woeful things with prime,
Things sinister with things sublime
    Alike dissolving.''

A queer, tender whimsicality is apparent in these
dramatic poems, most of which are novels in little, as
that " facing the worst " of which Hardy is so often
accused.   Think of "A Woman's Fancy"—of the
woman coming to live in the house of strangers and
being mistaken for the erring wife of the man who
had died there :

" So often did they call her thuswise
Mistakenly, by that man's name,
So much did they declare about him,
That his past form and fame

Grew on her, till she pitied his sorrow
As if she truly had been the cause—
Yea, his deserter; and came to wonder
What mould of man he was."

And ultimately when she died, "this kinless woman,
As he had died she had grown to crave," she besought
the neighbours to bury her in his grave.

Is this an ironic example of the variety of human
wishes? I think not. Hardy himself calls it "the
strength of a tender whim." We count it a grace in
her to have given the man's soul rest; we count it
human, lovably human, in her to grow to crave for him.

There is much talk of singing in this volume. He
talks about that August—full-rayed, fine—"When we
lived out of doors, sang songs, strode miles."

"Joyful lady, sing!" is the note of another refrain.
On Stinsford Hill he "glimpsed a woman's muslined
form sing-songing airily . . . that kind of note I need."

> "One pairing is as good as another
> Where all is venture!"

he cries in "The Contretemps," where two couples with
assignations at the same place get mixed up in the
dark—

> "Why not? Well, there faced she and I—
> Two strangers who'd kissed, or near,
> Chancewise. To see stand weeping by
> A woman once embraced will try
> The tension of a man the most austere."

Isn't this the care-free spirit of youth speaking?
"Is wary walking worth much pother?" he cries,
surely light-heartedly.

> "If I have seen one thing, [he sings in early years]
> It is the passing preciousness of dreams"—

and for that reason the eyes that smiled and the lips
that lured ought neither to be resisted nor forgotten.

The chimes play *Life's a Bumper*—it is as well to answer their call while we can. We cannot tire of too much loving; the passing preciousness of dreams must not be denied because of their impermanence. Even the convict at Upway Station "suddenly sang uproariously, ' This life so free is the thing for me ! ' " in spite of his handcuffs.

It is as well to remember this mood of Hardy. It is just as common as the mood which portrays the estranged husband and wife accidentally thrust together in one pew in church :

> " Her fringes brushed
> His garment's hem
> As the harmonies rushed
> Through each of them : . . .
> And women and men
> The matins ended,
> By looks commended
> Them, joined again.
> Quickly said she,
> ' Don't undeceive them—
> Better thus leave them.'
> ' Quite so,' said he."

While the mood depicted in " The Dream of the City Shopwoman " ought to be sent broadcast into every suburban home :

> " 'Twere sweet to have a comrade here,
> Who'd vow to love this garreteer,
> By city people's snap and sneer
> Tried oft and hard !
> We'd rove a truant cock and hen
> To some snug solitary glen,
> And never be seen to haunt again
> This teeming yard. . . .
> Our clock should be the closing flowers,
> Our sprinkle-bath the passing showers,
> Our church the alleged willow bowers,
> The Truth our theme.

And infant shapes might soon abound :
Their shining heads would dot us round
Like mushroom balls on grassy ground . . .
   —But all is dream !
O God, that creatures framed to feel
A yearning nature's strong appeal
Should writhe on this eternal wheel
   In rayless grime. . . ."

It is written from a boy's heart, when the prison of London first closes on him. Hardy escaped. He was once of the luky few.

In " The Child and the Sage " we get a point of view that puts Hardy as the world's greatest optimist. In the guise of the child he demurs against the sage's suggestion that it is only reasonable to expect a dash of cross, sickness and sorrow in a life full of pleasure :

   " And thus you do not count upon
      Continuance of joy :
   But, when at ease, expect anon
      A burden of annoy.
   But, Sage—this Earth—why not a place
      Where no reprisals reign,
   Where never a spell of pleasantness
   Makes reasonable a pain ? "

That is one of Hardy's secrets. He has all the child's wisdom and little of the sage's. He will not accept the world's judgments. He is always looking for and expecting something better. This it is to be an optimist. And all the time he is looking for and finding unexpectedly melodious rhythms, hammering the English tongue into something exquisitely limpid :

   " He was leaning by a face,
   He was looking into eyes,
   And he knew a trysting-place,
   And he heard seductive sighs :

But the face,
And the eyes,
And the place,
And the sighs,
Were not, alas, the right ones—the ones meet for
    him—
Though fine and sweet the features, and the feelings
    all abrim."

He plays with equal skill on that as on the heavier
tragic string. Think of " The Chapel Organist " with its
story of the girl whose passion for music was so great
that she sold herself to afford the fares to and from
the chapel where she gave her services :

" Yet God knows, if aught He knows ever, I loved
    the Old-Hundredth, Saint Stephen's,
Mount Zion, New Sabbath, Miles-Lane, Holy Rest,
    and Arabia and Eaton,
Above all embraces of body by wooers who sought
    me and won ! . . .
I have never once minced it. Lived chaste I have
    not. Heaven knows it above ! . . .
But past are the heavings of passion—it's music
    has been my life-love ! "

This long poem has just the metre to carry the effect ;
so have all the ghost poems, the poem about Sir
Nameless and the yawning boys in church rubbing their
heels into his nose on the brass on the floor, and the poem
about the grey-haired woman returning to the church
alone where she was married. All Hardy characters
are fond of doing that sort of thing. And then just
when you are attuned to a procession of tragic reminiscences you chance upon a lovely lyric like " First
or Last " :

" If grief come early
Joy comes late,
If joy come early
Grief will wait :
Aye, my dear and tender !

> Wise ones joy them early
> While the cheeks are red,
> Banish grief till surly
> Time has dulled their dread.
>
> And joy being ours
> Ere youth has flown,
> The later hours
> May find us gone :
> Aye, my dear and tender ! "

It is good to have that note emphasised in the midst of poems accentuating the horror of old age, of the haggard crone.

And yet it is this extreme sensitiveness to pain that gives us those wonderful lines to a dumb friend :

> " Never another pet for me !
> Let your place all vacant be ;
> Better blankness day by day
> Than companion torn away.
> Better bid his memory fade,
> Better blot each mark he made,
> Selfishly escape distress
> By contrived forgetfulness,
> Than preserve his prints to make
> Every morn and eve an ache. . . .
> Strange it is this speechless thing,
> Subject to our mastering,
> Subject for his life and food
> To our gift, and time, and mood :
> Timid pensioner of us Powers,
> His existence ruled by ours,
> Should—by crossing at a breath
> Into safe and shielded death,
> By the merely taking hence
> Of his insignificance—
> Loom as largened to the sense,
> Shape as part, above man's will,
> Of the Imperturbable."

If anything could make a cat-hater understand the feeling that lovers of the " Purrer of the spotless hue, plumy tail, and wistful gaze " have for their pets, it is this splendid elegy. A man who feels like that about the loss of an animal is likely to dread more than others the death of a love. Again and again he dwells on the deaths of lovers—of the anguish which impels deserted and betrayed lovers to kill themselves. Often and often we read along quite cheerfully of the conversation between a man and a woman, only to be fetched up short, as in " The Second Night," with the discovery that one of them is a ghost.

This ballad, " The Second Night," is typical. A man misses seeing his beloved for one night and goes the second :

> " She was there, with the look of one ill content,
>   And said : ' Do not come near ! ' "

She accuses him of deserting " the old love " for " the new Fair," and disappears. When he reaches the ferryman again he is told that she threw herself over the cliffs and was picked up dead on the shore the night before.

Often we get a sense of reading Wordsworth in this book, nowhere more than in " The Old Workman," where the old man, bent before his time, points to the stones of the quoin on the mansion front :

> " ' Those upper blocks,' he said, ' that there you see,
>   It was that ruined me ! ' "

He is proud to think that though he is unknown to the inhabitants of the house—

> " ' . . . Good I think it, somehow, all the same,
> To have kept 'em safe from harm, and right and tight,
>   Though it has broke me quite.' "

I recommend this poem to those who imagine that Hardy takes every opportunity to look on the gloomiest side possible. Here was a chance to grouse about inequality, sweated labour, witless, malign Nature —all Hardy does is to call attention to the man's fortitude.

He may give his ghosts a thin time, but that is, after all, in the English tradition — after the school of *The Mistletoe Bough.* Think of "A Sound in the Night." It is as good a legend as you could wish, this story of the bride of Woodsford Castle in the year 17—, with her

" ' What do I catch upon the night wind, husband ?—
What is it sounds in this house so eerily ?
It seems to be a woman's voice : each little while I
hear it,
And it much troubles me ! ' "

After suggesting all kinds of solutions ("It may be a tree, bride, that rubs his arms acrosswise ") the husband goes out, comes back and tells her that he was right, it was "the tree that taps the gargoyle head." A little too quick for him, the bride wishes to know why it is now silent, and why his heart is thumping so hard.

Suddenly he rises from her and tells her the truth :

" ' There was one I loved once : the cry you heard was
her cry :
She came to me to-night, and her plight was passing
sore,
As no woman . . . Yea, and it was e'en the cry
you heard, wife,
But she will cry no more.' "

"And now," he goes on, "I can't abide thee : this place it hath a curse on't." So he leaves her. A woman's body is found the next day, and the bride goes to a far-away country where she sleeps alone,

" And thinks in windy weather that she hears a woman
crying,
And sometimes an infant's moan."

That is a story very much after Hardy's own heart, and beautifully does he treat it.

That a soldier son of a whipper-in, returned from foreign lands, should see his father's red coat in the distance and go forward to greet him, only to find that the coat adorns a scarecrow, is exactly fitting for a Hardy story, as is the story of the knight's widow of Estminster who swore to forgo " Heaven's bliss if ever with spouse should she again have lain." She set that down in brass, and then fell in love with a man who urged her to marry him even if the price were hell. In the end she denied her passionate need, and was found gibbering in fits in front of her brass in the church.

All these stories and legends, all the reminiscences of past good days lead one irresistibly to the conclusion that Hardy would have us snatch at happiness with clear eyes, expecting nothing to last.

We could not part from him on a better note than that expressed most lyrically in " Best Times " :

" We went a day's excursion to the stream,
  Basked by the bank, and bent to the ripple-gleam,
        And I did not know
        That life would show,
  However it might flower, no finer glow.

I walked in the Sunday sunshine by the road
That wound towards the wicket of your abode,
        And I did not think
        That life would shrink
To nothing ere it shed a rosier pink.

Unlooked for I arrived on a rainy night,
And you hailed me at the door by the swaying light,
        And I full forgot
        That life might not
Again be touching that ecstatic height."

It is this note of ecstasy that needs to be emphasised in Hardy's poetry.

The emotions which he has recollected in tranquillity are neither passive nor grey : they are passionate and full of colour.

III

A. E. HOUSMAN

NO one can continue to suggest that poetry is unpopular in the face of Mr Housman's *Last Poems*. Reprint after reprint appears and still the public demand is not satisfied. Why is Mr Housman successful when the louder claimants fail? There was never less publicity, less preparation than that concerned with *Last Poems*. The book simply appeared, without any flourish, with an apologetic short preface: "I can no longer expect to be revisited by the continuous excitement under which in the early months of 1895 I wrote the greater part of my other book, nor indeed could I well sustain it if it came; and it is best that what I have written should be printed while I am here to see it through the press and control its spelling and punctuation."

The amazing thing is that in the very first poem we feel that we are back in *A Shropshire Lad*: the very same note is struck and maintained; the miracle has happened. *Last Poems* is merely a continuation. It is queer that the two poets of our time to last best are the two oldest and the two most fatalistic. Still to Housman's muse "the soldier's is the trade": he sings of grenadier and lancer:

> " I 'listed at home for a lancer,
> Oh who would not sleep with the brave?
> I 'listed at home for a lancer
> To ride on a horse to my grave."

And he sings of the virtue of fortitude:

> " We for a certainty are not the first
> Have sat in taverns while the tempest hurled

238

Their hopeful plans to emptiness, and cursed
Whatever brute and blackguard made the world.
It is in truth iniquity on high
To cheat our sentenced souls of aught they crave,
And mar the merriment as you and I
Fare on our long fool's-errand to the grave.
Iniquity it is ; but pass the can.
My lad, no pair of kings our mothers bore ;
Our only portion is the estate of man :
We want the moon, but we shall get no more.
The troubles of our proud and angry dust
Are from eternity, and shall not fail.
Bear them we can, and if we can we must.
Shoulder the sky, my lad, and drink your ale."

Not much need to ask who is the author of that.
There is the same clear-eyed courage in both Hardy
and Housman : the same refusal to accept false
comfort : the same spare, clean, well-knit style.

" Yonder see the morning blink :
   The sun is up, and up must I,
To wash and dress and eat and drink
And look at things and talk and think
   And work, and God knows why."

There is a glorious expression of the outlawry of
poets in the poem which begins :

" The laws of God, the laws of man,
He may keep that will and can ;
Not I."

—and ends with reluctant resignation :

" I, a stranger and afraid
In a world I never made. . . .
And since, my soul, we cannot fly
To Saturn nor to Mercury,
Keep we must, if keep we can,
These foreign laws of God and man."

" The Culprit " and " Eight o'Clock," with their
simple description of the last hours of a man about

to be hanged, are absolutely Hardyesque. Yet there is always the unconquerable spirit of man :

> " Half the night he longed to die,
>   Now are sown on hill and plain
> Pleasures worth his while to try
>   Ere he longs to die again.
>
> Blue the sky from east to west
>   Arches, and the world is wide,
> Though the girl he loves the best
>   Rouses from another's side."

Most of us would have taken 100,000 words of bad prose to convey the idea that he concentrates into those eight lines. The same thought recurs in these lines :

> " The skies, they are not always raining
>   Nor grey the twelvemonth through ;
> And I shall meet good days and mirth,
> And range the lovely lands of earth
>   With friends no worse than you."

There is no man living who can convey so much in so little space. What an exquisite lyric is the following, and how packed with matter :—

> " The fairies break their dances
>   And leave the printed lawn,
> And up from India glances
>   The silver sail of dawn.
>
> The candles burn their sockets,
>   The blinds let through the day,
> The young man feels his pockets
>   And wonders what's to pay."

It is almost more by virtue of what he omits than of what he includes that he is so fine a poet. He tries all sorts of experiments in metre : he achieves a true Elizabethan touch in " Epithalamium " : he sings less often about Ludlow : more often he philosophises in this fashion :

> " When first my way to fair I took
> Few pence in purse had I,
> And long I used to stand and look
> At things I could not buy.
>
> Now times are altered : if I care
> To buy a thing, I can ;
> The pence are here and here's the fair,
> But where's the lost young man ?
>
> —To think that two and two are four
> And neither five nor three
> The heart of man has long been sore
> And long 'tis like to be."

It is with extraordinary regret that we come at last to his final poem, " Fancy's Knell," and take our leave of him—and yet how much of the whole of him we get in these few verses, with the unforgettable beginning :

> " When lads were home from labour
> At Abdon under Clee,
> A man would call his neighbour
> And both would send for me.
> And where the light in lances
> Across the mead was laid,
> There to the dances
> I fetched my flute and played."

—and that magnificent finish :

> " Wenlock Edge was umbered,
> And bright was Abdon Burf,
> And warm between them slumbered
> The smooth green miles of turf ;
> Until from grass and clover
> The upshot beam would fade,
> And England over
> Advanced the lofty shade.

Q

The lofty shade advances,
I fetch my flute and play :
Come, lads, and learn the dances
And praise the tune to-day.
To-morrow, more's the pity,
Away we both must hie,
To air the ditty,
And to earth I."

Our only regret is that he sings less often of the
cherry hung with snow and the gold-cup flowers in
the lovers' lane and the mist blowing off from Teme.
We miss, too, this lovely note :

" Oh, when I was in love with you,
Then I was clean and brave,
And miles around the wonder grew
How well did I behave."

We miss the bells of Bredon . . . though we get
variants on the story there told of lovers lying alone.
We miss the nostalgia implicit in—

" 'Tis time, I think, by Wenlock town
The golden broom should blow ;
The hawthorn sprinkled up and down
Should charge the land with snow."

We miss the lament of the

" . . . soul that lingers sighing
About the glimmering weirs."

The apologia of the Shropshire Lad serves well
enough for both volumes, his answer to the critics
who say,

" Pretty friendship 'tis to rhyme
Your friends to death before their time
Moping melancholy mad :
Come, pipe a tune to dance to, lad,"

is :

" . . . since the world has still
Much good, but much less good than ill,
And while the sun and moon endure
Luck's a chance, but trouble's sure,
I'd face it as a wise man would,
And train for ill and not for good.
'Tis true, the stuff I bring for sale
Is not so brisk a brew as ale :
Out of a stem that scored the hand
I wrung it in a weary land.
But take it : if the smack is sour,
The better for the embittered hour ;
It should do good to heart and head
When your soul is in my soul's stead ;
And I will friend you, if I may,
In the dark and cloudy day."

Sixty-three short lyrics in one volume and forty-one
in another—just over one hundred in all—but every
one wrought like a Toledo blade, exquisitely polished,
a thing of eternal beauty, not in any sense a plaything
of the fancy, but stern, relentless truth-seeking.
Nature is " heartless, witless "; love is more brittle
than porcelain ; all too soon man goes to his long
home, but these things inspire us to waste less time—
to get out on our quest of beauty while we can.

PART V

SOME MODERN DRAMATISTS

GRANVILLE BARKER
J. M. BARRIE
CLEMENCE DANE
St JOHN ERVINE
JOHN GALSWORTHY
SOMERSET MAUGHAM
EUGENE O'NEILL
ARTHUR PINERO
BERNARD SHAW
ALFRED SUTRO

I

GRANVILLE BARKER

IT is the essence of drama that the playwright
says something. In most modern plays no one says
anything. Perhaps there isn't time. There are
so many frocks to admire, friends to talk to (where
are we going to meet if not in a theatre?), dramatic
situations to be worked out, that the majority
of dramatists do not worry overmuch to make their
characters do more than indulge in the small talk
of the drawing-room or in the farcically unreal
language of conventional melodrama. With what
relief do we turn to a play like *Waste* and find
wit, common sense, passion, political intrigue and,
most of all, an interpretation of life, wild anger at the
sloppy thinking that destroys any possibility of right
living. Unlike Shaw, Barker does not imagine that he
has found the truth : he is, as Dixon Scott says, simply
the pierrot on pilgrimage. In *The Voysey Inheritance*
he tackles the problem of dishonesty in business : in
Waste he lays bare the absurdity of a world in which
" one natural action, which the slight shifting of a
social law could have made as negligible as eating a
meal, can make one incapable . . . takes the linch-pin
out of one's brain." In *The Madras House* he tackles
the whole problem of women. Philip and Jessica are
two of Barker's most loved characters. In one of
those illuminating passages in italics which are not
the least beautiful part of his plays he likens Jessica
to a race-horse. " Come to think of it, it is a very
wonderful thing to have raised this crop of ladyhood.
Creatures, dainty in mind and body, gentle in thought
and word, charming, delicate, sensitive, graceful,
chaste, credulous of all good, shaming the world's

247

ugliness and strife by the very ease and delightsomeness of their existence ; fastidious—fastidious—fastidious . . . salted by the addition of learning and humour. Is not the perfect lady perhaps the most wonderful achievement of civilisation, and worth the cost of her breeding ? "

Jessica and Philip are at one in their hatred of the farmyard world of sex—they are at one in their wants : " I want an art and a culture that shan't be just a veneer on savagery."

" Male and female created He them . . . and left us to do the rest. Men and women are a long time in the making."

Philip is consumed with an intellectual passion. Whatever he thinks is worth giving expression to. " There's something wrong with a world," he begins, " in which it takes a man like me all his time to find out that it's bread people want, and not either cake or crumbs."

" There's something wrong," says Thomas, the " good fellow," " with a man while he will think of other people as if they were ants on an ant-heap."

The worst of it is that Thomas is right about Philip. There is Miss Yates under his dissecting knife. Miss Yates, a replica of Fanny in *Hindle Wakes*, only less attractive—" I took the risk. I knew what I was about. I wanted to have my fling. And it was fun for a bit "—which rather startles Philip, who confesses to having unconventional opinions, " but I don't do unconventional things "—regarding Miss Yates very much as if she was one of an ant-heap to be regarded with the eye of Henri Fabre.

Philip may not do unconventional things, but he is ready to face and to hurry on a new and more rational order of living. When Thomas remonstrates that " you can't behave towards women as if they were men," and Philip replies, " Why not ? . . . I always do," he shocks Thomas, but anticipates his wife's " I want to be friends with men. I'd sooner be friends with them. It's they who flirt with me. Why ? "

Most of the opinions in this play are those of
Constantine, Philip's father, who has deserted Philip's
mother and turned Mohammedan. It is he who is
most emphatic in his hatred of the Western views on
women. " Europe in its attitude towards women is
mad. . . . It's a terrible thing to be constantly conscious of women. They have their uses to the world
. . . their perpetual use . . . and the world's interest
is best served by keeping them strictly to it. . . . [In
Europe] wherever he turns he is distracted, provoked,
tantalised by the barefaced presence of women.
How's he to keep a clear brain for the larger issues
of life ? Why do you soldiers volunteer with such
alacrity for foreign service . . . every public question
. . . all politics, all religion, all economy is being
brought down to the level of women's emotion . . .
softening, sentimentalising, enervating . . . lapping
the world, if you let it, in the nursery cotton-wool of
prettiness and pettiness. . . . Justice degenerates into
kindness. . . . Religion is a pretty hymn tune to keep
us from fear of the dark. . . . Women haven't morals
or intellect in our sense of the words. . . . Shut them
away from public life and public exhibition. It's
degrading to compete with them. . . . I ask you all
. . . what is to happen to you as a nation . . . what
with the well-kept women you flatter and æstheticise
till they won't give you children, and the free women
you work at market rates till they can't give you
children . . ."

In the end Philip sums up the situation : " If we
can't love the bad as well as the beautiful . . . if we
won't share it all out now . . . fresh air and art . . .
and dirt and sin . . . then we good and clever people
are costing the world too much. Our brains cost too
much if we don't give them freely. Your beauty costs
too much if I only admire it because of the uglier
women I see . . . even your virtue may cost too
much, my dear."

Philip is out to produce a spiritual revolution, and
that is exactly what Granville Barker achieves with

each of his plays. He makes us think, he pays us the compliment of taking it for granted that we can think. His beauty is the beauty of clear crystal.

In *Waste* there is an acid clarity about the relations of the statesman, Trebell, with the flirtatious Mrs O'Connell. Trebell allows that there are " three facts in life that call up emotion—Birth, Death, and the Desire for Children."

In the second act he is interrupted in his grandiose schemes for reforming the country—disestablishing the Church to provide schoolmasters—" Teaching our children . . . nothing else matters . . . presume that the world will come to an end every thirty years if it's not reconstructed. Therefore give responsibility . . . give the children power "—by Amy O'Connell: " There's a danger of my having a child—your child— some time in April." He is quite ruthless when she pleads with him : " That night we were together . . . it was for a moment different to everything that has ever been in your life before, wasn't it ? " she asks.

" Listen," he replies. " I look back on that night as one looks back on a fit of drunkenness." She can't understand that he neither did nor does love her. " You've been talking a lot of nonsense about your emotions, and your immortal soul," he says. " You don't seem to have any personal feelings at all," she retaliates. When she implores him to marry her he is staggered. " Marry you ! I should murder you in a week." And she refuses to go through with it. Trebell indulges in metaphysical speculations which drive her to fury.

" Faith in what ? " she asks at the end of a long disquisition.

" Our vitality," he replies. " I don't give a fig for beauty, happiness or brains. All I ask of myself is— can I pay Fate on demand ? " She turns back to the all-important (to her) question of how she is to escape the consequences of their mad half-hour. " Won't you tell me whom to go to ? " she pleads. Trebell refuses, and goes back to governing the country—

"We must do away with text-book teachers "—"the wish to know is going to prevail against any creed "— while Amy goes away and kills herself—and Trebell is ruined. "D'you think if the little affair with Nature," he cries, "her offence and mine against the conveniences of civilisation, had ended in my death too . . . then they'd have stopped to wonder at the misuse and waste of the only force there is in the world . . . come to think of it there is no other . . . than this desire for expression . . . in words . . . or through children . . . the little fool, the little fool. . . . Why did she kill my child? What did it matter what I thought her? We were committed together to that one thing. Do you think I didn't know that I was heartless, and that she was socially in the wrong? But what did Nature care for that? And Nature has broken us."

And so he too kills himself.

"No," says Walter, "I don't know why he did it . . . and I don't care. And grief is no use. I'm angry— just angry at the waste of a good man."

Barker states the problem and offers no solution, but he leaves us determined to face facts a little more clearly, to alter, in so far as in us lies, some of the more glaring errors and superstitions to which we have been prone.

He has the essence of the playwright in him because he does realise the necessity of giving us a conflict. He has no magic poetry of phrase, no humour of a technical kind. He does not let us down lightly. He demands that we shall rise to his intellectual level.

II

J. M. BARRIE

BARRIE is a very imp of mischief. Most dearly does he love tantalising his audiences. In *Shall We Join The Ladies?* he gave us one of his most finished works of art and pretended that it was only the beginning. For years we have sighed for the chance of reading *Dear Brutus*—sighed in vain. If we wished to refresh our memory we had to see it acted. Only now can we get it in book form, and it is the publication of this best of all his plays that leads me to write about him at all.

M. Recouly places him as "something apart, exceptional, almost miraculous" because of his ability to raise the drama up to visionary heights by the magic wand with which he touches both characters and audience. "At once they leave the real world and go out into another." He likens Barrie's touch to that of an aeroplane leaving the ground. We never quite know the moment that the aeroplane actually leaves the ground. We never quite know the moment that Barrie switches us away from reality. In *The Admirable Crichton* we are shown the fragility of caste by the simple process of wrecking his characters on a desert island.

This island craze of Barrie—most strongly developed of course in *Mary Rose*—is like the Arabia craze of Walter de la Mare : it is the craving of the poet. It is curious how much more of a poet Barrie is by instinct than any living practitioner of that art (except perhaps three or four). M. Recouly calls him a great poet. "He discerns at once in men and things their deepest and most intimate qualities. As a poet, he is endowed with an exquisite Virgilian sweetness, which he scatters broadcast over characters and situations like a rain of precious stones." The miracle in Barrie lies in the blending of the poetic gift with a staggering craftsmanship. "No one," says Recouly, "surpasses Barrie in the art of . . . calling up his characters before his audience in a way that will never be forgotten ; of adjusting and fitting situation into situation, and of constructing a solid framework for his play. . . . Add to these gifts the inborn sense of dialogue and conversation, wit and sense of humour, and you will have a summary of Barrie's genius." He then analyses in detail the detective play, *Shall We Join The Ladies?* which contains an absolutely original idea—Barrie is always original, as Pinero never is— the unmasking of a criminal by asking all the suspects of the murder to dine together, and submitting them to the ordeal of a judicial inquiry as they eat and drink. The whole cream of the jest lies in the method of investigation, in the chase, not in the kill, and those of his audiences who were more at home in the hunting field than in the office of dramatic criticism instinctively got the atmosphere and finality of the play, while the non-sportsmen were left floundering. We hear a pistol shot. The curtain goes down, and we are left in ignorance whether there was a kill or not. The point that matters is that we had an amazing run for our money. As a superb piece of stagecraft even Barrie has not excelled that excellent trifle.

Dear Brutus is a very different affair. It has the power to infuriate us more than any play of modern times, not because it is so bad, but because it is so good. No one, we feel, has the power to tug at our heart-strings like this. Barrie knows too much about the things we strive like mad to keep hidden, even from our children, our wives, or our parents. In despair we take refuge in cynicism and turn on the seer with a cry of "Sentimentalist!" It is true : Barrie is eaten up with Sentiment, but oh, how many poles removed from the wishy-washy sentiment of Ian Hay ! It is most unfair of Barrie to give us a glimpse of those

woods where we may live our lives over again. It will
be remembered that at the end of Act I. all the characters are on the way to their second chance. In the
entr'acte between Act I. and Act II. it will be noticed
that people do not talk. In every other play there
is a buzz of conversation. In *Dear Brutus* old men
settle more deeply into their chairs and think, young
couples hold hands (sentimentally) in silence. It is
lucky for them all that they cannot anticipate the
pain they are going to feel. They give themselves up
to an exquisite anguish, hopelessly unreal, but very
soothing. This first act is full of moonshine : not so
the characters who take part in it.

Mrs Dearth, for instance (the wife of du Maurier is
the way all theatre-goers think of her, meaning—must
I say it ?—the wife of the weak-willed artist Dearth,
into whose skin du Maurier so marvellously projects
himself)—Mrs Dearth is " tall, of smouldering eye and
fierce desires, murky beasts lie in ambush in the laby-
rinths of her mind . . . a white-faced gipsy with a
husky voice, most beautiful when she is sullen, and
therefore frequently at her best." Lady Caroline
Laney is sufficiently described as the woman who
pronounces *r* as *w*. " Every woman who pronounces
r as *w* will find a mate : it appeals to all that is
chivalrous in man."

Lob, of course, is the Puckish side of Barrie, " so
light that the subject must not be mentioned in his
presence," whose greatest amusement is suddenly to
whirl round in such a manner as to make his guests jump.
There is symbolism here, could we but see it. There
is much talk of a movable wood, a sort of pleasant
Birnam. Lob dances in and above and under the table,
making sweet little clucking noises, while his house-
party sort themselves out, misunderstood husbands
with other men's unloved wives. Joanna and Purdie
are caught in the act of kissing by Mabel, Purdie's
wife, who quietly asks Joanna to return to her the
pieces of her husband's love when she has finished with
them. After forty-four pages of waiting (how clever

of Barrie, this), Will Dearth (du Maurier) is allowed
to shamble in, scarcely intoxicated, watery-eyed, the
relic of a good man, who had once been clear-eyed,
merry, a singer at his job. "Alice [Mrs Dearth] has
had a rather wild love for this man, or for that other
one . . . but somehow it has gone whistling down
the wind." Yet he can still say, "Crack-in-my-eye
Tommy," though his hand shakes ; he can still
"Wonder why I have become such a waster. . . .
Crack-in-my-eye Tommy, how I used to leap out of
bed at six A.M. all agog to be at my easel . . . and
now I'm middle-aged and done for."

Yes, there ought to be a close season for reminiscences. It is this sort of thing that makes us so angry
with Barrie. We all talk about the time when we got
up at six. It never happened except in the wood.

"It wasn't till I knew you had no opinion of me
that I began to go down-hill. . . ." Oh no ; oh no ;
one oughtn't to talk like that.

Alice is more honest : "I found I didn't care for
you, and I wasn't hypocrite enough to pretend I did."

But even that rouses an unpardonable retort from
Dearth. "The bluntness of you, the adorable wildness of you, you untamed thing ! . . . kiss or kill was
your motto . . . I felt from the first moment I saw
you that you would love me or knife me." It is the
stage direction here that catches us up, not the spoken
word :

"Memories of their shooting star flare in both of
them for as long as a sheet of paper might take to burn."

You can gauge your own sensitiveness by recalling
what passed through your mind during the silence of
the couple here.

"I didn't knife you," says Alice at last.

"I suppose it's too late to try to patch things up ?"
She agrees that it is.

DEARTH (*whose tears would smell of brandy*) :
"Perhaps if we had had children . . ."

"If I hadn't married you what a different woman I
should be," says Alice.

The sententious Dearth describes three things that
do not come back to men and women : "the spoken
word, the past life and the neglected opportunity."
If they did, he agrees (avoiding a hiccup) that they
would not make any better a show. After warning
her against the attentions of the dishonourable
Honourable Freddy Finch-Fallowe, he allows the brief
connubial chat to die away. Lob returns to tell his
guests that in the wood there awaits every one of
them his or her second chance, and off they go. It
would be hard to imagine a more intriguing first act,
but it is only the faintest foretaste of the glories
of that amazing second act. There is not in our
literature another dialogue quite so poignant as that
between Dearth and his daughter that-might-have-
been. As a prologue to that we have the joyous sight
of the philanderer Purdie now caught by Joanna (his
wife in this other world) kissing Mabel. "Then I
met you," says Purdie. "Too late," says Mabel,
"never—for ever—for ever—never." We have had
scarcely time to recover from the audacity of this when
the hobbledehoy—all legs, with brambles adhering to
her—leaps through the woods like an escaping nymph
from her singing father. "She has as many freckles
as there are stars in heaven. She is as lovely as
you think she is, and she is aged the moment when
you like your daughter best." How much theatre-
goers miss who miss such stage directions as this.
You now see how much Barrie adores this Margaret
of his that he has conjured down from the skies.
"Daddy" Dearth is "ablaze in happiness and health
and a daughter." He is almost a living incarnation
of what Francis Thompson thought Shelley to be.
But no sooner are we allowed to escape into the land
of sheer delight, where we all have such fathers and
such daughters, than "Hold me tight, Daddy, I'm
frightened. I think they want to take you away from
me . . . it's too lovely . . . things that are too
beautiful can't last . . . to be very gay, dearest dear,
is so near to being very sad. . . ." We can't stand

much of this, but she doesn't spare us a syllable.
"Daddy, what is a 'might-have-been'?" That sort
of thing. It gives Dearth a chance to lacerate us.
"I 'might-have-been' a great swell of a painter. . . .
I might have been a worthless, idle waster of a fellow
. . . some little kink in me might have set me off on
the wrong road. And that poor soul I might so easily
have been might have had no Margaret."

This is where we implore him to stop—we
clutch and scream under the anæsthetic—but no :
we are in the surgeon's hands, and he is well away,
ripping us open mercilessly. "The poor old Daddy,
wandering about the world without me," says Margaret.
It becomes more and more unbearable. We shift
uneasily in our seats. "I think men need daughters,"
says Margaret. We wallow in it. "Hie, Daddy, at
what age are we nicest?" We are spared nothing.
"When you were two, and knew your alphabet up to
G, but fell over at H . . . the year before she puts up
her hair . . ." Oh, stop! stop! "Daddy, do you
remember . . .?" "Daddy, do you remember . . .?"
He even tells her how he robbed her of her baby laugh.
"The laugh that children are born with lasts just so
long as they have perfect faith. To think it was I who
robbed you of yours!"

"Oh, how you love me, Daddikins," says Margaret.
(A vagrant woman has wandered in their direction,
one whom the shrill winds of life have lashed and bled ;
here and there ragged graces still cling to her, and
unruly passion smoulders, but she, once a dear, fierce
rebel with eyes of storm, is now first of all a whimperer.
She and they meet as strangers.)

We try to get up and go. We cannot bear this.
Alice Dearth — now the Honourable Mrs Finch-
Fallowe—is a beggar who curses her husband : she
envies Dearth his Margaret. When she goes, Dearth
talks about "we lucky ones." "Margaret, always
feel sorry for the failures . . . especially in my sort of
calling. Wouldn't it be lovely to turn them on the
thirty-ninth year of failure into glittering successes?"

R

Alice's parting remark has been "shuddery" enough—"Take care of her; they are easily lost "— but worse, far worse is to come. "It would be hard for me," says Margaret, "if you lost me, but it would be worse for you. I don't know how I know that, but I do know it."

Dearth sees a light . . . he decides to go and rouse the people in the house and get food for the beggar-woman. "I shall be back before you can count a hundred," he says gaily, and disappears in the blackness.

"Daddy," cries the fading daughter, "come back! I don't want to be a might-have-been."

It is like that agonising cry of "Mary Rose!" It is hard enough to bear the passing of lilac and laburnum, the end of a great day in the open air, but to try to lay hold on the skirts of death, to keep love at bay— to try to ensure permanency to material things—how impossible, how futile, how heart-breaking! But Barrie tries to secure permanence for things of the spirit. Charles Lamb's "Dream-Children" are safely in the air; Barrie brings Margaret to life; she is flesh and blood.

We are reduced to limp rags by the end of Act II. If we were silent at the end of Act I.—at the end of this we are reduced to tears, not altogether silent. One really audible sob—and the whole theatre would be submerged. Surely, surely we feel the third act will be an anti-climax. We are back in Lob's house. The house-party come in dazed from the wood. First, Mabel and Purdie—still with the outside influence on them. They gradually come to themselves.

PURDIE (*at last*): "Don't let go! . . . Hold on. . . . 'If the dog-like devotion of a lifetime . . .' which of you (Joanna or Mabel) was I saying that to?" Later—"I say, I believe I'm not a deeply passionate chap at all: I believe I am just . . . a philanderer!" The trio look on themselves without approval. ". . . The wood has taught me one thing, at any rate," he continues. "It isn't accident that shapes

our lives . . . it's not Fate. . . . What really plays
the dickens with us is something in ourselves. Something that makes us go on doing the same sort of
fool things, however many chances we get. . . . Something we are born with. . . . It isn't very pleasant to
discover that one is a rotter. . . . My whole being is
corroded."

To Purdie is given the moralising, the interpretation
of the core, of the spirit of the play : to him is given
the quotation from Shakespeare which gives the play
its name. We have the power to shape ourselves :
the question is, have we the grit ? Having decided
that they are rather laughable characters, Joanna,
Mabel and Purdie watch the others return. Husband
and wife in Mr and Mrs Coade have found that what
they got was what they wanted. Alice comes in and
lies about having given her sandwiches to a poor girl
and her father in the wood. Barrie is none too
merciful to Dearth's wife.

" The last of the adventurers draws nigh, carolling a
French song as he comes "—so runs the stage direction.
We try to slink like snails into imaginary shells—no ;
we cannot put off the pain—we shrink back and further
back and the menace comes nearer. We could howl
to warn the unhappy man to keep away—to stick to
his dream Margaret—anything to spare him the disillusion that is about to shatter him. He is here !
" I am sorry to bounce in on you . . ." he begins.

He sees Alice. They both become frightened as
they see that their clothes are not the same as those
which they were wearing outside.

In words that send a cold shiver down the spine
Barrie gives us another stage direction.

(The hammer is raised.)

" I am . . . it is coming back," says Dearth. " I
am not the man I thought myself. . . . I didn't know
you (to Alice) when I was in the wood with Margaret.
She . . . she . . . Margaret. . . ."

(The hammer falls). " O my God ! "

ALICE : " I wish—I wish——"

(She presses his shoulder fiercely and then stalks by the door.)

"I thank thee for that hour," says Dearth, and he too goes.

"If we could wait long enough," runs the final stage direction, "we might see the Dearths breasting their way into the light."

We don't believe it. That is the sentimental Barrie, having harrowed our feelings for three hours, sending us away with " It's only a play." It isn't only a play : it is very much more. It is a true interpretation of life ; only we are so afraid that we harden our hearts. We have to harden our hearts, or we could not endure the agony of living.

The Purdies of this world will go on with their amorous intrigues, the Dearths drift helplessly for want of a steadying child.

I return to Recouly's metaphor. In the first act we leave the ground in our aeroplane, uncertain of the moment of losing contact with the actuality; in the second act we fly over Elysian fields in perfect happiness, with just a twinge of terror here and there for the insecurity of our position ; in the third we make a graceful and perfect landing.

Recouly reminds us that we have to keep the wind of logic away from this voyage : it would break up the aeroplane.

Barrie has a perfect understanding with his audience which is open to auto-suggestion, and ready to abandon itself entirely to the magic of his charm.

He has an extraordinary capacity for writing a full play in one act. He have all revelled in the irony of *The Twelve-Pound Look*, with its perfect " curtain." How many of those who have seen it acted have read the stage directions ? They are a little upsetting for the complacency of those who always see themselves as the heroes and their enemies as the villains.

"If quite convenient (as they say about cheques), you are to conceive that the scene is laid in your own house, and that Harry Sims is you. . . . It pleases us

to make him a city man, but (rather than lose you) he
can be turned with a scrape of the pen into a K.C.,
fashionable doctor, Secretary of State, or what you
will. . . . It is that day in your career when everything went wrong just when everything seemed to be
superlatively right. In Harry's case it was a woman
who did the mischief. She came to him in his great
hour and told him she did not admire him. Of course
he turned her out of the house and was soon himself
again, but it spoilt the morning for him."

No, " stage directions " is wrong: this is a full
synopsis written by the author.

What fun it is to watch the pompous Harry rehears-
ing the ceremony of the accolade before his peaky-
faced wife. . . . Enter the typist (a new girl) . . .
later re-enter Harry . . . of course — the mutual
recognition: once she had been his wife. Kate the
typist and Harry the success are left to discuss life
and each other. He is anxious to know who the man
was for whom she forsook him fourteen years ago.
When she tells him, he doesn't like it at all: " There
was no one, Harry; no one at all." An appalling
idea: she left him not for the sake of a lover, but to
get away from the swaddling bands of luxury. " Your
success was suffocating me."

" I tell you," says Sir Harry, " I am worth a quarter
of a million."

" To me," answers Kate, " exactly twelve pounds.
With my first twelve (earned) pounds I paid for my
machine. Then I considered that I was free to go,
and I went. . . . If only you'd been a man, Harry.
. . . Haven't you heard of them? They are something fine: and every woman is loath to admit to
herself that her husband is not one. When she
marries, even though she has been a very trivial person,
there is in her some vague stirring toward a worthy
life, as well as a fear of her capacity for evil. She
knows her chance lies in him. . . . I didn't give you
up willingly, Harry. I invented all sorts of theories
to explain you. Your hardness—I said it was a fine

want of mawkishness. Your coarseness—I said it goes with strength. Your contempt for the weak—I called it virility. Your want of ideals was clear-sightedness. Your ignoble views of women—I tried to think them funny . . . but I had to let you go. You had only the one quality, Harry, success.''

Yes, Barrie can lash out when he is moved, as here, to righteous wrath.

" If I was a husband "—here is her Parthian shaft— " it is my advice to all of them—I would often watch my wife quietly to see whether the twelve-pound look was not coming into her eyes." She goes. Lady Sims comes in, has a look at the typewriter, says (inconsequentially), " Are they very expensive ? " and the curtain falls. " We have a comfortable feeling, you and I, that there is nothing of Harry Sims in us." Have we ? I think not. Never, after seeing this.

There is *The Will* with the devoted young couple : "I leave everything of which I die possessed to my beloved wife." Philip is earning £170 a year. He and Emily only strive to outdo the other in generosity . . . everything augurs well . . . but Surtees, the lawyer's clerk, has a strange disease . . . ominous this, and symbolic, " always in me, a black spot, not so big as a pin's head, but waiting to spread and destroy me in the fullness of time. . . . The doctor says there's a spot of that kind in pretty nigh all of us, and if we don't look out it does for us in the end . . . he called it the accursed thing." The curtain falls for a second : Philip and Emily are middle-aged, prosperous : " seventy thou." is Philip's term : they wrangle over bequests : they are no longer generous. The curtain again falls, to rise on Sir Philip at sixty, " strong of frame, but a lost man." He is in mourning. " Things went wrong," he confesses to the old lawyer ; "I don't know how. It's a beast of a world. . . . The money I've won with my blood . . . if I bring it to you in sacks, will you fling it out of the window for me ? " He is reminded of " the spot no bigger than a pin's head." " I wish," he says, " I could help some young things before that spot has time to spread and destroy them as it has destroyed me and mine . . ." (summing up his life). "It can't be done with money. . . ." (He goes away : God knows where.)

How Barrie does loathe success: to him money is truly a curse. Is this the cry of a sentimentalist ? It can't be sour grapes. He is by far the most prosperous dramatist of our time.

He is easily the first to whom we apply the word " genius," if by that strange word we mean a man whose mental processes completely evade us. He has the gift, not only of making the sentimental palatable, but almost of making us believe that to be sentimental is a virtue. As a tear-monger and a laughter-monger, better still, as a tear-and-laughter-in-one-monger, he stands absolutely alone.

III

CLEMENCE DANE

A BILL OF DIVORCEMENT and *Will Shake-speare* are in many respects two of the most significant plays of our time, the former because of its dramatic problems. For once the problem is actual; it really hurts : we feel that Margaret Fairfield is a door-mat, a fluffy, mindless, incompetent creature, completely at the mercy of the opinion of the person nearest to her. We feel that she has no right to turn her husband down when he returns to her sane after fifteen years in an asylum, and we also feel that she has a right to some ounce or two of happiness to make up for the years of misery she has endured. She is impaled on the horns of a hopeless dilemma. Hers is a really dramatic situation. To suggest that Clemence Dane is contributing anything to the solution of the problem of " Divorce for Insanity " is ludicrous. The problem never crops up. Margaret is already divorced when the play starts : her one-time husband is no longer mad.

We are solely concerned with individual agonies : whether it really is expedient that one man should die for the people : if so, what an infamously constructed world : whether daughters of men who have suffered mentally should deny themselves the chance of becoming mothers for the sake of eugenics : whether moral contracts are binding : how far sensitive men and women can go on hurting one another—and a thousand other things.

Clemence Dane is a queer creature. She has a wonderful capacity for sensing people's thoughts, and yet she is quite inhuman. It is simply impossible for her to create a man who is more than a wooden block. The husband is merely a mass of nerves, jumpy, quick, crazy for affection; Sydney's lover is just a walking suit of clothes, while Gray (Margaret's lover) might have stepped straight out of an Ethel Dell novel; he is so ludicrously unlike any man who ever lived. There are moments (not a few) when he rants like a Lyceum villain : we feel a little cheated when he fails to knock Margaret down.

I found the spinster aunt, Miss Fairfield, staggeringly unreal—as unreal as the Christmas bells and the Christmas snow and the Christmas holly and the Christmas presents. She is used to unfold the plot. That seems to be the dramatist's great difficulty—how to let the audience know what has gone before without making the elucidation as hopelessly unreal as the " rag " elucidation in *The Critic.*

Clemence Dane is a maddening writer. She has all the gifts and then exhibits a lack of *savoir-faire* that savours of the " Housemaid novelettes."

" Wouldn't it warm the cockles of Aunt Hester's heart to hear you ! " says the seventeen-year-old Sydney, and then adds archly : " What are cockles, Gray ? "

When I saw the play first I thought Meggie Albanesi had mischievously interpolated that as a gag because she had forgotten her part. I was shocked. But there are few things we would not forgive this glorious actress. Then on reading the play I saw the ghastly irrelevant flippancy and shivered. What would Ibsen say, what would William Archer say, what A. B. Walkley and what St John Ervine ? But one and all they missed it. I who am obtuse enough, heaven knows ! to many things, had my æsthetic sense shattered by the phrase : " What are cockles, Gray ? "

When Margaret keeps on reiterating " I hope I'm doing right " because she is so certain that she is doing wrong in trying to snatch at personal happiness, we merely want to take her by the scruff of the neck and kick her. Then we think again, realise what an amazing fool she is going to live with, and let it go at that. We could not think of any punishment better adapted to fit the crime.

The worst of Gray Meredith (what a name !) is that Clemence Dane likes him. He is her idea of a man. " He is about forty, tall, dark and quiet, very sure of himself, and quite indifferent to the effect he makes on other people (as if most men . . . well, well !). As he is a man who never has room in his head for more than one idea at a time, and as for the last five years that idea has been Margaret, the rest of the world doesn't get much out of him." So runs Clemence Dane's own description of him.

He is about as entertaining as a volume of *The Graphic* for 1853, and about as heavy.

While we are gnawing our gums with wrath over the futility of Gray and Margaret, the telephone bell rings, and all is forgiven. It is ominous of dreadful things. At the same moment the church bells stop.

Margaret (*in a strange voice*): " Yes, they stopped when that other bell rang."

With a shiver she goes off to church. The audience is delighted. That telephone bell is going to mean something. All telephoning on the stage thrills the house : everyone cranes forward a little to hear the other man talking. Watch your neighbour next time you are in a theatre and you will see that I am right. Young playwrights should always begin with a telephone scene : it is far more effective than a bedroom, even in a farce.

To get back to *The Bill*. Sydney is now left to conduct one of those modern love scenes in which young people cry " Owl ! " " Idiot ! " " old thing," " old man " in heart-rending accents to show how much reticence expresses the overflowing heart. " You're as hard as nails," says Kit to Sydney. We know better, and Clemence Dane knows that we know better. It is a trick to make us love Sydney more.

After a love scene which makes Kit uncomfortable, and makes us realise that there is nothing new under the sun, not even the seventeen-year-old cheeky modern girl of 1932, as seen by Clemence Dane, the telephone bell rings again, and we come back to the main issue, as we do when the judge dons the black cap after days of irrelevant chatter. Something is going to happen. We really want to know what the fellow on the other end of the line is saying to Meggie Albanesi, who is superb in her dialogue with the invisible man. Perhaps it is easier to act with a telephone than a man. I at any rate have never seen anyone fail to " get away " with a telephone scene. But this is certainly one of the best. From it we learn that while Margaret and Gray are in church Margaret's erstwhile husband, Sydney's father, is lurking close, escaped from his asylum, sane. It now all depends on Hilary, the father. When he arrives he reminds us of Lob. Now that I know Malcolm Keen better, I know that he reminds me of Malcolm Keen. I do not like Malcolm Keen's acting. It is unreal. He is too full of sensibility, too empty of real energy. His treatment at the hands of the invertebrate Margaret is simply barbaric. She realises that " he's like a lost child come home," and all she can do is to tell him point-blank that she never loved him. Gray is even more asinine and without feeling than she is. He (God knows for what reason, except that he is one of these " quiet " men who are for ever talking) gets angry because Margaret prefers to discuss the situation with her own husband rather than leave it to him, the lover. Being the fool she is, Margaret tells the truth to Hilary in such a way as nearly to send him back to his asylum. What he has to hear, and the way he hears it, would be enough to turn any sane man's head, if he loved the woman as Hilary obviously loves the worthless Margaret. One of the most staggering people in this staggering play is Dr Alliott, another man much beloved of his creator, who wishes us to visualise in him " a pleasant, roundabout, clean little old man, with a twinkling face . . . he understands you better than you do yourself."

It is this creature, if you please, into whose mouth

is put the " hard word, but the true one " that " It is
expedient that one man should die for the people "—
without anyone having the common sense to contradict
him. A long explanation of the new laws is gone into,
and his wife asks her husband to agree that they are
good ones, giving that second chance which even the
sentimental Barrie denies to men.

The trouble with Margaret is that she finds out
that she does not love the man she married. He has
to suffer for her blunder. It really has nothing to
do with his sanity or insanity. Margaret's outburst
proves that. " Think of it—to want so desperately
to feel—and to feel nothing. Do you know what it
means to dread a person who loves you ? To stiffen
at the look in their eyes ? To pity and—shudder ? "

That is the problem, and it is a real one. Partner-
ships can be dissolved by mutual agreement, but if one
party is fretting to go, and the other fretting to stay,
there is something to be said for holding to the contract.

Margaret, like most selfish people, can't see it.

" Knowing his history," she says, " knowing mine,
is it possible that you expect me to go back to him ? "

Then follows that terrible scene in which her poor
demented husband throws himself upon her mercy.
" I'll not get in your way—but—don't leave me all
alone. Give me something—the rustle of your dress,
the cushion where you've lain—your voice about the
house. You can't deny me such little things, that you
give your servant and your dog."

Margaret keeps on telling him that she doesn't love
him, that she can't think of anybody but Gray, but
the white heat of his fury drives her back to her last
defences.

" You can't leave me. You can't drive me out—
the wilderness—alone—alone—alone," he moans, and
" like a crucified moth " she gives in.

That is a fine curtain to Act II. : it might well be
the end of the play. It seems impossible even in the
best of plays to have three adequate acts.

The first part of Act III. is calculated to drive most

intelligent audiences into Hilary's asylum. Sydney's noble heroics in dismissing the boy she adores because she is afraid lest their children might be tainted with an insane trait would be all right if only they were not made all wrong by Kit's " old thing " reiterated most damnably, a vice only a little less evil than Sydney's damnable reiteration of " old man."

As soon as the callow Kit receives his *congé*, the tailor's dummy, Gray, comes to receive his. In a moment of passion he throws, quite recklessly, a whole cigarette in the fire, and then charmingly proceeds to bully the women he is supposed to be in love with. He taunts Margaret with not loving him, and Margaret (" very white, but her voice is steady ") says : " I love you. I ache and faint for you. I'm withering without you like cut grass in the sun. I love you. I love you. . . . I *am* you. But he's—he's so defenceless. It's vivisection—like cutting a dumb beast about to make me well."

Gray calls her twice a fool. " To deny me, that's a little thing. I'll not go under because you're faithless. But what you're doing is the sin without forgiveness. You're denying—not me—but life. You're denying the spirit of life. You're denying—you're denying your mate."

Sydney, the dutiful daughter, has happily played the eavesdropper up to this point, and now breaks in to urge her mother to go. She has the sense to tell Margaret that " You're no good to him. You're scared of him. . . . I'll make him happier than you can." After a quite maddening bit of play-acting on Gray's part, Margaret falls into his arms and off they go, to the intense relief of the audience. The curtain descends with Sydney attempting to make up to Hilary for the loss of his wife, with the Victorian aunt as usual misinterpreting everything.

Clemence Dane's second play, *Will Shakespeare*, was almost completely a failure on the stage. To read it takes one's breath away. The poetry is pure Elizabethan : the drama poignant : there is nothing on the

modern stage to compare with that amazing speech of
Queen Elizabeth to Shakespeare at the end of the play :

" I tell you, you shall toss upon your bed
    Crying ' Let me sleep ! ' as men cry ' Let me live ! '
And sleeping you shall still cry ' Mary ! Mary ! '
This will not pass. Think not the sun that wakes
The birds in England and the daisy-lawns,
Draws up the meadow fog like prayer to heaven,
And curls the smoke in cottage chimney-stacks,
Shall once forget to wake you with a warm
And kissing breath ! The four walls shall repeat
The name upon your lips, and in your heart
The name, the one name, like a knife shall turn.
These are your dawns. *I* tell you, I who know.
Nor shall day spare you. All your prospering years,
The tasteless honours for yourself—not her—
The envy in men's voices, (if they knew
The beggar that they envied !) all this shall stab,
Stab, stab, and stab again. And little things
Shall hurt you so ; stray words in books you read,
And jests of strangers never meant to hurt you ;
The lovers in the shadow of your fence,
Their faces hid, shall thrust a spare hand out,
The other held, to stab you as you pass :
And oh, the cry of children when they play !
You shall put grief in irons and lock it up,
And at the door set laughter for a guard,
Yet dance through life on knives and never rest,
While England knows you for a lucky man."

There is no question that this is fine poetry and also
finely dramatic. We are tortured as the poet is tortured at the loss of the only thing in life that matters.
Only out of suffering is great work born.
    But there is suffering in Anne Hathaway too:

" Am I your wife, so close to you all day,
    So close to you all night, that oft I lie
Counting your heart-beats—do I watch you stir
And cry out suddenly and clench your hand

Till the bone shows white, and then you sigh and
   turn,
And sometimes smile, but never ope your eyes,
Nor know me with a seeking touch of hands
That bids me share the dream—am I your wife,
Can I be woman and your very wife
And know not you are burdened ?   You lock me out,
Yet at the door I wait, wringing my hands
To help you."

Anne's tragedy is the tragedy of many women—
that of not being able to hold her man. Shakespeare's
heart is elsewhere, a traveller:

               " . . . I've dreamed of others—tall,
Warm-flushed like pine-woods with their clear red
   stems,
With massy hair and voices like the wind
Stirring the cool dark silence of the pines.
Know you such women ?—beckoning hill-top women,
That sway to you with lovely gifts of shade
And slumber, and deep peace, and when at dawn
You go from them on pilgrimage again,
They follow not nor weep, but rooted stand
In their own pride for ever—demi-gods."

It is indeed true, as Henslowe says :

" Not once in a golden age love's scale trims level."

Shakespeare at the thought of getting away is

" As a man stifled that wildly throws his arms,
   Raking the air for room, for room to breathe,
   And so strikes unawares, unwillingly,
   His lover ! "

Anne wants to go with him ; " for we have been such
lovers as there's no room for in the human air and
daylight side of the grass."
Shakespeare then learns for the first time that Anne
tricked him into marriage with a tale of a child to
be born, and with the sharp cruelty of the satiated

sensualist turns on her with " I never loved you." So
cruel does he become that in her agony Anne cries,
" Pitiful God ! if there be other lives . . . let me not
be a woman . . . let me not again be cursed a woman
surrendered to the mercy of her man ! " And when
at the end of Act I. he breaks away from her, Anne
cries, clinging to him :

" Remember ! See, I do not pray ' forgive ' !
Forgive ?   Forgiving is forgetting, no,
Remember me !. . . Husband, when harvest comes,
Of all your men and women I alone
Can give you comfort, for you'll reap my pain
As I your loss. . . . Ah, but when you're old
(You will be old one day, as I am old
Already in my heart), too weary old
For love, hate, pity, anything but peace,
. . . Come back to me when all your need
Is hands to serve you and a breast to die on."

In Act II. we see Shakespeare already in the toils
of Mary Fitton, writing *Romeo and Juliet* to prove to
her that he is more than a fantastic weaver of gossamer.
In the second scene of this act Anne's mother comes
to tell him that his son (of whose existence he was
ignorant) is dying, and he arranges to go back to Stratford with her. Mary Fitton, at a moment's notice,
takes the part of Juliet, and is swept off her feet in her
sudden ecstasy, and falls into Shakespeare's arms—and
Stratford and the world are forgotten.

In Act III. there is rivalry between Marlowe and
Shakespeare, not only in the writing of plays, but for
the favour of Mary Fitton, and in the second scene
Shakespeare murders Kit in the private room of an
inn at Dartford, where he finds him with Mary. After
the deed is done he upbraids his mistress, who in her
turn tells him that she never loved him :

" I could have loved if you had taught me loving,
Something I sought and found not ; so I turned

From searching. I have clean forgotten now
That ever I sought . . .
You should have loved me less, my fool, and less."

In Act IV. Elizabeth banishes Mary from the Court
and in a long interview with Shakespeare points the
way to greatness:

" I know the flesh is sweetest, when all's said,
And summer's heyday and the love of men :
I know well what I lose . . ."

Shakespeare, " being in hell, paying the price, alone,"
is also made to realise what he loses:

" The years before me ! And no Mary ! Mary ! "

—only the ghost of Anne's voice calling on him to
remember her when he is old and all his need is hands
to serve him and a breast to die on.

Not since the days of Elizabeth has there been a
play dealing with the riotous passions of youth so
feverishly.

Clemence Dane was herself once an actress. She
has a magnificent sense of stagecraft and of the
dramatic: her unduly developed brain has made her
a little inhuman, much in the way that poets are inhuman in politics—Spenser, for instance, in Ireland.
Her potentiality is greater than that of any other living dramatist, for she never repeats herself. She is
possessed of infinite variety.

IV

ST JOHN ERVINE

ST JOHN ERVINE is an amusing person. In 1912 he wrote in a paper called *The Citizen*, under the title of "The Day's Illusion," a glorious article about Sir Arthur Pinero, in the course of which he said : " If a poll of playgoers were taken to decide who is the greatest dramatist in England, it is certain that Sir Arthur Pinero would be elected to that position. . . . The plain truth is that Sir Arthur Pinero is neither a thinker nor a wit nor a stylist. You may search his plays from the first to the last without finding a single original thought, a single saying full of wit, or a single beautifully written phrase. You will not find any expression of noble emotion in any of his characters: he has not put one man or woman on the stage who has any of the qualities of greatness."

Of Pinero's heroines he says : " They are common theatrical women. . . . They are without reticence or dignity, balance or courage. . . . The Pinerotic heroes are cads : not one of them is a man of fine fibre or worthy impulse : there is about them the taint of the Piccadilly prowler." He denies him wit as he denies him style and craftsmanship.

It would be, I say, cruel to remind Ervine of what he says about Pinero in these modern days. Even a critic has a right to change his opinions as he changes his paper.

I am not, however, at the moment concerned with Ervine the dramatic critic, who pontificates so Sabbatically in *The Observer*, but Ervine the dramatist, over whose *Mixed Marriage* as an undergraduate I raved. He has written many plays which are not good. I could not summon up much enthusiasm over the

274

story of the man whose soul was bound up so much in his ship that he sent his son to his death in her. And yet *The Ship* is a late play. Let me get back to *Mixed Marriage*, a straightforward drama about Roman Catholics and Protestants in Belfast in the year 190-. The year matters so much in Ireland.

There will be many people unable to stomach (in the reading) the very conscientious manner in which Ervine keeps the brogue up. English dialects in print are bad : Belfast brogue is the very devil. Synge had the sense to avoid spelling every word awry. The main business of Act I. is to watch John Rainey the workman reiterate his gospel that " a Cathlik's a Cathlik, an' a Prodesan's a Prodesan," while we watch Hughie his son fall in love with Nora Murray, a Catholic. " Ye cudden tell the differs atween a Cathlik an' a Prodesan if ye met them in the street an' didden know what their religion wus," says one of his sons. His wife also is of the "live and let live " school. They try to get Rainey to speak on behalf of a strike : he refuses to if they persist in using a Roman Catholic hall. His sons and his son's friend, Michael, urge him to put the brotherhood of the workmen before sectarianism in religion. " What a fine thing it 'ud be if the workin' men o' Irelan' was to join their han's thegither an' try an' make a great country o' it. There wus a time whin Irelan' wus the islan' o' saints. By God ! da, if we cud bring that time back again." Rainey denies that that can ever be again because " there's such a quare differs atween a Cathlik an' a Prodesan."

In Act II. we learn that Rainey did speak on behalf of the strike. Hughie is asking his mother whether she would object to his marrying the Catholic Nora. " She's not goan t' change her religion, an' A'm not goan t' change mine. If there's an' childher . . . we'll let them choose fur themselves whin they're oul' enough. . . . Half the religion in the wurl' is like a disease that ye get thrum yer father."

His mother sees deeper than that. " Whin ye come til bring up yer childher, it's quare how ye don't think like that. . . . Ye can't say, this chile's me an' that chile's her. They're jus' like as if ye wur both lumped thegither. It's very difficult. . . ." They are interrupted in the middle of their argument by Michael, who tells them that there is an Orangemen and Catholic riot which only Rainey will be able to quell. Nora comes in and talks to Mrs Rainey about Hughie. " Men make a quare fuss about religion, an' wan thing an' another, but A'm thinking it's more important fur a wumman t' be able t' make a good dinner fur her man nor t' be able t' pray in the same church. An' sure it's the same God annyway," says Mrs Rainey, with her complete common sense. Ervine is at his best with mothers. It is his sobriety, his complete rather aged common sense coming out. Everyone remembers the sanity of the old mother in *The Ship*, steadying the two inflammatory opposites, father and son. They discuss the stupidity and lovableness of men in an irrelevant manner, as Mr and Mrs Rainey quite irrelevantly in the third act discuss the times they've had together ; there is a passionate outburst of feeling on Nora's part for Hughie : " A'd let Irelan' go til hell fur ye, Hugh ! " They go on proclaiming their love for each other, while Rainey descends the stairs listening. He turns on Nora like a bull, " they wur right whin they said the strack wus a Papesh plot."

He threatens and implores until Mrs Rainey enters to act as usual as mediator. Rainey refuses to continue his support of the strikers. Michael turns to Nora and asks her to believe that " Irelan's a bigger thing nor you an' me an' Hugh an' all o' us rowled thegither."

" A don't belave it," retorts Nora. " A'm in the wurl' t' be happy, an' A'll be happy wi' him." Rainey says : " It's onnacherl fur a man an' a wumman til live in the same house an' worship in a differ'nt church." In the end, after terrific argument, Nora and Hughie leave the house together and Rainey refuses to stir a hand for the strikers. In the last act (ten days later) there are stones being thrown at the windows of Rainey's house : in about three minutes there is

shooting. Nora is terrified at the result of her obstinacy
in clinging to Hughie ; she hears the soldiers shoot,
rushes out on them and is killed. As a play it is much
too wordy, but the conflict is a real one, and we are
made to realise the desperate earnestness of Ervine.
It is comparable in dramatic effect with Galsworthy's
Strife. The stupidity of men in quarrelling over
religion, over economics, is made equally clear in both
plays, but the Irishman scores in making the Irish
girl's passion deep, true and real. The sense of waste
of love is really remarkably well presented.

Jane Clegg is another of his pre-war plays which has
been recently revived.

Jane is thirty-two, waiting at the beginning of the
play with Johnnie and Jenny (her ten- and eight-year-
olds) and her husband's mother (stout, coarse, very
sentimental and querulous) for the return of her fur-
tive, mean husband, Henry. Jane is defending Henry
(who is a commercial traveller) from his mother's
tongue. He is, we learn, a man of *affaires.* There is
an interlude during which we see the headstrong nature
of Jenny and the interfering habits of the grand-
mother. Jane, we gather, is capable of firmness with
her children, but also capable of making allowances
for a weak husband. She tells his mother that she
didn't leave Henry when he was unfaithful to her
because of the children. " A woman who leaves her
husband on moral grounds is treated as badly as a
woman who runs away with another man." The
older woman stirs up in her the spirit of rebellion.
" Why shouldn't I leave him ? " she repeats. " I
hadn't any money, so I couldn't. . . . It isn't right to
ask a woman to take a man for worse. . . . I don't
believe in putting up with things unless you can't help
yourself." We learn that she is economically free
owing to a relative's bequest—that she is restless.
" I'm not certain of Henry. That's what's so hard.
I give him everything, and he isn't faithful." Henry
comes in and tries to wheedle some of her private
money out of her. Mrs Clegg, senior, weeps at her

daughter-in-law's hardness. Henry talks acidly about
" Seven hundred pounds she has, eating its head off in
a bank, and won't lend me two hundred of it." The
argument is interrupted by the advent of Mr Munce
(" a weedy person of the race-course type "), who is left
alone to dun Henry for money. He does not mince
matters. He accuses Henry of owing him twenty-five
pounds, and spending his debt on a woman, not his
wife, who is expecting a child of his. " If I could only
raise a bit, I'd take her off to Canada or somewhere.
I'm damned fond of her, that's what I am. I can't
stick my wife. She's hard, Munce, hard as hell." He
lets slip the fact that his wife won't let him have her
seven hundred pounds. Munce taunts him with
being less than a man : he puts the screw on by suggesting that he will tell Jane about the other woman.
    In Act II. a Mr Morrison calls on Jane with a story
about a missing cheque of one hundred and forty
pounds which Henry has apparently taken. He
comes in while they are talking, blusters badly and
suggests that he left the cheque in his bag at a cloak-
room. Jane reminds him that he took no bag with
him in the morning. He confesses, and Jane agrees
to pay : Morrison is sent away.
    In Act III. Morrison is paid, but unfortunately the
story that Henry had told about having had to spend
the one hundred and forty pounds on bad debts is
discredited. Jane refuses to pay until she hears how
the money was spent. Having detected him in
gambling, thieving and lying, " I wonder if you're
worth saving," says Jane. Mr Munce then reappears,
and the fat is well in the fire. He reveals the existence
of the " fancy woman " and the " fancy child," and at
last leaves Jane alone with her husband, whose defences
are at last all down.
    " I'm not a bad chap, really," he says, " I'm just
weak. I'd be all right if I had a lot of money and a
wife that wasn't better than I am . . . it doesn't do
a chap much good to be living with a woman who's his
superior. . . . I ought to have married a woman like

myself, or a bit worse. That's what Kitty is. She's
worse than I am, and that sort of makes me love her.
I always feel mean here . . . it makes me meaner
than I really am to be living with you." To which
Jane replies: "I used to think you were so fine before
I married you. You were so jolly and free and
light-hearted."

At last he tells her that he spent the money on
tickets to Canada for Kitty and himself. "She didn't
want to have a child, and she's scared." In the end
he gets up and goes.

It is a sombre but quite sincere play, singularly
(in the reading) undramatic. Henry is scarcely worth
writing about. He is so absolutely of the Reuben
nature. Jane is too rigid. It is hard to find a
central core, a theme. It certainly is not a problem
play of the "Ought-Wives-to-Stay-with-Unfaithful-
Husbands?" sort.

On the other hand, it is courageous of Mr Ervine to
have eliminated all the glittering display of the unfaithful rich. *Jane Clegg* has to win through on its
merits. No one goes to see it on account of the frocks.
Poverty hath its problems no less severe than wealth,
even where the erotic passions are concerned. The
difficulty is to rouse interest on the part of those who
can afford to pay for seats. They want to see themselves.

V

JOHN GALSWORTHY

BACKING plays is exactly on a par with backing horses. Galsworthy produces *Loyalties*, a play remarkable mainly for the fact that it is a good detective police-court melodrama, and it runs for— well, long enough to be called "a great play," and almost simultaneously *Windows*, in which he really has something to say, and no one goes to listen to him. That very able Frenchman, M. Recouly, summed up the defect of *Loyalties* admirably when he suggested that the problem which de Levis the Jew had to solve, whether to follow the lure of money or the lure of caste, was a worthy and dramatic one, which Galsworthy deliberately avoided in order to give the public something more suitable to their palate. Most of us got a little restive at the unnecessary police inspector and solicitor's office scenes, excellently as they were produced; they were irrelevant. Almost the entire play was irrelevant. It is always pleasant to see a country house dressing-room, the card-room of a London club, and a solicitor's office on the stage : it is always a joy to watch J. H. Roberts and Meggie Albanesi act, but it is a greater satisfaction to see Galsworthy in his own element, holding the balance in *Strife*, where we see both Capital and Labour naked, each cutting each other's throats for no purpose; in *The Silver Box*, where we are made to realise the difference in the interpretation of the law between the rich and the poor; in *Justice*, where the futility and barbarity of our penal code are mercilessly revealed; in *The Fugitive*, where his extraordinary tenderness rather runs away with him in his anxiety to show how clipped are the wings of the dainty

girl of the period when she tries to exist outside her
cage.

In *Windows* he is writing to please himself; in
Loyalties he is offering a sop to Cerberus quite needlessly.

" Prejudices—or are they loyalties, I don't know
—criss-cross: we all cut each other's throats from
the best of motives." Loyal—the Jew to his love
of money, the Englishman to his class and his queer
codes of honour—is that the idea ? It is a rather
poor one, and incidentally quite wrong. There are
not, I imagine, many Jews quite so unpleasant as de
Levis ; even in these days very few Englishmen who
rob their fellow-guests. There is one interesting
point. De Levis in a fit of anger says : " You called me
a damned Jew. My race was old when you were all
savages. I am proud to be a Jew." No one dreams
of replying to that that most Englishmen are quite
proud to be savages, but don't talk about it, whereas
quite a number of Jews seem to be anything but proud
of belonging to a much older and more honourable
race than ours. Now there is a play in that. But
these are straws. I am told by those who acted in
it that *Loyalties* was an extraordinarily " actable "
play—good drama, and so on. That is what I
felt when I first saw it (except for the policemen).
It is only on rereading it that the melodramatic
qualities appear, the falsities of characterisation, and
the strained effort to bring in a dozen " loyalties."
" Keep faith ! " cries Margaret, the wanton. " We've
all done that. It's not enough." There is a big
theme there, but again Galsworthy didn't tackle it.

In *Windows*, which seemed to upset a great number
of people, he did tackle his problem—or rather he
presented it fairly.

Bly, the window-cleaner, with his philosophy (" What
do *you* think of things, Mr Bly ? " " Not much, sir.")
and his reprieved young daughter (" Ah ! she was
famous at eighteen. *The Sunday Mercury* was full of
her, when she was in prison . . . she's out now ; been
out a fortnight. I always say that fame's ephemereal.

But she'll never settle to that weavin'. Her head got turned a bit. . . . They sentenced 'er to be 'anged by the neck until she was dead, for smotherin' her baby"). Yes, with Mr Bly and his daughter we are back among the characters who matter to Galsworthy: fugitives, pigeons, wasters, forgers, the down-and-out, the feckless, the jail-birds; these are his province. There is a sweet reasonableness about these creatures of his imagination which endears them to us always. " Take my daughter," says Mr Bly. " If I was a blond beast, I'd turn 'er out to starve; if I was an angel, I'd starve meself to learn her the piano. I don't do either. . . . What is up and what is down ? . . . Is it up or down to get so 'ard that you can't take care of others ? . . . Is it up or down to get so soft that you can't take care of yourself ? " There is something far more attractive in the philosophy of Mr Bly than in the chatter of the horse-racing, wealthy, card-playing crowd in *Loyalties*.

" In my opinion Nature made the individual believe he's goin' to live after e's dead just to keep him living while 'e's alive—otherwise he'd 'a' died out." That one sentence is worth the whole of *Loyalties*.

Mr Bly works on Mr March's feelings to get his daughter a job : " You see, in this weavin' shop—all the girls 'ave 'ad to be in trouble, otherwise they wouldn't take 'em. It's a kind of disorderly 'ouse without the disorders."

Then Faith Bly appears, demure, pretty, " her face an embodiment of the pathetic watchful prison faculty of adapting itself to whatever may be best for its owner at the moment." March engages her as parlourmaid and then struggles with his wife to keep her. Even Cook has to be inveigled into giving her views : " Of course, it's a risk, sir; but there ! you've got to take 'em to get maids nowadays. If it isn't in the past, it's in the future." " We ought to have faith," says March; " faith in human nature, Cook."

Cook (*scandalised*) : " Oh no, sir, *not* human nature. I never let that get the upper hand."

This is our own Galsworthy, tender, ironic, witty,

with more than a little spice of the Comic Spirit, which blows upon men when they get distorted. There was very little of it in *Loyalties*. To laugh when we are searching for clues to the burglary is to offend against the law of theatrical make-believe ; one must be serious to carry off the artificial. *Windows* is not artificial, so we can laugh in the midst of tragedy—as we do in life. Mrs March manages to put her common-sense views in an amusing way. When Johnny, her son, wants her to give Faith her chance, she retaliates : " I can't understand this passion for vicarious heroism. . . . Where do you come in ? You'll make poems about the injustice of the Law. Your father will use her in a novel. She'll wear Mary's blouses, and everybody will be happy—except Cook and me."

But it is Cook who reconciles her to the idea : " It's wonderful the difference good food'll make, ma'am."

Faith is engaged and left alone with Cook.

" Forget all about yourself," says she comfortably, " and you'll be a different girl in no time."

" Do you want to be a different woman ? " asks Faith surprisingly.

" Oh . . . and here's the sweets," says Cook. " You mustn't eat them."

" I wasn't in for theft," comes the sharp rap over the knuckles.

Bly, the window-cleaner, sums up the situation for the end of Act I. : " Fact is her winders want cleanin'," he says of Faith, " she 'ad a dusty time in there."

In Act II. a fortnight has passed and the inevitable complication has arisen : Johnny and Faith. Bly as usual philosophises. " Policemen, priests, prisoners, Cabinet ministers, anyone who leads an unnatural life, see how it twists 'em. You can't suppress a thing without it swelling you up in another place. . . . Follow your instincts."

That is Bly's constantly reiterated motto : " Follow your instincts . . . trust 'uman nature, I say, and follow your instincts." When he is left alone with his daughter he tries to jockey her into joviality :

" You shouldn't brood over it," he says. " I knew a man in Valpiraso that 'ad spent 'arf 'is life in prison —a *jolly* feller: I forget what 'e'd done, somethin' bloody."

Faith tells him that life's "right enough, so long as I get out "—which inclines her father to be frightened lest she should follow her instincts too far in the streets. " It's 'ardly worth while to do these winders. You clean 'em, and they're dirty again in no time. . . . And people talk o' progress. . . . All this depression comes from 'avin' 'igh 'opes. 'Ave low 'opes, and you'll be all right."

Faith and Johnny have a chance to disclose to each other their wants in life, she her want of windows: " I love the streets at night—all lighted. . . . I used to walk about for hours. That's life! Fancy! I never saw a street for more than two years. Didn't you miss them in the war ? "

They follow their instincts well enough to be caught red-handed kissing with emphasis by Cook. Mrs March immediately dismisses Faith. Johnny, raging, talks about " saving " her, and goes in for direct action by taking post in an arm-chair with its back to her bedroom door, armed with a pipe, a pound of chocolate, three volumes of *Monte Cristo*, and an old concertina. Nobody can get up and Faith can't get down. He tells his sister that he intends to stay there till his mother capitulates. The curtain descends to the wailing of the concertina. In the third act Johnny is still outside the girl's bedroom door hours afterwards on hunger strike. Mrs March calls a truce and there is a parley. Faith and Johnny come downstairs, Faith morose, because it's her evening out, and she wants to go. Bly, drunk, comes in to fetch her away. There is one horrible moment when, having seen two Cooks, he sees two Faiths and selects the apparition. " You're the one that died when my girl was 'ung," he says, and Faith says, " I *did* die." For Galsworthy the hit is clumsy, but as his intention is to hurt he cannot afford to be delicate.

Then there enters a young impudent *souteneur*, with whom Johnny picks a quarrel. Faith breaks in. " Why can't you let me be ? I don't want to be rescued. . . . I want to be let alone. I've paid for everything I've done—a pound for every shilling's worth. And all because of one minute when I was half crazy. Wait till *you've* had a baby you oughtn't to have had, and not a penny in your pocket ! It's money—money—all money ! . . . I'll have what I like now, not what you think's good for me." She elects to go with the bullying blackguard who has come for her, when a plain-clothes man comes in to warn the *souteneur* and recounts the fact that he has already been had up several times for living on the earnings of immoral women. Up to this moment Faith had kept her faith in him : he goes out and she gives way to her wrath. Johnny offers to marry her. "Don't be silly," she replies. " I've got no call on you. You don't care for me and I don't for you. No ! You go and put your head in ice. . . . There's nothing to be done with a girl like me."

She goes. Mrs March suddenly drops her formality, and, as if she had seen a vision, keeps on repeating : " She—wants—to—be—loved. She—just—wants— to—be—loved. . . . Don't—have—ideals ! Have— vision—just simple—vision ! . . . Open the windows ! Open ! " Mrs March has by this time consumed five little glasses of brandy . . . hence her slow speech and sudden enlightenment. To Cook is given the last word : " We must look things in the face," she says ; " there isn't a millehennium. There's too much human nature. We must look things in the face."

Windows was a failure : *Loyalties* was a striking success. Why ? Is the standard of mentality shown by an audience in a theatre so much lower than that of the readers of novels ? The best novels do not attract so many readers as those of Ethel Dell, Nat Gould and Garvice, but the audiences that flock to *Loyalties* are surely readers of Wells, Bennett and Shaw. The truth must be that in the privacy of their own homes the ordinarily comfortable leisured masses of people do not mind facing real problems; on the stage they must have the happy ending—the exciting dénouement, the triumph of virtue, stereotyped ideas, things that will not disturb their stomachs, which are sufficiently occupied in the business of digesting heavy dinners. To watch a burglar being hunted down is always fun. To watch a servant of no moral fibre following her instincts is only interesting to those interested in sociology. If the stage is merely meant to be a variety entertainment, *Loyalties* is the sort of play we want. If we agree that it is a place in which fundamental problems ought to be thrashed out, then *The Fugitive, The Silver Box, Justice* and *Windows* are the plays that we want to keep alive.

No one wants to see less of the healthy instinct which keeps plays like *Polly, The Beggar's Opera* and *Treasure Island* going; there can never be too many pirates, smugglers, light songs, dainty dancers; every sane person wants to see very much less of the sentimental rubbish that Ian Hay and writers of his stamp put on so successfully. Ian Hay, like A. A. Milne, is most entertaining so long as he keeps right on the surface; his *métier* is the superficial. He can be bright, breezy and witty, as can Arnold Bennett, but there are few shocks so miserable as to have to sit through such a medley of ineptitude as we had to endure in *Sacred and Profane Love*, and some other Bennett productions, when he imagined that he had something serious to say. All great artists—and Bennett is emphatically among the very great ones—seem to suffer from temporary aberrations. Galsworthy has never written a bad novel. He has written some quite indifferent plays, but *Windows* is not, *pace* the critics, one of them. It is in his best vein. And it is so because of its sincerity. Galsworthy's business is to interpret pain; his place is with the weak, the helpless; there is no more sympathetic artist living. His sense of humour never deserts him : he faces all facts unflinching : he knows men and women inside out, particularly those who have got on the wrong side of the law. So great are his gifts that he can deceive even the elect, as in *Loyalties*, perhaps because so few among his audiences could know well enough whether he was transcribing from the life those who spend their time at country-house parties. The old aristocracy is dead; he portrays the transitional period: it is hard to believe that Dancy's type exists, though Galsworthy would doubtless say that the Law Courts have of late given proof of it.

Galsworthy's plays will always be worth going to see, because he has an unerring sense of stagecraft, his dialogue is always natural, full both of feeling and wit, his characters live, there is always a conflict of real emotions, and (best of all) there is a sincerity and a sensitiveness in him that are singularly beautiful.

VI

SOMERSET MAUGHAM

THE plays of Somerset Maugham are, up to the moment, fourteen in number — *The Explorer, Mrs Dot, A Man of Honour, Penelope, Jack Straw, Lady Frederick, The Tenth Man, Cæsar's Wife, Landed Gentry, The Land of Promise, The Unknown, Smith, The Circle* and *East of Suez.*

East of Suez is in seven scenes, a melodrama totally devoid of merit, to which people flock in hundreds of thousands under the impression that it is a revised *Chu-Chin-Chow.*

The first scene is by far the best. No one speaks. It is simply a living representation of a street in Peking. There is colour, there is life.

In scene two we meet Harry Anderson, of the British American Tobacco Company, a good-looking man of thirty, and George Conway, of the Legation. The former tells his friend that he is engaged to a young and beautiful widow whose mother was Chinese, and hopes that it won't make any difference to their friendship. George becomes reminiscent and tells Harry that he too was once awfully in love with a half-caste, a Eurasian girl, but that the Minister in Peking had threatened to sack him if he married her. Daisy, Harry's fiancée, then enters. She is an extremely pretty woman, with a pale, very clear, slightly sallow skin and beautiful dark eyes. " There is only the very faintest suspicion in them of the Chinese slant. . . . George stares at her. At first he is not quite sure that he recognises her, then suddenly he does." Naturally he does not let Harry know. George and Daisy are soon left alone, and he tells her that he proposes to inform Harry of her past. She in turn accuses him of being the cause of her going rotten, and unfolds the story of her life. She makes it clear that he was the real passion of her life, and when he went her mother had sold her to an ancient Chinaman, Lee Tai Cheng, for two thousand dollars. She went from Shanghai to live with Rathbone, an American trader, in Singapore. After four years as his mistress she returned to her Chinaman. She extracts a promise from George that he will not betray her.

In scene three we see her married to Harry and deadly bored, shadowed by her procuress of a mother, whom she keeps with her as her ayah, who brings her presents from Lee Tai Cheng and a note from George Conway, with whom she is now hopelessly in love. When he comes to her after an absence of ten days she can scarcely contain her joy. He confesses that he loves her, but he must be loyal to his friend.

Lee then enters, and he too tells Daisy that he wants her and waits for her. Daisy's charms are of such a kind, it will be noticed, that even to have lived with her is not to have tired of her. Lee and the ayah now suggest that she should poison Harry. Harry comes in and suggests that they leave Peking, as no one calls on them. Daisy demurs passionately. He then tells her that he has been transferred to Chung-King, whereupon she has hysterics . . . the ayah tempts her . . . and goes up to ask Buddha whether it is right that she should murder Harry.

In the fourth scene the ayah extracts the cartridges from Harry's revolver. Harry makes Daisy put on a full Manchu dress, which changes her completely into an Oriental. Husband and wife argue about leaving Peking and then settle down to play chess. Suddenly there is a shriek for help in the street. Harry rushes out with the cartridgeless revolver. Daisy, stricken with remorse, tries to prevent him : the ayah holds her back and tells her that she cannot help Harry in any way. Lee Tai has arranged to have his throat slit. Suddenly Harry reappears with a coolie : a crowd come in, and George Conway is brought

T

in wounded. Daisy flies at her mother in a fiendish
temper and tries to throttle her. Harry suddenly
becomes suspicious of the ayah. He begins to bully
her, when Daisy at last is driven to confess that the
old Chinawoman is her own mother.

In scene five we see George convalescent alone
with Daisy. Harry is called away for the night. She
implores George to stay the night with her. For the
first time in the play we approach reality. " Harry
doesn't exist. I've loved you always from the first
day I saw you. The others were nothing to me—Lee
Tai and Harry and the rest. I've loved you always.
I've never loved anyone but you. All these years I've
kept the letters you wrote to me. I've read them
till I know every word by heart. . . . Do you think
I'm going to let you go now ? . . . You can't leave me
now. If you leave me I shall kill myself. . . . There's
no room in my soul for anything else. You say that
love is like a wild beast gnawing at your entrails.
My love is a liberator. . . . There's nothing in the
world now but you and me and the love that joins us.
I want you, I want you." George puts up a goodish
fight, but is of course beaten in the end.

In the sixth scene Daisy is happy and gay in a
Chinese house waiting for George. Lee Tai comes in and
tells her that China is waiting to reclaim her. " What
have you to do with white men ? You are not a
white woman. What power has this blood of your
father's when it is mingled with the tumultuous stream
which you have inherited through your mother from
innumerable generations ? . . . There is in your heart
a simplicity which the white man can never fathom
and a deviousness which he can never understand.
Your soul is like a rice patch cleared in the middle of
the jungle. . . . One day your labour will be vain and
the jungle will take back its own. . . . You will come
back to China as a tired child comes back to his
mother." George comes in while he is still talking,
and Lee Tai continues to air his views on East and
West civilisations. " You have appealed to the

machine-gun and by the machine-gun shall you be judged. . . . You have shattered the dream of our philosophers that the world could be governed by the power of law and order . . . you have thrust your hideous inventions upon us. Fools. Do you not know that we have a genius for mechanics ? Do you not know that there are in this country four hundred millions of the most practical and industrious people in the world ? . . . And what will become of your superiority when the yellow man can make as good guns as the white and fire them as straight ? "

Irrelevant to the action of the play, but interesting none the less. What is more to our purpose is the fact of Daisy's confession—" I've been happy for the first time in my life. At last I've known peace and rest. Oh, George, I'm so grateful for all you've given me. In these three months you've changed the whole world for me ": and George's—" I've never known a single moment's happiness. . . . I'm a low, rotten cad. . . . I've loved you so that there was room for nothing else in my soul . . . and I've hated myself for loving you. I've hated you for making me love you. . . . You're stronger than I am. . . . I want you to believe that I love you. But I can't go on with this deceit."

He then tells her that he wants to finish it. He doesn't love her any more. He is going on leave almost at once for three or four months. He then leaves her, and Lee Tai, who has listened to every word, returns to tell her that George has lied to her, that he is really engaged to an English girl. She then sees red, takes the letters that George had written to her and tells Lee Tai to let Harry have them.

In scene seven Daisy shows her true nature to George, how she will do anything to bind him to her, and he turns in revulsion from her—" this love has been a loathsome cancer in my heart." She shows him the Chinese side of her nature. George goes out and shoots himself. Daisy reverts to her Chinese dress. Harry bursts in with the letters in his hand, and the curtain falls finally with the completely disillusioned husband in a storm of sobs kneeling at Daisy's feet, while " motionless she contemplates in the glass the Chinese woman of the reflection."

There might easily have been a good play in *East of Suez* : the tug between East and West, the passion-ridden Daisy are both excellent. But there is too much complication — too much melodramatic tension. A far better play is *The Circle*, which alienated a great number of people because of its cynical attitude. In point of fact, it is healthy for once to find the wife and *tertium quid* going off when the curtain falls and risking something. The play is not altogether good. The husband, Arnold, has few faults beyond his Christian name and a certain finicky tidiness. He is a trifle bloodless. He likes ornaments to be free of dust. Elizabeth, his wife, is a dear. "If you're not going to say ' Damn ' when a thing's damnable, when are you going to say ' Damn '? " she asks when Arnold objects to her use of the oath. We learn that his mother thirty years before deserted her five-year-old child (Arnold) and a husband who adored her and gave her all the money she could want. Elizabeth defends her action.

" Some of us are more mother and some of us more woman. It gives me a little thrill when I think that she loved that man so much. She sacrificed her name, her position and her child to him." Elizabeth creates in her mind a fantastic vision of the romantic woman, which is sadly shattered when she suddenly turns up, fussy, affected, behaving as if she were twenty-five, outrageously dressed. She is accompanied by Lord Porteous, her snappy, gruff, second husband. She turns to a young man staying in the house, Teddie, and greets him effusively as Arnold, her son. "My boy ! my boy ! I should have known you anywhere."

Elizabeth points out to her her mistake, and without any hesitation she flings herself on Arnold with "the image of his father ! I should have known him any-where ! " Her first husband, Champion-Cheney, comes in, having picked up Lady Kitty's lip-stick. It is thus that husband and wife meet for the first time for thirty years.

In Act II. Lady Kitty and Porteous are quarrelling over the cards. Elizabeth has a long talk to Champion-Cheney, who tells her that Lady Kitty's " soul is as thickly rouged as her face. She hasn't an emotion that's sincere. She's tinsel. You think I'm a cruel, cynical old man. Why, when I think of what she was, if I didn't laugh at what she has become I should cry." Having made her disillusion complete, Elizabeth is left alone with Teddie, and there follows a jerky love scene after the modern manner in which Elizabeth calls him an owl, so great is her love for him. "What are we going to do about it ? " she asks. " I'd love you just as much if you were old and ugly," he replies. " And it's not only love ; love, be blowed. It's that I *like* you so tremendously. I think you're such a ripping good sort. I just want to be with you." " Teddie," she says a little later, " nothing in the world matters anything to me but you. I'll go wherever you take me. I love you."

The whole of the love-making in this scene is conducted on a level of boyish and girlish high spirits, both of them overcharged with emotions that are in danger of breaking loose at any moment. It is impossible to regard Teddie as a wife-snatcher, or Elizabeth as an unfaithful wife. They are a couple of delicious children giving rein to midsummer madness.

As a contrast to them we are given a cynical scene between the footling Lady Kitty and the husband from whom she ran away. " My dear Clive," she says, " I don't mind telling you that if I had my time over again I should be unfaithful to you, but I should not leave you."

Champion-Cheney explains his rule of life :

" I love old wine, old friends and old books, but I like young women. On their twenty-fifth birthday I give them a diamond ring and tell them they must no longer waste their youth and beauty on an old fogy like me. We have a most affecting scene, my technique on these occasions is perfect, and then I start all over again."

LADY K.: "You're a wicked old man, Clive."

C.-C.: "That's what I told you. But, by George! I'm a happy one."

Elizabeth tackles Arnold and tells him that she wants her liberty: "We've been married for three years and I don't think it's been a great success. . . . I don't love you." To which Arnold fatuously replies: "You've made your bed and I'm afraid you must lie on it."

"Why should you lie on the bed you've made if you don't want to?" she retorts. "There's always the floor. . . . I'm sorry, but if you're not in love with a man his love doesn't mean very much to you." She confesses that she is desperately in love with Teddie.

In the third and last act Lady Kitty does her best to make Elizabeth see reason: "It breaks my heart to think that you're going to make the same pitiful mistake that I made." She becomes reminiscent: "The first two years were wonderful. People cut me, you know, but I didn't mind. I thought love was everything. . . . One sacrifices one's life for love and then one finds that love doesn't last. The tragedy of love isn't death or separation. One gets over these. The tragedy of love is indifference."

Arnold, coached by his father, changes his tactics and tells Elizabeth that he won't stand in her way if she must go. He will let her divorce him. He becomes the soul of generosity. Teddie comes to fetch her away and she tells him that she cannot come. (It is exactly like *The Bill of Divorcement*.) She tells him of Arnold's noble self-sacrifice.

"I should never forgive myself," she says, "if I profited by his generosity."

"If another man and I," said Teddie, "were devilish hungry and there was only one mutton chop between us, and he said, 'You eat it,' I wouldn't waste a lot of time arguing; I'd wolf it before he changed his mind. . . . It's idiotic to sacrifice your life for a slushy sentiment."

"What would you do," goes on Elizabeth, "if I were married to you and came and told you I loved somebody else and wanted to leave you?"

"You have very pretty blue eyes, Elizabeth. I'd black first one and then the other. And after that we'd see."

"You damned brute," she sighs contentedly.

This is the only sort of talk that appeals to women in novels and on the stage and—perhaps in real life.

"Let's say good-bye," she says. "Have pity on me. I'm giving up all my hopes of happiness."

TEDDIE: "But I wasn't offering you happiness. . . . I should be fed to the teeth with you sometimes, and so would you be with me. . . . Often you'd be wretched and bored stiff and lonely, and often you'd be frightfully home-sick, and then you'd regret all you'd lost. . . . I don't offer you peace and quietness. I offer you unrest and anxiety. I don't offer you happiness. I offer you love."

ELIZABETH: "You hateful creature, I absolutely adore you!"

Porteous and Lady Kitty have been privileged to be witnesses of this shameless and unedifying conversation.

"You're damned fools, both of you," says Porteous, "damned fools. If you like you can have my car." And off the pair of love-lorn lunatics go to drive through the dawn and through the sunrise, leaving Porteous to moralise:

"If we made rather a hash of things perhaps it was because we were rather trivial people. You can do anything in this world if you're prepared to take the consequences, and consequences depend on character."

Such is ever the Maugham theory. *The Circle* is most typically a Maugham play. It is Maugham at his very best. There are things in it that are hateful, but its brilliance cannot be denied.

One's first impression is that it is a Comedy of Manners, scintillating, witty, but artificial. A better acquaintance with Maugham decides us that it is true sound philosophy. It hurts, it disturbs, its acidity eats into us. It is extraordinarily scarifying.

VII

EUGENE O'NEILL

C. E. BECHHOFER has written an introduction to O'Neill's first plays to be printed in England. Just as Sherwood Anderson leads America in the art of novel-writing, so Eugene O'Neill leads in drama. *The Emperor Jones* is like no other play that ever was. Its author has been a clerk, a gold prospector in Honduras, an actor, a reporter and an able seaman. The influence of the sea is very strong. The first play in the first series is *The Straw*, a long drama about consumption, in which the heroine, Eileen, is deserted by one lover because she has to go into an asylum. While there she falls in love with another patient, Murray, who recovers, goes away unable to reciprocate her passion, returns to find her dying and to please her says that he will marry her, and suddenly finds that he really is in love with her. It is a purely conventional drama, not very interesting.

Diff'rent is a vastly superior play. Emma Crosby at the age of twenty, romantic and dreamy, is in love with a sailor, Caleb Williams, aged thirty, accustomed to go off on two-year whaling voyages. She regards him as "diff'rent," a sort of Sunday-go-to-meeting Saint. She finds out that he had once had an affair with a brown girl on some island and immediately turns him down, in spite of his explanation that everything is "diff'rent" down in the islands. "Them native women—they're diff'rent."

Thirty years afterwards we see Emma withered and scraggy, with "something revoltingly incongruous about her, a pitiable sham, a too-apparent effort to cheat the years by appearances. The white dress she wears is too frilly, too youthful for her: so are the

296

high-heeled shoes and clocked silk stockings. There is an absurd suggestion of rouge on her tight cheeks and thin lips . . . the black of her hair is brazenly untruthful. Above all there is shown in her simpering, self-consciously coquettish manner that laughable— and at the same time irritating and disgusting— mockery of undignified age snatching greedily at the empty similitude of youth. She resembles some *passé* stock actress of fifty made up for a heroine of twenty." We see her flirting with Caleb's nephew, then pleading with the coarse boy, who is only concerned to play up to her to get money out of her. He even goes so far as to let her think that he would marry her, and she is wild with joy. Then he discovers that Caleb will give him more money if he doesn't marry her, tells her what he really thinks of her and goes. Caleb, finding that his thirty years' wait for this sex-repressed woman has changed her to something evil, hangs himself in her barn. The curtain falls as she goes to imitate him. It is an extremely unpleasant play, but treats of a problem of great importance sensibly, candidly and without straining one's credulity. There is neither wit nor humour in it, but plenty of good sense and great sincerity.

The Emperor Jones is vastly superior to either of these plays. It consists of eight very short scenes set "on an island in the West Indies as yet not self-determined by white mariners."

In scene one we are in the palace of the Emperor, Brutus Jones, nigger, one-time Pullman car attendant on an American railway. On the stage are a negro woman and Henry Smithers, a Cockney trader of forty, bald, pasty-faced, with washy-blue eyes like a ferret's. "His expression is one of unscrupulous meanness, cowardly and dangerous." He catches the woman stealing: she shakes her head. "Bloody liar," he begins. "But tell me what's up. There's something funny goin' on . . . you blacks are up to some devilment. This palace of 'is is like a bleedin' tomb." She tells him that all the niggers have left—run away to

the hills. The woman goes. Jones comes in. "His
features are typically negroid . . . his eyes are alive
with a keen, cunning intelligence. . . . He wears a
light blue uniform coat, sprayed with brass buttons,
heavy gold chevrons on his shoulders." To Smithers
he indulges in a little self-adulation : " From stow-
away to Emperor in two years ! Dat's goin' some ! "
He has worked out a system of philosophy for himself :
" For de little stealin' dey gits you in jail soon or late.
For de big stealin' dey makes you Emperor and puts
you in de Hall o' Fame when you croaks. If dey's one
thing I learns in ten years on de Pullman ca's listenin'
to de white quality talk, it's dat same fact. And when
I gits a chance to use it I winds up Emperor in two
years." Smithers accuses him of having had all the
luck. " But I makes dat luck, you heah ? . . . When
dat murderin' nigger Ole Lem hired to kill me takes
aim ten feet away and his gun misses fire and I shoots
him dead, what you heah me say ? "

SMITHERS : " You said you'd got a charm so's no lead
bullet'd kill yer. You was so strong only a silver
bullet could kill yer, you told 'em. Blimey, wasn't
that swank for yer, and plain, fat-'eaded luck ? "

" From dat time on," says Jones, " I has dem all eatin'
out of my hand. . . . Ain't a man's talkin' big what
makes him big—long as he makes folks believe it ? "

Smithers makes him realise that his Emperor days
are over, that his subjects have retired to the hills
to make silver bullets to kill him. While Jones tells
the trader the way he proposes to escape through the
forest to the French gunboat a tom-tom sounds faint
and steady from the hill-side. " It starts at a rate
exactly corresponding to normal pulse-beat—seventy-
two to the minute — and continues at a gradually
accelerating rate from this point uninterruptedly to
the very end of the play. Jones starts at the sound.
A strange look of apprehension creeps into his face for
a moment as he listens."

" You'll find yer bloody 'air'll be standin' on end
before ter-morrow mornin'," says Smithers. " It's

a bleedin' queer place, that stinkin' forest, even in daylight."

"De Baptist Church done pertect me and land dem all in hell," says the nigger. "And I'se got little silver bullet o' my own, don't forgit."

In the second scene, "Nightfall," Jones is at the edge of the great forest sweating with exertion. "Dat soft Emperor job ain't no training for a long dash ovah dat plain in de brilin' sun. . . . Feet, you is holdin' up yo' end fine an' I sutinly hopes you ain't blisterin'."

He gradually loses his confidence: his landmarks get mixed. "How come all dese white stones come heah when I only remembers one?" He begins to light matches. Little Formless Fears creep out from the deep blackness of the forest. They are black, shapeless, and only their glittering little eyes are to be seen. "If they have any describable form at all it is that of a grubworm about the size of a creeping child. They move noiselessly, but with deliberate, painful effort, striving to raise themselves on end, failing and sinking prone again." When he sees them Jones yells with terror and fires at them. They disappear. The beating of the tom-tom quickens. He plunges into the forest.

In the third scene it is nine o'clock, in the forest: the moon has risen. A negro, Jeff, dressed in Pullman porter's uniform, is throwing a pair of dice. Jones comes in foot-weary, starts to whistle, stops. "What's dat odder queer clickety sound I heah? . . . Sound like—sound like—fo' God sake, sound like some nigger was shootin' dice!"

He sees Jeff, really believes that it is a living man that he sees, and is happily relieved. "Jeff! . . . Dey tol' me you done died from dat razor cut I gives you. . . . Ain't you gwine—look up—can't you speak to me? Is you—is you—a ha'nt?" Again he fires. The tom-tom beats louder and quicker. He plunges wildly into the underbrush.

In the fourth scene it is eleven o'clock. Jones' uniform is now ragged: he is melting with the heat:

he argues with himself that it was hunger that made him imagine that he had seen the ghost of Jeff. A small gang of negroes enter, dressed in convict suits, shackled, carrying picks and shovels. Jones suddenly sees them and sinks back too numb with fright to move. " Lawd Jesus ! " he murmurs. The guard points sternly at Jones, motioning him to take his place. He raises his whip and lashes Jones across the shoulders. Jones winces with pain and cowers abjectly. Then when the guard turns his back the nigger springs at him and brings an imaginary shovel down on the man's head. He realises that he has no shovel, and fires point-blank at the guard. " Instantly the walls of the forest close in from both sides."

In scene five it is one o'clock. Jones is on his knees praying. A crowd of figures in Southern costumes come in—an auctioneer, white planters, black slaves. They bid for Jones, who fires at the auctioneer. " I shows you I'se a free nigger, damn yo' souls." Jones then rushes off, crying with fear, the tom-tom growing ever louder.

In scene six it is three o'clock. Jones is chattering with fear. " Ain't got no bullet left on'y de silver one." Gradually we discern two rows of seated figures as if rowing at sea. He looks up, sees the figures, shudders with terror and then joins them in their swaying motions backwards and forwards.

In scene seven it is five o'clock, and we see the hunted man kneeling before an altar, when a figure of a Congo witch-doctor appears and completely hypnotises Jones by a pantomimic performance in which he shows that the forces of evil demand sacrifice. Jones howls for mercy. A huge crocodile appears and Jones in agony uses his last, his silver bullet.

In the last scene of all it is dawn. The tom-tom is now so loud that it sounds as if it were " on the very spot." Lem, followed by a squad of his soldiers and Smithers, comes in. Smithers is disgusted to find that Lem is not going to hunt his quarry. The " ape-faced old savage " squats and waits.

" 'E's miles orf by this an' safe to the coast, damn 's'ide!" says the Cockney in contempt. " I tole yer yer'd lose 'im, didn't I?—wastin' the 'ole bloomin' night beatin' yer bloody drum and castin' yer silly spells!" A sound of snapping twigs is heard. Lem's followers creep noiselessly into the forest. Smithers continues: "Blarsted fat'eads! . . . Still, after all, it might 'appen. If 'e lost 'is bloody way in these stinkin' woods 'e'd likely turn in a circle without 'is knowin' it. They all does."

Shots are heard from the forest. Lem grins with satisfaction and tells Smithers that his men are using silver bullets. "You was scared to put after 'im till you'd moulded silver bullets, eh?" says the trader. "If yer don't beat all 'ell! . . ."

The soldiers come in with Jones's body. Smithers continues: "Silver bullets! Gawd blimey, but yer died in the 'eighth o' style any'ow." The body is taken out and he goes on sneering at Lem. "And I s'pose you think it's yer bleedin' charms and yer silly beatin' the drum that made 'im run in a circle when 'e'd lost 'imself, don't yer? . . . Stupid as 'ogs, the lot of 'em! Blarsted niggers!"

It is of course partly the theme that makes this play so important. Never before, certainly, has the peculiar temperament of the modern nigger been so closely studied. The tricks picked up from the white man, the vices, the religious veneer, the deep-seated superstitions, the quite definite moral superiority over the degenerate, mean, cowardly white Smithers are all wonderfully brought out. Then there is the harrowing sense of impending tragedy in the insistent, ever-quickening beat of the tom-tom. Even when we read we feel the horror of the closing mesh of the net : on the stage the effect must be almost paralysing to the easily moved. As in all good dramas (Ibsen, for instance), there is so much implicit that isn't said.

As in *The Pilgrim's Progress* and *The Faerie Queene*, the allegory can easily be worked out, but the story can stand by itself. Each member of the audience may apply it as he likes. He cannot escape the sense of universality in it. It has something of the *Everyman* spirit pervading it. We all try putting a bluff over on life, we have extraordinary, quite undeserved good luck, we bid higher stakes, stay at the tables a little too long, suddenly panic, and then run in circles to avoid the inevitable.

From the point of view of stagecraft, O'Neill has done something quite new. The old three-act convention is discarded. *Diff'rent* is in two acts, and the eight scenes of *The Emperor Jones* are all part of one act. It ought to be played straight through, with no intervals at all, or very short ones, all of the same length. The tension is like that in the porter's scene in *Macbeth*. We don't want to have to talk or drink during intervals. We want the whole of it undisturbed by any outside influence, just as we want to read it through without interruptions.

We are luckily able at last, through the energy, vigilance and acumen of Mr Cochran, to see *Anna Christie, The Hairy Ape* and others of O'Neill's plays in London. It should give a fillip to our own younger writers to go on breaking with tradition. O'Neill may well spur on C. K. Munro, Noel Coward and the rest not to give in to the demands of the men with the money-bags.

VIII

ARTHUR PINERO

M RAYMOND RECOULY, the famous French critic, differs very considerably from St John Ervine in his estimate of Pinero. Of *The Second Mrs Tanqueray* he says: "No simpler and more dramatic theme could be imagined. . . . The greatness of Pinero's art and his supreme cleverness is shown in the way he has reduced to its simplest and clearest expression a conflict of wills which arises between two or three characters. It is for this reason that his play defies the action of time. It contains no problem, no description of manners. It is satisfied with stating and solving by the simplest means a dramatic situation which is infinitely human and deeply touching. Moreover . . . the play is admirably constructed. The action is perfectly combined and perfectly ordered."

Not many Englishmen would agree entirely with this criticism, but it is of great interest put by the side of Ervine's. Immediately upon reading this criticism and after rereading a couple of Ervine's plays I reread *Mrs Tanqueray*. It reads better than any other play of its time: it is thirty years old. The quiet beginning of the three men dining, of Aubrey the forty-two-year-old widower of a cold-blooded saint announcing his second marriage (to a girl with a very lurid past), is skilfully conceived. We sympathise at once with the man who had thrown in his lot with an iceberg, whose daughter at nineteen had elected to stay in a convent, who at his second venture undertakes to be chivalrous to a woman whose warmth of soul has led men to be anything but chivalrous in the past. Paula's age is

303

twenty-seven : she is "beautiful, fresh and innocent-
looking ": she is intensely lovable, and infernally
jealous and moody. The curtain falls on Act I. at
a magnificent juncture. Ellean, Aubrey's daughter,
has decided to leave her convent and come back to
her father, exactly as he decides to marry Paula,
who has seen her letter of confession burnt by the
priggish, rather too heavily benevolent man who is
honouring her with his name. In Act II. we see
Paula and Aubrey in their country house, the father
absorbed in Ellean, Paula bored to distraction.
"You'll kill me with this life," she says passionately.
(Really Aubrey had no luck to turn from the Ant-
arctic frost of his first to the volcanic furnaces of
his second wife.) "In the morning, a drive down to
the village, with the groom, to give my orders to the
tradespeople. At lunch, you and Ellean. In the
afternoon, a novel, the newspapers : if fine, another
drive—*if* fine ! Tea—you and Ellean. Then two hours
of dusk ; then dinner—you and Ellean. Then a game
of bezique, you and I, while Ellean reads a religious
book in a dull corner. Then a yawn from me, another
from you, a sigh from Ellean : three figures suddenly
rise—' Good-night, good-night, good-night ! ' . . . And
so we shall go on here, year in and year out, until the
sap is run out of our lives, and we're stale and dry and
withered from sheer, solitary respectability. Upon my
word, I wonder we didn't see that we should have
been far happier if we'd gone in for the devil-may-care,
café-living sort of life in town ! "

It is hard to do other than sympathise with Paula
here. She has reason, logic, all common sense and
instinctive right on her side. Unfortunately her
stultified emotions find an outlet in a thoroughly un-
wholesome jealousy of her stepdaughter. "Aubrey,"
she says, "there are two sorts of affection—the love
for a woman you respect, and the love for a woman you
love. She [Ellean] gets the first from you : I never
can." So great, so uncontrollable is her passion that
she blurts it out to the sober, calm, pure, innocent,

nun-like Ellean, who is almost unbelievably cruel in her coldness to the woman who is thirsting for her affection. Aubrey in a peculiarly priggish manner tells his friend Drummle of his fear lest Paula should inoculate his saintly Ellean with some of her warped, curious doctrines. There is a powerful scene where Paula (driven, one would say, frantic by Ellean's aloofness and Aubrey's priggishness) is suburbanly catty to Mrs Cortelyon on learning that she has a scheme afoot for taking Ellean to Paris. To revenge herself for the loss of the girl whose affection she has striven so hard to win she invites a drunken fool and his mincing, doll-like, immoral wife to stay with them against Aubrey's wishes. In Act III. we see Paula thoroughly unhappy in their presence, having quarrelled with Aubrey on their account. "I—I've outgrown these people," she confesses to Drummle. "This woman— I used to think her 'jolly'—sickens me. I can't breathe when she's near me : the whiff of her handkerchief turns me faint ! "

To our intense surprise she also confesses that she has, "out of malice, pure devilry," intercepted the letters that have been coming for Aubrey from Ellean. Drummle makes her tell Aubrey about this. While she is telling him she pins him down to confess that he had sent Ellean away " because you don't consider me a decent companion for her, because you're afraid she might get a little of her innocence rubbed off in my company." To date the play and damn it, this desperately silly man then insults her by maundering on about the time when she too was as innocent as his daughter. Just when she has the sense to upbraid him for preaching, Ellean unexpectedly returns to announce that she has fallen in love with a " boyish, high-spirited " V.C. Her father asks her to be very gentle with Paula, and she even goes to the extent of going up to her stepmother and kissing her, which drives the impulsive Paula into an ecstasy of joy until Ellean confesses that she is in love. Paula immediately reverts to her mockery : " *You* in love ! You ! Oh,

u

this is why you've come home ! Of course, you can
make friends with me now ! You'll leave us for good
soon, I suppose ; so it doesn't much matter being
civil to me for a little while ! " How all " step "
and " in-law " relationships are caught up in that
one bitter remark. Then the characteristic *volte-face* :
" Ellean dear ! Ellean ! I didn't mean it. I'm so
horribly jealous, it's a sort of curse on me."

Captain Ardale, Ellean's lover, comes in : he and
Paula stare at one another, and something of the horror
that crosses their faces on recognising each other
spreads to the audience. They are left alone to curse.
" You—you beast ! " shouts Paula, " to crop up in
my life again like this." She decides that she is
going to tell Aubrey that she was once mistress of
the man whom his daughter wishes to marry, and in
the fourth act, in a most moving and dramatic moment,
she reveals the truth. In a singularly silly interview
with Ellean, Aubrey tells her that he will not let her
marry Ardale because he wanted to keep her ignorant
of evil—and she decides to go against her father's
wishes until she is left alone with Paula, when she
discovers the truth. " From the first moment I saw
you I knew you were altogether unlike the good
women I'd left : directly I saw you I knew what
my father had done. You've wondered why I've
turned from you ! There—that's the reason ! Oh,
but this is a horrible way for the truth to come home
to everyone ! "

When Aubrey and Paula come together finally, to
fight out what shall be done, Paula says : " I believe
the future is only the past again, entered through
another gate. . . . To-night proves it. You must see
now that, do what we will, go where we will, you'll be
continually reminded of—what I was. . . . The only
great distances the world contains are those we
carry within ourselves—the distances that separate
husbands and wives." She goes out and kills herself,
an inevitable conclusion, bravely faced, leaving Ellean
to bemoan the fact a little late that she wishes that

she had been more merciful. It is, as a play, of course,
much too moral for our modern taste. If there is one
adage in which to-day we do not believe it is that of
being sure that our sins will find us out. But *The
Second Mrs Tanqueray* is so finely dramatic, contains in
Paula so human and so interesting a personality, that
we are willing to forgive the *naïveté*.

Pinero has been accused, times without number, of
being derivative, almost a plagiarist, of colouring his
ideas from his immediate predecessors. So in *Mrs
Tanqueray* everyone saw Ibsen; in *The Enchanted
Cottage* there was a touch of Barrie: there was—
so much that the play failed. The central idea was
excellent : the transforming power of love, so that a
nervous wreck of a warrior and an ugly girl should
appear to each other the embodiment of physical
strength and beauty. That even plain women have
their dreams is a subject for the fantastic dramatists.
Pinero has tried his hand at everything : in fantasy
he is heavy-handed.

Barrie has called *Iris* the most notable play of our
time. Barrie does not go to the theatre. It is a little
on the bitter side. Iris herself is, of course, a sort of
Mrs Tanqueray in her unregenerate days.

When we are first introduced to her she is robust,
happy, sweet, " beautiful, with a soft, appealing voice
and movements instinct with simple grace and dignity."
In view of her latter end it is worth noticing those
stage directions. She is a very wealthy widow condemned under her husband's will to lose all her money
if she remarries. At the time of the play, at the age of
twenty-six, she has been five years a widow. Her time
and affections are divided between Laurence Trenwith,
aged twenty-eight, who has no money or prospects
beyond that of cattle-ranching in British Columbia
("What career is there, apart from the criminal, for
engaging but impecunious incapacity ? . . . It begins
with a beggarly secretaryship, passes through the
intermediate stages of a precarious interest in a wine
business and a disastrous association with the Turf and

the Stock Exchange, and ends with the selling, on
commission, of an obsolete atlas or an unwieldy Bible "),
and Frederick Maldonado, "a tall massive man of
about forty, with brown hair and beard, handsome
according to the Jewish type"—"a pawnbroker with
imagination," a financier. As Iris is one of those
women to whom comfort is a necessity, we are not
surprised to find her announcing her engagement to
the wealthy Jew, in spite of the fact that the pauper
Laurence implores her to go out with him to British
Columbia and rough it. She cannot bear to let him
go—and yet she cannot bear to let her money go.
She tells Maldonado that she hasn't the love for
him that a woman ought to have for a husband, and
rouses his anger.

"What an ass! I really imagined—for three mortal
hours!—that it was reserved for me to escape the
proverbial fate of the millionaire where the love of
women is concerned!" He goes out. Laurence
returns, and she tells him that she is not fit for the
life he asks her to lead, but that she cannot live without him. She throws over Maldonado and becomes
Laurence's mistress, taking him out with her to
Switzerland, where, in the second act, we see them
both very happy, though Iris is taunting herself with
her cowardice in not being capable of risking poverty
with her lover. "Your poor, weak, sordid Iris, who
must lie in the sun in summer, before the fire in winter,
who must wear the choicest lace, the richest furs :
whose eyes must never encounter any but the most
beautiful objects—languid, slothful, nerveless, incapable almost of effort." Laurence tries to convince
her that they would be happier still if they married.

"I hadn't the recklessness on the one hand," she
demurs, "nor the power of self-denial on the other.
And so I treat your love as the poet did the fruit—I
steal it : greedily and lazily I steal it."

Laurence tells her that he is ashamed of the thought
of living on her. He insists on going out to work. He
is of the type that cannot accept money from a woman.

" Why should we try to escape from the current ? "
asks his siren. " We love each other ; we've been
happy, we *are* happy." A bombshell bursts to disturb
their Elysian delights : Iris's solicitor decamps with
all her money. Laurence determines to waste no
more time, but to go out to Canada alone, and come
back and fetch Iris when he has succeeded in making
a home for her. Maldonado steps in at this juncture
in true Mephistophelian style and speeds Laurence off
to Canada. There is one last scene between Laurence
and Iris in which he implores her to go out with him
poor, but she decides that she must conduct her own
struggle with poverty alone. " After I have proved to
you that I can live patiently, uncomplainingly, without
luxury . . . content with the barest comfort," then
she will go out to him. When he has gone Maldonado
comes back to her, thrusts a cheque-book on her, and
in the fourth act, with something of a shock (even
knowing her as we do), we see her installed in a West
End flat as Maldonado's mistress. " I wish you had
been merciful and had taken me out on to the lake and
drowned me," says Iris. He proposes to make amends
by marrying her. " It's too late," she says. " I'm
down, beyond recovery. I've lost heart. I no longer
care."

Maldonado's passion is, however, by no means dead.
" I love you more than ever, my dear. . . . You're
extraordinary. By the common rule of life I ought to
be chafing to be rid of you ; the fizz should have gone
entirely out of what remains of the liquor by this time.
. . . I say it's wonderful, considering what's behind
us, that we should stand here as we do—I again en-
treating you to be my wife . . . for a soft word, a
spark of warmth, just a little tenderness. I shall never
be able to do without you . . . you devil in marble."
She learns that Laurence is back in England, sends for
him, and in the last act sees him : he is passionately
adoring in his manner until she makes him realise to
what depths she has sunk. . . . " He never left me alone.
There's no palliation in that, perhaps, no excuse—but

he never left me alone. Oh, I meant to be poor! I meant to be poor!"

The play at this stage becomes extraordinarily melodramatic. All Laurence can do is to repeat the phrase "I'm sorry," and edge his way to the door. As soon as he has gone Maldonado reappears, with necktie disarranged, eyes bloodshot and face livid, shouting: "You rag of a woman! You double-faced trull: you liar! . . . You're the sort of woman that sends a hot-blooded man to the gallows." Instead of killing her, as we expect him to, he simply sends her out into the night. Again, like *The Second Mrs Tanqueray*, this is a very moral play, pointing the fact that the way of transgressors is hard. To-day we are inclined to forget all about sin, and wonder more why Laurence is quite so blatant a foot, so unbending a moralist and unforgiving a Christian as to turn his back on the girl whose misfortune it had been really to love him, so far as her weak nature allowed her to love anyone.

The difficulty both with *Iris* and *Mrs Tanqueray* is that we simply do not believe in the things that people in their day believed. If we love people we are not likely to kick them out for infidelity.

Our love may be rougher, better able to stand shocks : it is certainly more honest.

IX

BERNARD SHAW

THE time, I should have guessed, must now be past when anyone could still seriously imagine Shaw to be a charlatan. "For ten years past," he wrote in his valedictory article for *The Saturday Review* on 21st May 1898, "with an unprecedented pertinacity and obstination I have been dinning into the public head that I am an extraordinarily witty, brilliant and clever man. That is now part of the public opinion of England ; and no power in heaven or earth will ever change it. I may dodder and dote. I may potboil and platitudinise. I may become the butt and chopping-block of all the bright, original spirits of the rising generation : but my reputation shall not suffer : it is built up fast and solid, like Shakespeare's, on an impregnable basis of dogmatic reiteration."

It is useful to see how accurate this prophecy of twenty-five years ago was.

It is true that, unlike many of his contemporaries, Shaw survived the war. It left him shaken. No one can read his latest plays with the same fervour that he brought to those early ones. We have been stunned with a large noise ; those delicious detonations of his early plays have now no longer the power to make us jump. He is witty, brilliant and clever; he has neither doddered nor doted, potboiled nor platitudinised, he is not the butt of the rising generation, and yet his reputation is not impregnable : it is by no means solid, like Shakespeare's.

In the old days, when the dons used to tell us that Shaw was a wind-bag, a shallow tub-thumper, an insincere clown, one who stood on his head in the

pulpit because no one would listen to his sermons
unless he threw in some sop of mental acrobatics, we
undergraduates smiled. That was ever, we thought,
the way of dons, to be pettily jealous of the man who
got the world to discuss his ideas. It was easy to say
that there was no originality in him, that he owed all
his revolutionary notions to Samuel Butler. That is
a simple truth upon which Shaw himself had insisted
for some years.

What so many people did fail to realise about Shaw
was that he was an extraordinary phenomenon—a
Puritan without hypocrisy. Even now it is hard to
realise that there could exist a man capable of reverencing a God and laughing at him almost at the same
time. G. K. Chesterton has been telling us for years
that it is no good reverencing a God until and unless
you can laugh at him, and we had accepted the statement as in the true Chestertonian manner, as though
we had read " the only way to walk forwards is to go
backwards "—" the only way to see the stars is to go
down a coal mine." Paradoxes are the easiest things
in the world to invent. They always happen to
possess more than a modicum of truth, and they
always give their originators a reputation for wit.
There are many weaknesses in Shaw, but one of them
is, in fact, his greatest strength. He never can resist
an attempt to shock, or a Johnsonian frisk. He is
the ascetic *farceur*. Again a paradox. For to see a
bishop unbend to a practical joke upsets our sènse
of propriety. Shaw is more saintly than any
living bishop. To watch him indulging in clown's
badinage at times disgusts us. When Granville Barker
introduces Constantine in *The Madras House* as a
Mohammedan we may, for a moment, be startled,
but when we begin to think at all we realise that our
being startled was an index of our narrowness. Constantine's Mohammedanism matters. It gives Barker
the chance to let in air on to the stuffy question of sex.
When the waiter in *You Never Can Tell* announces
that his son is a K.C. you may be momentarily

jerked into irrational laughter, but you are very
soon angry with yourself for having been trapped.
It is one of Shaw's little japes. It means nothing.
With Shaw, as with Wordsworth, rigid selection is
necessary. There is much in his work that does not
wear well. *Pygmalion*, written for Mrs Pat Campbell,
and *Captain Brassbound's Conversion*, written for
Ellen Terry, have little more than local interest.
Heartbreak House has isolated lines of great power.
Arms and the Man showed us soldiering as it really is,
but it took a European holocaust to prove how right
he was. *How He Lied to Her Husband* is an exquisite
trifle. *John Bull's Other Island* held the mirror up
to the Englishman. *Fanny's First Play* is brilliant.
Getting Married is dull. *You Never Can Tell* is a trifle
light as air, midsummer madness, the somersault of a
brainy madcap. When all is said, it is probably *Man
and Superman* (because it contains most of his ideas
best expressed) and *Candida* that will last. *Candida*
is a truly amazing play. Think of Shaw's description of Morell. At last the stage parson (prolific of
children, stammering of tongue, nervous in manner,
with shuffling feet and snuffling nose) is discarded.
Another convention goes by the board. " The
Reverend James Mavor Morell is a Christian Socialist
clergyman of the Church of England, and an active
member of the Guild of St Matthew and the Christian
Social Union. A vigorous, genial, popular man of
forty, robust and good-looking, full of energy, with
pleasant, hearty, considerate manners, and a sound
unaffected voice, which he uses with the clean athletic
articulation of a practised orator. . . . He is a first-
rate clergyman, able to say what he likes to whom he
likes . . . his well-spring of enthusiasm and sympathetic emotion has never run dry for a moment : he
still eats and sleeps heartily enough to win the daily
battle between exhaustion and recuperation trium-
phantly. Withal, a great baby, pardonably vain of
his powers and unconsciously pleased with himself."
Such is the man that Shaw is going to humble to the

dust through the mouth of an eighteen year-old poet
and his wonderful wife. Candida is a woman "who has
found that she can always manage people by engaging their affection, and who does so frankly and instinctively without the slightest scruple. So far, she is
like any other pretty woman who is just clever enough
to make the most of her sexual attractions for trivially
selfish ends ; but Candida's serene brow, courageous
eyes, and well-set mouth and chin signify largeness of
mind and dignity of character to ennoble her cunning
in the affections."

What induced Shaw to give so fine a woman so
grotesque a father as Mr Burgess, " a man of sixty,
made coarse and sordid by the compulsory selfishness
of petty commerce, and later on softened into sluggish
bumptiousness by overfeeding and commercial success.
A vulgar, ignorant, guzzling man, offensive and contemptuous to people whose labour is cheap, respectful
to wealth and rank, and quite sincere and without
rancour or envy in both attitudes. Finding him
without talent, the world has offered him no decently
paid work except ignoble work : and he has, in
consequence, become somewhat hoggish " ?

In Marchbanks, the poet who is to open Morell's
eyes to his own shortcomings, Shaw has tried to create
a Shelley. As Shaw has about as much of the poetic
in his composition as a crayfish, he does nothing more
than say that Marchbanks is a Shelley. He puts no
words into his mouth which could in any circumstances
have been used by the poet. The scene is exquisitely
done in which Marchbanks disturbs Morell's serenity
for the first time. Marchbanks works upon his mind
almost as Iago works on the mind of Othello. Marchbanks tells Morell that he is in love with Candida
and the parson comes out with some of those high-
sounding phrases on which he has lived all his life.

" Let us put aside all that cant," says Marchbanks,
almost beside himself with rage. " It horrifies me
when I think of the doses of it she has had to endure
in all the weary years during which you have selfishly

and blindly sacrificed her to minister to your self-sufficiency."

When Morell tells the boy that he is making a very great fool of himself he replies with one of those flashes of inspiration for which Shaw is so remarkable :

" Do you think that the things people make fools of themselves about are any less real and true than the things they behave sensibly about ? They are more true : they are the only things that are true."

That is perhaps the finest moment in the play, when Morell is first really staggered. He goes on preaching at Marchbanks, but the poet rounds on him at the end of all his fine phrases, and they are fine. " Is it like this for her here always ? A woman, with a great soul, craving for reality, truth, freedom : and being fed on metaphors, sermons, stale perorations, mere rhetoric."

Morell tells him in reply that his talent is the gift of finding words for divine truth, and Marchbanks, ever with the last word, impetuously retorts : " It's the gift of the gab, nothing more and nothing less.' Scarcely less real is Morell's typist, Prossy, that " brisk little woman of about thirty, of the lower middle class . . . pert and quick of speech, and not very civil in her manner, but sensitive and affectionate." Whoever saw Ada King take that part has a memory of as perfect a bit of acting as we are likely to see in our time. Prossy bridling at Burgess, Prossy really angry with Marchbanks, who discovers her wild passion for Morell by disclosing his own. " All the love in the world is longing to speak : only it dare not, because it is shy ! shy ! shy ! That is the world's tragedy."

PROSSY : " Wicked people get over that shyness occasionally, don't they ? "

But Marchbanks is not going to be put off by her defensive wit. When she tells him that it's not proper to be saying the sorts of things that he is saying he counters her with, " Nothing that's worth saying is proper." When she tells him to talk about in-different things he replies : " Would you stand and talk about indifferent things if a child were by, crying bitterly with hunger ? . . . I can't talk about indifferent things with my heart crying out bitterly in its hunger."

When Candida teases him about her having to clean the lamps and blacklead the stove, he breaks into a Shavian attempt at Shelleyan talk which is merely ludicrous.

" No," he says, " not a scrubbing-brush, but a boat —a tiny shallop to sail away in, far from the world : where the marble floors are washed by the rain and dried by the sun : where the south wind dusts the beautiful green and purple carpets."

No—this simply will not do. Even worse follows. " Or a chariot ! to carry us up into the sky, where the lamps are stars, and don't need to be filled with paraffin oil every day."

Shaw is not of those who are at home on Mount Parnassus. Humour was a closed book to Milton, Wordsworth and Shelley : why should not poetry be denied to Congreve, Swift and Shaw ? Shaw's mistake was in daring to create the character, and then in making him speak any but the baldest prose. So swiftly are we carried along by the main theme, however, that we forget and forgive. We are too engrossed in watching the disintegration of Morell. Candida begins to take a hand in the game. She tells Morell that she would give both her goodness and her purity to Eugene as willingly as she would give her shawl to a beggar dying of cold if there was nothing else to restrain her. " Put your trust in my love for you, James : for if that went, I should care very little for your sermons—mere phrases that you cheat yourself and others with every day."

Shaw again goes all to bits in the third act, when Eugene is left alone with Candida and asks her whether he may say some wicked things to her, and is left with the cold comfort of repeating the name Candida five times. Things perk up again for a moment in the final scene, when Candida is given her

chance. " Oh ! I am to choose, am I ? I suppose
it is quite settled that I must belong to one or the
other. . . . I am up for auction, it seems. What do
you bid, James ? " And Morell offers her his strength,
and Marchbanks his weakness, and she chooses the
weaker—her spoilt husband. Eugene grows up in a
moment : he has learnt to do without happiness.
Candida sends him out into the night with two
sentences ringing in his ears : " When I am thirty
she will be forty-five. When I am sixty she will be
seventy-five."

" In a hundred years," he says, in his farewell speech
to her, " we shall be the same age. But I have a
better secret than that in my heart."

And he leaves the parson cured (we hope but do not
believe) and Candida in his arms, but ignorant of the
secret in the poet's heart.

One does not come back to all of Shaw with a great
zest. Mingled with his great common sense there is a
vast amount of nonsense, particularly about education
and doctors. Whenever he sees a vested interest,
following in his father's (Samuel Butler's) footsteps,
he attacks it, and for the most part his attacks are
deserved. He has, I think, led us to expect too much
from him. Like Milton, he suffers from having wisdom
at one entrance quite shut out. He is not versatile.
He is as incapable of tragedy as he is of poetry.
His business is lashing out at stupidity, bursting the
balloons of bombastic nonsense with which we abound.
There is a devastating clarity about him ; his prose
style is as perfectly adapted to the medium in which
he works as Swift's is. A very little of him will last
a very long time.

Who could help revering and remembering the man
who advises us to wear out, not rust out, and so live
that when we die God shall be in our debt.

Puritanism has its points when it discards the visor
of hypocrisy.

X

ALFRED SUTRO

IN *The Laughing Lady* Sutro hit upon an exceedingly good idea. In the first place he begins with a delicious telephone conversation—even the dullest telephone titillates us on the stage. The genial Playgate is rung up by Lady Marjorie Colladine. We gather that she has been divorced during the afternoon, and that her friends have cut her, and that she wishes to dine with him. No sooner has he sympathised with her and asked her to come at once than he remembers that he has asked the barrister who had cross-examined her earlier in the day. By the time that he got her number again she had left her house for his. Playgate's wife is as furious as he is.

"To have at my table—the same night—a woman who has just been divorced—and the counsel who—this very afternoon—has flayed her alive—in the witness-box."

They are immediately joined by Cynthia Dell, a forty-five-year-old scandalmonger.

"In court all day!" she begins. "Saw Marjorie in the box. . . . I wouldn't have missed it for worlds! Bertie Walton goes into her room—in his pyjamas—half-an-hour after midnight. . . . At half-past twelve at night in a Folkestone hotel. He stops there till two. And she swears they only—talked!"

They are joined by Sir Harrison Peters, another guest, who is delighted at the prospect of the eminent barrister, "the shyest man in the world with women," having to meet his victim of the afternoon.

CYNTHIA : "He positively undresses them—in court."

PETERS : "In private life he'd be puzzled to—button their glove. . . . His admirable wife runs him

and regulates him ; winds and unwinds him. . . . (It's
a terrible thing to say about any man—and I beg that
you won't repeat it—but I've the profound conviction
that Daniel—in the twenty odd years that he has been
married—has never once been unfaithful to his wife.) "
Farr and his wife then come in, immediately followed
by the twenty-five-year-old Marjorie.

During dinner she is enlightened about the Einstein
theory by the barrister. Conversation among the
ladies afterwards turns on the character of Peters,
the war profiteer. " Is he married ? " asks one girl.
" Not technically," answers Cynthia, " but there are
one or two ladies—real ladies—who are not—sisters
to him." Sutro finds it easy to scintillate with that
artificial sparkle. " Lord Humperley, who's so often in
the bankruptcy court that it's almost a club to him,"
is another of Cynthia's witticisms.

Cynthia's character was worth enlarging upon :
" The most malicious woman in London," who
would do anything to help a friend and say anything
to hurt her. We hear more of Marjorie's former
husband after dinner. " Rather a dear . . . in a
wooden-headed sort of way " is her description of him,
" a born soldier . . . for ever running off somewhere
where there was a scrap on. . . . I didn't hear from
him much, you know—he had a Public School education,
University and so forth—and finds writing letters very
difficult." The man she was accused of living with,
Bertie Walton, is stigmatised by her as " a fashion-
plate with a giggle, a manikin with a glass in its eye."

When the men come in they cut out for bridge, and
Marjorie is left to talk to Farr, who is enormously
attracted by her. She gives him leave to call on her,
and is rung up by her husband, who wants also
to call on her the next day. This first act is a real
triumph of stagecraft. Sutro is not a great enough
writer to keep up this pace. Our interest rapidly
subsides. First Peters calls on Marjorie, and in a
singularly unpleasant and unnecessary scene proposes
to give her ten thousand pounds, a motor car and a

flat in Cavendish Square. Hector, her husband, comes
in at the right moment to kick the man out : he then
tells her that he wants her back. " My dear Hector,"
says Marjorie, " this is too lovely ; too magnificently
idiotic . . . you can't divorce your cake and eat it !
We're divorced, Hector—we are—beautifully divorced.
And in six months we can marry again." He tries to
tempt her to go abroad with him. " I'm not going
to be your wife any more, thank you." He then
demands whether there is any other man, and Farr
immediately comes in—a delightful comedy situation :
husband wanting the wife he had just divorced back
again, faced by the barrister he had paid to convict
her, who is now, in his turn, in love with her. Hector
abuses Farr for being so brutal to her the day
before, and then takes his leave. Farr then pleads
for him. " Lady Marjorie, women are bored by
merely good men, and made unhappy by merely clever
ones. Marriage is often a condition of brilliant misery,
often one of happy dullness. Of the two the latter is
preferable."

" Thank you," she replies. " As we're exchanging
platitudes, let me say that, having tried happy dullness,
and not liking it, I'll have brilliant misery next time,
please, the *least* bit underdone."

When he accuses her of being cruel she retaliates
with : " Oh, you men ! Your idea of feminine cruelty !
Let me tell you, Mr Farr, through the length and
breadth of this country there are women being bored
by their husbands to such a degree of flattened pulp
that one must go back to Chinese torture to find a
parallel of suffering."

As the curtain falls on the second act Farr has
declared his passion for her, is kissing her, and the
telephone again rings.

In the last act Mrs Farr comes in and suggests that
to save her husband's reputation it would be better
for Marjorie to become his mistress than to do him
harm in his work by a public marriage. " What need
is there for a divorce ? Do what you can for him—

you who have won. . . . I am old, and you're young :
I'm plain, and you're beautiful. I ask you—not to
—break him ! " Farr enters as his wife goes out.
Marjorie tests him, finds that he is willing to give up
his children and work for her sake. She confesses
that she loves him, but she refuses to go away with
him. She tells him that he doesn't love her.
" There's an ugly word for it . . . But if that's all
I mean to you—take me ! . . . Why go away ? I'll
be your—mistress."

That staggers him back to respectability, and the
play closes on the note of—" Why make people
suffer ? " It is Marjorie talking. " We'll do the fine
thing, the big thing ! We love each other, Daniel
. . . but there's life—and it's greater than love—oh,
my dear, my dear—good-bye."

It would be hard to imagine a more false or lame
conclusion. They are all puppets, incapable of expressing or feeling any real emotion.

The same is true of *The Great Well*, in which secret
information is betrayed by an erring wife to the man
who wishes to be her lover.

It is an artificial play from start to finish : all the
characters are stereotyped.

There is the " very pretty girl of twenty," Annette,
who reads *Married Love*, one of those " unpleasant
books " in the aged Simon's eyes. I wonder if Simon
ever read it. There is the thirty-year-old Camilla,
whose idea of living dangerously is to refuse to occupy
the same bedroom with her husband and allow herself
to lunch at the Ivy with a major, who says that he has
no moral sense—a " loose liver " is Simon's phrase
for him. There is a sixty-five-year-old voluble Aunt
Eleanor, extraordinarily tedious, to provide comic relief. There is the thirty-five-year-old Peter (he would
be called Peter), the tall, heavily built husband with the
shy, sensitive face. "His clothes hang rather loosely
on him, and his movements are apt to be somewhat
awkward and abrupt." He makes me want to scream.

The Aunt Eleanor type of wit is altogether too cheap.

x

" It's a mistake to compromise yourself, my dear.
Be good ; it comes much cheaper in the end. You
can be as bad as you like as long as you're good "—
that is by far the best of her sentences. Peter is
director of an oil company which is rapidly going
under. He has a secret which he shares only with
the other directors and his wife. The secret is that
the Great Oil Well has dried up.

Major Arnold Darenth, the handsome, well set-up
villain of thirty, tries to wrest the secret from Camilla.
Her conscience is too Nonconformist for her to become
his mistress, but it is elastic enough for her to betray
her husband's secret in order to save Darenth from the
Canadian Mounted Police. Darenth is a delicious
myth. This is how he talks : " I'm a waster . . .
not my fault—the war. I'd have been a snuffy,
respectable don at Balliol if it hadn't been for the
blooming war—or a rising young barrister perhaps.
But you can't go on killing Germans and Turks for
four years and a half and then placidly read for the
Bar or sit on a stool in a merchant's office."

Oh, Mr Sutro, Mr Sutro, where are your eyes ? A
few hundred thousand men are giving the lie direct to
that peculiarly false statement.

Darenth caught Peter asleep on duty at Albert
and that (of course) made them friends for life.
Unfortunately in peace time Peter is rarely caught
napping : Darenth always is. He gambles and always
loses. With Camilla he would have won if only he
had been less clumsy. " I can't bear the thought,"
she says to him, " really I can't—of the emptiness—
without you." Then she divulges to him the great
secret, assured that he will use the information in such
a way as not to harm Peter. She then goes to her
dinner at the Ivy and the Galsworthy play with
Darenth, leaving Annette to console Peter for having
married a girl who doesn't love anything that is his
except his money.

In Act II. we are privileged to see the offices of the
Stratton River Oil Company. To many of us who

believed that " the City " was simply a convenient illusion to enable men to get away from home it comes with something of a start to find that it is a wildly exciting place, where even men of the Peter stamp rush up and down shouting : "By Heaven, I'll expose him ! By God, he shall pay ! "

The secret is out. Darenth tells Camilla that he sold it for £2000 to a low-down man who causes a ramp (is that the term ?) on the oil market. Everyone rushes to sell their old shares for any sum. Then Camilla says that she is going to divulge Darenth's infamy. He then makes it quite clear to her that if she does reveal the truth everyone will take it for granted that she is his mistress. Peter tells Camilla that he has spies at work, to find out who the culprit is. The directors have a stormy meeting, during which they accuse each other in a manner that must be unpopular even in the city. Then comes the inevitable cable saying that the Great Well is flowing better than ever (wonderful things, oil wells), and Peter is in the seventh heaven when that muddling old fool Simon comes in to tell him that Darenth was the man who sold the secret.

In the next act Peter goes home and faces Camilla with the fact, which she stoutly denies. Her lying is the only creditable or credible thing about her. She is on the point of convincing him when his co-directors swoop down and accuse Peter himself of selling his own shares, using the secret for his own purpose. Camilla can't stand this, so confesses to them, whereupon Peter contradicts her and says that they are right—he did use the secret for his own ends. Luckily Milford, the man who employed Darenth, came in and told the truth. The directors realise that Peter is only defending Camilla and leave him to tackle her. Unfortunately Darenth arrives and there is an almost unendurably silly conversation between them. Peter cannot believe that Camilla is not Darenth's mistress. He sends for her : offers her £2000 a year and her release. In the end Camilla produces a letter to prove her technical loyalty to her husband. She of course gives Darenth his *congé* and tells Peter that she is really glad that she is going to bear his child.

This last act is so silly that it doesn't bear thinking about. Sutro has a sense of the stage, but very little of life. He is bound by the traditions. He must have stock figures, stock plots. He is clever at manipulation. He has nothing to say that matters, but his stagecraft is good. He entertains, but leaves no permanent impression on the mind.

He represents, best of all contemporary writers, what is bound to happen when you compel men of intelligence and ideas to limit their output to inconsequential and wholly artificial themes. Mr Sutro has wit ; he appears also to have sufficient wits to go with the stream and give the actor-managers what they think the public likes.

PART VI
SOME MODERN ESSAYISTS

MAX BEERBOHM
ALICE MEYNELL
G. S. STREET

I

MAX BEERBOHM

IN *And Even Now* we get a collection of ten years' work, as precious, as inimitable, as quietly humorous in the main as ever. Not all are worthy. " How Shall I Word it ? " might have been a contribution to *Punch*.

But *And Even Now* would be memorable if it contained only "No. 2 The Pines," a model fragment of biography. Swinburne lives again by reason of it. " Here, suddenly visible in the flesh, was the legendary being and divine singer. Here he was, shutting the door behind him as might anybody else, and advancing —a strange small figure in grey, having an air at once noble and roguish, proud and skittish . . . the first impression he made on me . . . was that of a very great gentleman indeed. Not that of an *old* gentleman, either. . . . There was yet about him something— boyish ? girlish ? childish, rather : something of a beautifully well-bred child. But he had the eyes of a god, and the smile of an elf . . . so small and sloping were his shoulders that the jacket seemed ever so likely to slip right off . . . his hands were tiny, even for his size, and they fluttered helplessly, touchingly, unceasingly . . . it made me unhappy to see what trouble he had in managing his knife and fork. . . . I have known no man of genius who had not to pay, in some affliction or defect either physical or spiritual, for what the gods had given him. Here, in this fluttering of his tiny hands, was a part of the price Swinburne had to pay. . . . So soon as the mutton had been replaced by the apple-pie, Watts-Dunton leaned forward and ' Well, Algernon,' he roared, ' how was it on the Heath to-day ? ' Swinburne . . . now threw back his head, uttering a sound that was like the cooing of a dove, and forthwith, rapidly, ever so musically, he spoke to us of his walk : spoke not in the strain of a man who had been taking his daily exercise on Putney Heath, but rather in that of a Peri who had at long last been suffered to pass through Paradise. And rather than that he spoke would I say that he cooingly and flutingly *sang* of his experience. The wonders of this morning's wind and sun and clouds were expressed in a flow of words so right and sentences so perfectly balanced that they would have seemed pedantic had they not been clearly as spontaneous as the wordless notes of a bird in song. The frail, sweet voice rose and fell, lingered, quickened, in all manner of trills and roulades."

The whole essay is pitched on this high note. It is amazingly sustained.

Even in his most trifling moments he is not only readable but polished. There is that passage in " Hosts and Guests " of his entertaining friends : " Somewhere in the back of my brain . . . was always the haunting fear that I had not brought enough money in my pocket. I never let this fear master me. I never said to anyone ' Will you have a liqueur ? '—always ' What liqueur will you have ? ' But I postponed as far as possible the evil moment of asking for the bill. When I had in the proper casual tone (I hope and believe) at length asked for it, I wished always it were not brought to me folded on a plate as though the amount were so hideously high that I alone must be privy to it. So soon as it was laid beside me, I wanted to know the worst at once. But I pretended to be so occupied in talk that I was unaware of the bill's presence ; and I was careful to be always in the middle of a sentence when I raised the upper fold and took my not (I hope) frozen glance. In point of fact the amount was always much less than I had feared. Pessimism does win us great happy moments."

On the subject of servants he gets more serious than is his wont.

" It is unseemly," he opens, " that a man should

let any ancestors of his arise from their graves to wait on
his guests at table."

"Convention," he finishes, "alone has forced me to
be anywhere a master. . . . When I was a king in
Babylon and you were a Christian slave I promptly
freed you. . . . Anarchistic? Yes; and I have no
defence to offer, except the rather lame one that I am
a Tory anarchist. I should like everyone to go about
doing just as he pleased—short of altering any of the
things to which I have grown accustomed. Domestic
service is not one of these things, and I should be glad
were there no more of it."

It is a powerful plea and should be widely read for
its complete common sense.

Compare Max Beerbohm on " Going Out for a Walk "
with Stevenson and Hazlitt. Max is essentially a
townsman : the urban touch is visible all through.

"Walking for walking's sake may be as highly
laudable and exemplary a thing as it is held to be by
those who practise it. My objection to it is that it
stops the brain. Many a man has professed to me that
his brain never works so well as when he is swinging
along the high road or over hill and dale. This boast
is not confirmed by my memory of anybody who on a
Sunday morning has forced me to partake of his adventure. Experience teaches me that whatever a fellow-
guest may have of power to instruct or to amuse when
he is sitting on a chair, or standing on a hearth-rug,
quickly leaves him when he takes one out for a walk.
The ideas that came so thick and fast to him in any
room, where are they now ? Where that encyclopædic
knowledge which he bore so lightly ? . . . The man's
face that was so mobile is set now : gone is the light
from his fine eyes. He says that A. (our host) is a
thoroughly good fellow. Fifty yards further on he
adds that A. is one of the best fellows he has ever met.
We tramp another furlong or so, and he says that
Mrs A. is a charming woman. Presently he adds that
she is one of the most charming women he has ever
known. We pass an inn. He reads vapidly aloud to

me : ' The King's Arms. Licensed to sell Ales and
Spirits.' I foresee that during the rest of the walk he
will read aloud any inscription that occurs. We pass
a milestone. He points at it with his stick, and says
' Uxminster, eleven miles.' We turn a sharp corner
at the foot of a hill. He points at the wall, and says
' Drive slowly.' I see far ahead, on the other side of the
hedge bordering the high road, a small notice-board.
He sees it too. He keeps his eye on it. And in due
course, ' Trespassers,' he says, ' Will Be Prosecuted.'
Poor man !—mentally a wreck."

That passage is worth putting by the side of all the
essays ever written on the subject. It may be urban ;
it is certainly urbane.

Then there is the unforgettable paper called " A
Clergyman," so exactly after Max's own heart :

" Fragmentary, pale, momentary : almost nothing ;
glimpsed and gone : . . . nothing is told of him but
that once, abruptly, he asked a question, and received
an answer. This was on the afternoon of April 7th,
1778, at Streatham, in the well-appointed house of
Mr Thrale."

Doctor Johnson is talking about sermons : suddenly—

"A CLERGYMAN, whose name I do not recollect: 'Were
not Dodd's sermons addressed to the passions ? '

" JOHNSON : ' They were nothing, sir, be they addressed to what they may.' "

This is just the sort of hare that Beerbohm loves to
start. He will write the biography of " A Clergyman."

" I know not," he begins, " which is the more startling
—the debut of the unfortunate clergyman, or the
instantaneousness of his end. . . . What drew the
blasting flash must have been not the question itself,
but the manner in which it was asked.

" Say the words aloud : ' Were not Dodd's sermons
addressed to the passions ? ' They are words which,
if you have any dramatic and histrionic sense, *cannot* be
said except in a high, thin voice. . . . You must pipe
them. Remember, now, Johnson was very deaf."

In a few moments Beerbohm has proved that he is a

young, shy curate of the neighbouring church, with high and narrow forehead, and mouse-coloured hair. He never rallied under the blow. "'A Clergyman' never held up his head or smiled again after the brief encounter recorded for us by Boswell. He sank into a rapid decline. . . . I like to think that he died forgiving Dr Johnson."

Delicious fooling, reminiscent of Savonarola Brown, Enoch Soames and other poor ghosts who for ever live owing to the craft of their creator.

There is a glorious chapter called "The Crime," where he burns a novel of which the critics (for whom Max has a supreme contempt) had said pleasant things, only to find that it really possessed "intense vitality," "immense vitality": it simply would not burn. Charred pages with fragments—"lways loathed you, bu " . . . "ning Tolstoi was right . . ."—worrying him. The fire went out : the book remained.

But "William and Mary" is the essay to which we all come back with the greatest pleasure. William was a reviewer of books extraordinarily happily married to Mary, whose laugh "was a lovely thing . . . as though she were pulling repeatedly a little silver bell." William wrote "extraordinarily gloomy plays about extraordinarily unhappy marriages." He had no success, nor did he need it. He was comfortable : they were both radiantly happy. Then Mary died in childbirth. William was killed in the Boer War. The essayist goes back to their cottage : "The latticed windows between had all been boarded up from within. . . . I stood looking at the door. . . . In the door-post to the right was a small knob of rusty iron—mocking reminder that to gain admission to a house one does not 'will' the door : one rings the bell. . . . My hand drew back, wavered, suddenly closed on the knob. I heard the scrape of the wire—and then, from somewhere within the heart of the shut house, a tinkle. It had been the weakest, the puniest of noises. It had been no more than is a fledgling's first attempt at a twitter. But I was not judging it by its volume. Deafening

peals from steeples had meant less to me than that one
single note breaking the silence—in there. . . . Again
my hand closed on the knob. . . . That was my answer ;
and the rejoinder to it was more than I had thought to
hear—a whole quick sequence of notes . . . like a
trill of laughter echoing out of the past. . . . It was so
like something I had known, so recognisable, and, oh,
recognising, that I was lost in wonder. And long must
I have remained standing at that door, for I heard the
sound often, often. I must have rung again and
again, tenaciously, vehemently, in my folly."

One cannot deny beauty to the artist who writes as
sensitively as that.

Fastidious, detached, moving among words with the
same delicacy and studied care that a superb dancer
adopts in an intricate country or sword dance, Max
Beerbohm is a salutary antidote to the modern idea
that haste is all. He has brought the polishing of the
sentence and the selection of the fittest word to a fine
art. Not only so, but the polished and selected idea
that he finally gives us is invariably original, invariably
memorable.

II

ALICE MEYNELL

" THEY leave a sense of stilled singing in the
mind they fill." That was George Meredith's
verdict on Mrs Meynell's essays. He made a
mistake over Samuel Butler : he made none over the
woman whom J. C. Squire describes as one of the great
half-dozen women writers England has yet produced.
Certainly no other woman and very few men have taken
quite such pains or been quite so sensitive about the
accurate word. To read her essays after those of
most of our contemporaries needs a margin of rest.
Our eyes are accustomed to skim a certain amount of
verbiage in their hunt for the core of a discourse.
Mrs Meynell has to be read slowly and not skimmed if
you would gain from her the sweetness and the strength
which are hers to give. " Without anxiety, without
haste, and without misgiving are all great things to be
done, and neither interruption in the doing nor ruin
after they are done finds anything in them to betray."
That is at any rate how her great things are done.

It is fitting and typical that Mrs Meynell should
praise, among exercises, " the effectual act of towing
. . . the ample revenge of the unmuscular upon the
happy labourers with the oar, the pole, the bicycle, and
all other means of violence. . . . To walk unbound is
to walk in prose, without the friction of the wings of
metre, without the sweet and encouraging tug upon
the spirit and the line. . . . Your easy and efficient
work lets you carry your head high and watch the birds,
or listen to them. . . . Here, on the long tow-path,
between warm, embrowned meadows and opal waters,
you need but to walk in your swinging harness, and so
take your friends up-stream."

Here is the sense of discipline, of unhurried ease, of the ability to keep your mind free to see, hear and love Nature's colours and sounds that one associates with all Mrs Meynell's work. She sees, as W. H. Davies sees, with a much keener vision than the rest of us.

" A field of tall flowers tosses many ways in one warm gale, like the many lovers of a poet who have a thousand reasons for their love : but the rushes, more strongly tethered, are swept into a single attitude, again and again, at every renewal of the storm."

We have all seen that ; how few of us have noticed it. Always on country delights her touch is exact. Who before has called our attention to the gipsy, outlaw qualities of rushes?

" A well-appointed country house sees nothing out of the windows that is not its own. But he who tells you so . . . is certainly disturbed . . . if his otherwise contented eyes should happen to be caught by a region of rushes. The water is his—he had the pond made ; or the river, for a space, and the fish, for a time. But the bulrushes, the reeds . . . though their roots are in his ground right enough, there is a something about their heads . . ."

The same delicate, fanciful criticism that she brings to bear upon the country-side is evident in her criticism of books. In an excellent essay on *Pathos* she puts in a powerful plea for the divine between literature and life. " Is not life one thing and is not art another ? Is it not the privilege of literature to treat things singly, without the after-thoughts of life, without the troublous completeness of the many-sided world ? Is not Shakespeare, for this reason, our refuge ? Fortunately unreal is his world when he will have it so : and there we may laugh with open heart at a grotesque man : without misgiving, without remorse, without reluctance. If great creating Nature has not assumed for herself she has assuredly secured to the great creating the right of partiality, of limitation, of setting aside and leaving out, of taking one impression and one emotion as sufficient for the day. . . . In some of his persons,

indeed, Shakespeare is as Nature herself, all-inclusive ;
but in others—and chiefly in comedy—he is partial,
he is impressionary, he refuses to know what is not to
his purpose, he is light-heartedly capricious."
     So in a few words does Mrs Meynell clear the air of a
thousand cobwebs of cant. It is the never sufficiently
recognised defence of the Restoration Drama, of the
Comedy of Manners, of Congreve and Wilde—irrefutable,
exact.
     Extraordinarily acute again is her attack on biog-
raphers who stress the pains, illnesses and death of
their subjects. She takes her text from Nature :
     " Where are they—all the dying, all the dead, of the
populous woods ? Where do they hide their little last
hours, where are they buried ? Where is the violence
concealed ? . . . Hunting goes on, but with strange
decorum. You may pass a fine season under the trees,
and see nothing dead . . . there is nothing like a
butcher's shop in the woods. But the biographers
have always had other ways than those of the wild
world. They will not have a man die out of sight. . . .
There never is a modern biography that has taken the
hint of Nature. One and all, these books have the
disproportionate illness, the death out of all scale. . . .
If death is the privacy of the woods, it is the more
conspicuously secret because it is their only privacy.
You may watch or may surprise everything else. The
nest is retired, not hidden. The chase goes on everywhere. It is wonderful how the perpetual chase seems
to cause no perpetual fear. The songs are all audible.
Life is undefended, careless, alert, and noisy."
     Modern biographers obviously do not read Mrs
Meynell, for the point has not even now been taken, in
spite of the unanswerable argument.
     One of Mrs Meynell's greater gifts is her sensitive-
ness to individual words. How she rhapsodises over
ensoleillé, " new as the sun, as remote as old Provence " !
She revels in the encountering " as gay strangers "
of two words of various origin and divided race,
as in " superfluous kings," "a lass unparalleled,"

"multitudinous seas," in the finely comic (to English ears) "il s'est trompé de defunte" and other French phrases of unrivalled mediocrity. Everyone will remember her essay in the first number of *The London Mercury* on the use of "in" and "un" in "An Article on Particles." "That 'un' implies, encloses so much, denies so much, refuses so much, point-blank, with a tragic irony that French, for example, can hardly compass. Compare our all-significant 'unloved,' 'unforgiven,' with any phrase of French . . . but in order to keep these great significances the 'un' should not be squandered as we squander it. And neither should the less closely embraced 'in' be so neglected. It has its right place and dignity and is, as it were, more deliberate. . . . Let us try to keep our 'un' in its right place by considering how, for instance, it makes of 'undone' a word of incomparable tragedy, surpassing 'defeated' and 'ruined' and all others of their kind. . . . The Teutonic 'un' comes more readily to the English pen than the Latin 'in,' and thus is joined habitually to the wrong kind of adjective and verb and adverb. Not only, moreover, to the Romantic word, but also to the Greek. . . . The misuse of 'less' is even somewhat more to be resisted than that of 'un,' because in the case first named the grammatical construction of our English words . . . is violated. And beautiful words that are neglected for 'quenchless' and 'relentless' pass out of use."

It is passages like this that make us realise the inestimable value of the work done by the purists to keep the well of English undefiled in a debased and vulgar age.

The same fastidiousness is to be observed in Mrs Meynell's commentaries on life. "It would be a pity," she says, "if laughter should ever become, like rhetoric and the arts, a habit." She would have us laugh less, as children laugh "because they must, and never by way of proof or sign . . . they laugh because someone runs behind them . . . and movement does so jog their spirits that their legs fail them, for laughter, without a jest." What Mrs Meynell objects to is the laugh that is given "thrice for the same thing—once for foolish surprise, and twice for tardy intelligence, and thrice to let it be known that they are amused." Laughter should be kept for its own unpremeditated act. In a delightful paper called *Have Patience, Little Saint*, she declaims against the prevalent manner adopted towards beggars. "Have Patience, Little Saint," is the graceful phrase of excuse customary in Portugal. "We have a strange way of vindicating our dignity when we refuse to man, woman or child the recognition of a simply human word. . . . The refusal of intercourse . . . (is) . . . the last outrage. . . . The merry beggar has lamentably disappeared. . . . It is significant of much."

In *Unstable Equilibrium* she puts in a plea for the beauty of the leg: "It is principally for the sake of the leg that a change in the dress of man is so much to be desired. . . . The leg is the best part of the figure, inasmuch as it has the finest lines and therewith those slender, diminishing forms which, coming at the base of the human structure, show it to be a thing of life by its unstable equilibrium. . . . In the case of the woman's figure it is the foot, with its extreme proportional smallness, that gives the precious instability, the spring and balance that are so organic. But man should no longer disguise the long lines, the strong forms, in those lengths of piping or tubing that are of all garments the most stupid. . . . It is hardly possible to err by violence in denouncing them. . . . When an indifferent writer is praised for ' clothing his thought,' it is to modern raiment that one's agile fancy flies."

One of the most charming essays is *The Colour of Life*. "The true colour of life," she says, " is not red . . . red is the colour of life violated . . . the true colour of life is the colour of the body . . . its very beauty is that it is white, but less white than milk : brown, but less brown than earth : red, but less red than sunset or dawn. It is lucid, but less lucid than

Y

the colour of lilies. It has the hint of gold that is in
all fine colour . . . under Sicilian skies, indeed, it is
deeper than old ivory ; but under the misty blue of
the English zenith, and the warm grey of the London
horizon, it is as delicately flushed as the pale wild
roses, out to their utmost, flat as stars, in the hedges
of the end of June." She sees " old ivory and wild
rose in the deepening midsummer sun in the colour of
the Cockney child bathing in the Serpentine." You are
inclined to wonder that, even undressed, he still shouts
with a Cockney accent. You half expect pure vowels
and elastic syllables from his restoration, his spring,
his slenderness, his brightness, and his glow. But for
an example of Mrs Meynell's style at its best this, I
think, from *The Horizon*, may serve :
    " It is the law whereby the land and the horizon
answer one another that makes the way up a hill
so full of universal movement. All the landscape is
on pilgrimage. The town gathers itself closer, and its
inner harbours literally come to light : the headlands
repeat themselves : little cups within the treeless hills
open and show their farms. In the sea are many
regions. A breeze is at play for a mile or two, and the
surface is turned. There are roads and curves in the
blue and in the white . . . but it is the horizon, more
than all else, you have come in search of . . . it is
to uplift the horizon to the equality of your sight that
you go high . . . so delicate and so slender is the
distant horizon that nothing less near than Queen
Mab and her chariot can equal its fineness. Here on
the edges of the eyelids, or there on the edges of the
world—we know no other place for things so exquisitely made, so thin, so small and tender. . . . On
the horizon is the sweetest light. Elsewhere colour
mars the simplicity of light, but there colour is effaced,
not as men efface it, by a blur or darkness, but by mere
light. . . . As the upspringing of all things at your
going up the heights, so steady, so swift, is the sub-
sidence at your descent. The further sea lies away,
hill folds down behind hill. The whole upstanding

world, with its looks serene and alert, its distant replies, its signals of many miles, its signs and communications, gathers down and pauses."

Comparable perhaps with this is her pæan in praise of clouds : " The privation of cloud is indeed a graver loss than the world knows. Terrestrial scenery is much, but it is not all. Men go in search of it ; but the celestial scenery journeys to them : it goes its way round the world. It has no nation, it costs no weariness, it knows no bounds. . . . The sea has no mood except that of the sky and of its winds. It is the cloud that, holding the sun's rays in a sheaf as a giant holds a handful of spears, strikes the horizon, touches the extreme edge with a delicate revelation of light, or suddenly puts it out and makes the foreground shine . . . but the cloud is never so victorious as when it towers above some little landscape of rather paltry interest — a conventional river heavy with water, gardens with their little evergreens, walks, and shrubberies . . . high over these rises, in the enormous scale of the scenery of clouds, what no man expected—an heroic sky. Few of the things that were ever done upon earth are great enough to be done under such a heaven. It was surely designed for other days : it is for an epic world."

It is obvious from these extracts what a feeling for Nature this fastidious lover has. The same tender observation leads her to rehabilitate the reputations of some famous women of the past who have been unfairly treated by the less observant and the less scrupulous.

She uses Mrs Lucy Hutchinson with her exquisite sense of style as a rebuke to the women of a later age, quoting this " lovely phrase of her grief " : " As his shadow, she waited on him everywhere, till he was taken to that region of light which admits of none, and then she vanished into nothing."

" Her power," says Mrs Meynell, " her integrity, her tenderness, her pomp, the liberal and public interests of her life, her good breeding, her education, her exquisite

diction, are such as may well make a reader ask how
and why the literature of England declined upon
the vulgarity, ignorance, cowardice, foolishness that
became 'feminine' in the estimation of a later age ;
that is, in the character of women succeeding her, and
in the estimation of men succeeding her lord. The
noble graces of Lucy Hutchinson, I say, may well
make us marvel at the downfall following—at Goldsmith's invention of the women of *The Vicar of Wake-
field* in one age, and at Thackeray's invention of the
women of *Esmond* in another. . . . What an England
was hers ! And what an English ! A memorable
vintage of our literature and speech was granted in
her day."

I have given this quotation at full length because it
would stand word for word as true if written about
Alice Meynell herself : all those qualities of tenderness,
good breeding, integrity, exquisite diction, all those
noble graces of refinement are the very qualities that
are Mrs Meynell's own.

In an essay on Mrs Dingley she puts in a lively plea
for that other half of " M. D." whom the world is
delighted to ignore. " M. D." in her argument, in
Swift's *Journal to Stella*, never stands for Stella alone.
" Dingley's half of the tender things said to M. D. is
equal to any whole, and takes nothing from the whole
of Stella's half."

I thought that most of us were agreed about that,
but I suppose for every real reader of the *Journal* there
are a hundred who talk as if they had read it, and it is
easier to suppose Stella to be the recipient of all those
tender messages and Dingley to have been a sort of
chaperon—a chaperon !   " The saucy, charming M. D.,"
" little monkeys mine," " dear little young women,"
" nautinautinautidear girls "—this does not sound like
chaperonage.

"Two hundred years," says Mrs Meynell at the
conclusion of her unanswerable proof, " is long for
her to have gone stripped of so radiant a glory as is
hers by right. ' Better, thanks to M. D.'s prayers,'

wrote the immortal man who loved her, in a private fragment of a journal, never meant for Dingley's eyes, nor for Ppt's, nor for any human eyes ; and the rogue Stella has for two centuries been made to steal all the credit of those prayers, and all the thanks of that pious benediction."

Another fallen dusty idol whom she strives to restore to her proper niche is Steele's Prue.

" It is painful to me to complain of Thackeray : but see what a figure he makes of Prue in *Esmond.*"

Mrs Meynell denies that Prue was dull, dowdy, exacting, jealous, neglected or evaded.

" She kept some four hundred of these little letters of her lord's. It was a loyal keeping. But what does Thackeray call it ? His word is ' thrifty.' . . . ' Thrifty ' is a hard word to apply to her whom Steele styled, in the year before her death, his ' charming little insolent.' She was ill in Wales, and he, at home, wept upon her pillow, and ' took it to be a sin to go to sleep.' Thrifty they may call her, and accurate if they will ; but she lies in Westminster Abbey, and Steele called her ' your Prueship.' "

On Dr Johnson's wife Mrs Meynell is equally charming. " This paper," she begins, " shall not be headed ' Tetty.' . . . Men who would trust Dr Johnson with their orthodoxy, with their vocabulary, and with the most intimate vanity of their human wishes, refuse, with every mark of insolence, to trust him in regard to his wife. On that one point no reverence is paid to him, no deference, no respect, not so much as the credit due to our common sanity. . . . If England loves her great Englishman's memory, she owes not only courtesy, but gratitude, to the only woman who loved him while there was yet time. . . . He chose, for love, a woman who had the wit to admire him at first meeting, and in spite of first sight. ' That,' she said to her daughter, ' is the most sensible man I ever met.' He was penniless. . . . She loved him, accepted him, made him happy, gave to one of the noblest of all English hearts the one love of its sombre life . . . well

for him that he married so young as to earn the ridicule
of all the biographers in England : for by doing so he,
most happily, possessed his wife for nearly twenty
years. I have called her his only friend. He was
' solitary ' from the day she died."

After Nature, Art, Literature and Biography Mrs
Meynell ascends to her best subject, *The Darling
Young*. She brings the same shrewd attentiveness
to bear here as she does everywhere else. More and
more she reminds us of W. H. Davies standing stock-
still, scarcely daring to breathe as he watches in ecstasy
some simple country scene.

" To attend to a living child," she says, " is to be
baffled in your humour, disappointed of your pathos,
and set freshly free from all the preoccupations. You
cannot anticipate him . . . you are the fellow-traveller
of a bird. . . . No man's fancy could be beforehand
. . . with a girl of four who dictated a letter . . . with
the sweet and unimaginable message : ' I hope you
enjoy yourself with your loving dolls.' " How deserved is the retort to that harassed father who tried
to snare sympathy by saying : " Do you know I have
been working hard, darling ? I work to buy things
for you." . . . " Do you work to buy the fat ? " she
asked. " I don't like fat."

It is only to be expected that the meticulous scholar
who listens for the timbre of a word, who worries over
the misuses of " un " and " in," will be entranced by
such child language as " Lift I up and let I see it not
raining."

But better than her child stories is her extraordinarily
acute summary of their unreadiness, a lesson to every
parent : " It is no doubt this unreadiness that causes
little children to like twice-told tales and foregone
conclusions in their games. They are not eager . . .
for surprises. If you hide and they cannot see you
hiding, their joy in finding you is comparatively small :
but let them know perfectly well what cupboard you
are in, and they will find you with shouts of discovery.
The better the hiding-place is understood between

you the more lively the drama. . . . When the house
is filled with outcries of laughter from the breathless
breast of a child, it is that he is pretending to be surprised at finding his mother where he bade her pretend
to hide."

" Their poor little slowness is so distinctively their
own . . . if, on a voyage in space, electricity takes
thus much time, and light thus much, and sound thus
much, there is one little jogging traveller that would
arrive after the others had forgotten their journey,
and this is the perception of a child. . . . We have
but to consider all that it implies of the loitering of
the senses and of an unprepared consciousness—this
capacity for receiving a great shock from a noise and
this perception of the shock after two or three appreci-
able moments—if we would know anything of the
moments of a baby. Even as we must learn that our
time, when it is long, is too long for children, so must
we learn that our time when it is short, is too short for
them." It would be hard to think of a more important
reminder than that. If only all educationists had
such common sense, allied with such vision, reformation
on rational lines might even come in our day.

Under the Early Stars is almost equally delightful.
" Play is not for every hour of the day, or for any hour
taken at random " is the burden of the refrain of this
paper. " There is a tide in the affairs of children.
Civilisation is cruel in sending them to bed at the most
stimulating time of dusk. Summer dusk, especially, is
the frolic moment for children, baffle them how you
may. They may have been in a pottering mood all
day, intent upon all kinds of close industries, breathing
hard over choppings and poundings. But when late
twilight comes, there comes also the punctual wildness.
. . . The kitten grows alert at the same hour, and
hunts for moths and crickets in the grass. . . . The
children lie in ambush and fall upon one another in the
mimicry of hunting. . . ."

And perhaps best of all is the final essay on *The
Illusion of Historic Time,* in which she reminds us that

" if there were no child there would be nothing old . . . it is by good fortune that ' ancient ' history is taught in the only ancient days. So, for a time, the world is magical. . . . By learning something of antiquity in the first ten years, the child enlarges the sense of time for all mankind. . . . The past of childhood is not single, is not motionless, nor fixed in one point : it has summits a world away from the other. Year from year differs as the antiquity of Mexico from the antiquity of Chaldea. . . .

" There is a long and mysterious moment in long and mysterious childhood, which is the extremest distance known to any human fancy . . . it is the moment of going to sleep . . . his nurse's lullaby is translated into the mysteries of time. She sings absolutely immemorial words."

" She sings absolutely immemorial words "—it is a good note on which to leave this exquisite artist. Her words leave " a sense of stilled singing." It is all singing, such clear pure notes as have not been heard in our time elsewhere.

III

G. S. STREET

IT is now almost thirty years since *The Auto-biography of a Boy* appeared to startle and delight a passionate few. Mr Street is not too prodigal of his art. At intervals of three years he is content modestly to produce a volume of essays : only the passionate few take any notice, but they are without doubt books with lasting power. *The Wise and the Wayward, The Trials of the Bantocks, A Book of Stories, A Book of Essays, Books and Things, The Ghosts of Piccadilly, People and Questions, On Money and other Essays, At Home in the War*—just ten books in thirty years and most of them out of print. Mr Street has all the qualities of the great essayist. He is quiet, unruffled, urbane, scholarly, humorous, introspective, and of course egotistic : "It is more agreeable to see a book on one's shelves than an awkward mass of cuttings in a drawer," is his apology for republishing the essays contained in *People and Questions*.

He defends the Early Victorians with care and scrupulous fidelity to fact. He finds their most characteristic note to be confidence—in politics particularly. "It cannot besadden us that the altruistic and freedom-loving spirit, which was the finest quality of old Liberalism, should have so utterly vanished. . . . Joined to this overwhelming confidence in the present and future was naturally a contempt of the past. It seemed ridiculous to the forties and fifties that people ever lived without gas and railways."

Again : "Confident and hard and fast was the theoretical morality of those days. (As for the practised morality, I decline altogether to believe in the swift change of which we are accused.) About the

345

virtues of women there was no hesitation. A line was drawn, on one side of which was a company so pure and holy that men must be abashed when they entered it, and on the other, poor creatures from whom everybody but clergymen recoiled in horror. . . . It was a simple distinction. A morality for women in which kindness, serviceableness, intelligence, count for nothing and conventional chastity counts for everything is inevitable in a society where the home is still the important unit."

The point he is trying to make clear is of course that we have " advanced," that we are " broader," that æsthetically we are nicer; but "I wonder if simple and profound effects of beauty, like that of a bare tree against a winter sky, stir the senses of an average Englishman now more surely than fifty years ago. I am not sure."

He is sure that intellectually we are inferior.

" There is strangely little interest at present in any abstract or intellectual subject whatever. I do not think I need modify that statement on account of popular lectures given to fashionable ladies. . . . In the forties and fifties and early sixties there was a great deal of interest in things of genuinely intellectual import. . . . It is something to our discredit if we have ceased in a measure to care for what cannot be touched or seen . . . it is not well to ignore the meaning of life and the things of the spirit. . . . Indifference and apathy seem to mark our generation . . . if intelligence be not wanting to us, certainly zeal and energy are."

He regards it as significant that Bernard Shaw " the most brilliant of our playwrights," should be altogether analytical and destructive. " He startles and disturbs the conventional and unthinking man with a fine effect, but he has little instruction to give the wise man."

" Happy forties and fifties and early sixties," he concludes, " when great questions were in the air and were discussed with fervour ! Men are happier when their souls are lifted above the little things of life, and talk about the eternal verities ' opens the heart and lungs ' almost as effectually as laughter. It may be that we live in an ebbing of the spirit now in England, and that the flow will come again in our time. . . . Meanwhile, apathetic, analytical creatures that we are, we invite the humour of the gods if we look down on the Early Victorians."

Many essays have been written of late on the Victorians, mainly commendatory. Asquith and Inge united to praise them, but Street, so long ago as 1910, had written an essay which got nearer to the root of the matter.

On slighter themes he brings the same shrewd judgment to bear, illuminating whatever he touches.

" The distinction," he says in his essay on " The New House," " between animate and inanimate is crude and superficial. . . . A man must be very fortunate or of abnormal sympathy if he has no acquaintance who is so much dead matter to him, and he is much to be pitied who has no living friends in stocks and stones."

In " Flags in the Rain " he enters a protest against the bedecking of the streets of London :

" With the dignity of its houses, and the tender green of its trees, Piccadilly is a fine and beautiful sight. To hang flags between the trees and the houses is to take a serene and comely matron and trick her out like a chorus girl. . . . You do not compliment a guest by painting your house purple and putting on a false nose. . . . The true note of London is its strength and dignity and age ; skimpy little flags and tawdry drapings are a discord."

He has wise things to say both of town and country : " The art of living in London is the art of not going about." On milk : " Surely it is an unlovely paradox that milk . . . should be given us in London with so much uproar. Every house in my street goes to a different shop for milk, and every milkman, yelling defiance, flings a hundred cans on the pavement and kicks them about, and the fury lasts from six to eight. . . . I believe that milkmen are really brewers

and wine merchants in disguise, and seek to disgust
us with our innocent drink." This thought occurs to
him while lying in bed remembering "the lanes of
my dear Sussex." "Tranquillity remembered in
emotion," as he cleverly paraphrases it. It is pleasant
to find that, unlike most writers who walk, his brain
does not function as he strides along. "I hope one
is more in tune with the grass and the trees and the
scurrying rabbit . . . when one thinks not at all."
His Sussex, too, is a fresh one. Not for him the
obvious Downs.

"Most of Sussex I know and love : the country has
all that I desire, cornfields and pasture and woods and
bleak downs and the sea ; but the stretch of it midway
or nearly between Tunbridge Wells and Lewes is the
fairest and kindest of all. Five-Ashes, Framfield,
Cross-in-Hand, the sweet names match the wandering
green lanes one walks to reach them, with here a
peaceful old homestead and there a beautiful old mill,
and ever, as one gains the higher ground, a noble view
over sloping fields and woods and the dark line of the
South Downs. . . . Since England chose to have a
few rich men rather than many strong men, and let the
country-side go hang, the stronger and the harder
have gone from it, and there is something parasitical
and unreal in the life which is left. But there is also
left humanity and kindness and natural courtesy.
There are places in Great Britain—I name them not—
where children scowl at a stranger and jeer behind his
back. Here they run to a cottage gate to tell you
your way and speed you with smiles and nods. . . .
Nature and man in Sussex are my friends."

He even finds in fogs matter for enjoyment because
the millionaire has to share the poor man's discomfort.
As befits the official Reader of Plays, his judgment on
the theatre is peculiarly thoughtful. He insists on the
necessity of team work among actors : "intelligence
and not sympathetic emotion must be the basis of
acting in the first instance."

On Education too he is wise. He states as a simple

fact that the average product of the Universities and Public Schools knows nothing at all. "It is not the case that he has been taught useless things, or has but a smattering of this or that—he knows nothing. Nothing. I do not say that this fact is necessarily bad. . . . It is still my opinion . . . that for a youth with brains the Greats school at Oxford . . . is by far the best education to be had in England, and might easily be made an ideal one. It may not give him riches, but it gives him a sense of perspective, and taste, and above all, the habit of considering the meaning of words. . . . In so far as my mind differs from a parrot's I believe it owes an incalculable debt to the turning of modern thoughts into thoughts . . . possible to ancient Romans and Greeks. . . . There were horrid gaps in our classical reading. We read our authors at an absurdly slow pace ; the clever and indolent had far too easy a time."

"As for the average boy," he says later, " if it is found impossible to give him the essence of education, which I take to be the desire of knowledge and the habit of thinking, I would suggest that he might at least be taught—unintelligently and by force if not intelligently—a few elementary facts about his own country."

These two paragraphs contain more wisdom about Education than I have read packed in the same space by any expert. He touches the very heart of the matter when he laments the fact that schoolmasters have now become the boys' natural friend, and therefore have to remain boys. " That cannot be wholesome, and I strongly question if it can be pleasant . . . to go on with the implicit pretence that playing cricket or football is the most important activity in life . . . what a life for the grown man is that of the contemporary schoolmaster."

Ironically he sums up the whole question : " The way to form a boy with a sane outlook on life and immune against its dangers of emotions is to keep him like a novice in a monastery, save for a quarter of the year, till he is nearly twenty." It is pleasant to find some man capable of preserving a detached attitude towards vested interests like schools and universities.

In an essay which is strangely reminiscent of Charles Lamb he writes in praise of the Cockney.

" I like the south more than the north," he says bravely. " Sturdy independence, grit, precision of mind—these are qualities I respect. But I am more at home with the South Countrymen. To me they seem softer and kindlier, less fit to battle with a rough world, of a mellower social habit—generally more sympathetic to one who never learned how to push." He confesses to being most at home with Cockneys. " I am but an amateur countryman at best." He calls his beloved Cockneys " the best-natured people under the sun. . . . A deliberately rude or offensive Cockney is hardly to be met. . . . He is not given to hearty peals of laughter, but his laughter, for all that, is near the surface." He does not credit the townsman with more intelligence than the countryman, but he does assert (and I agree entirely) that " some of the best-looking women in England you may see any weekday evening . . . going down Bond Street or St James's Street from the shops where they are employed to the trains and omnibuses, but I doubt you could not say a like thing of their brothers."

He is delightful at the expense of " superior people " who know things. Again he sums up the matter freshly and perfectly : " I know a ' musical comedy ' makes no appeal to my intellect and knowledge of life, but I don't want to say so every minute while I watch one. The superior person does, and that is why he is one of our minor discomforts. . . . I am inclined to think that inferior people are, on the whole, a more serious inconvenience."

By inferior people he means those who damage the soul. " Inferiority," he says, " is catching." He is excellent too in his damnation of enthusiasts, reserving the lowest place in his inferno for the enthusiastic egoist " who, with all the energy and appealing force with which other enthusiasts speak of their causes and sports and missions and hobbies, calls on you to exult with him in the lucky speculation he has made," but the enthusiast comes out of the ordeal highly compared with the " level-headed."

" When you hear the expression ' level-headed,' it is ignorance crying to ignorance, stupidity applauding stupidity. . . . It is the complacent belief of the dull that the lively—of the prosaic that the imaginative—lack soundness of judgment."

It is characteristic of Mr Street to make play with the expression. " No one with a sense of humour would use it in praise. As one hears it, one thinks of a low forehead, a flat surface above it, and straight staring eyes—eyes, in fact, which must be always level, which may never look down for memory, or upwards for inspiration. It does not suggest a noble nature or even a wise one. And as one thinks of the level-headed collectively one remembers that they of all people, with all their prejudice and caution, are the prey of the charlatan and the swindler, their sentimentality exploited in the theatre and the book-shop, their greed in the city ; and one sees an absolutely level surface of close-packed heads, with the swindler and the charlatan dancing aloft on it." Such it is to have a lively sense of the exact values of words. We had, many of us, accepted " level-headed " before. We shall scarcely be able to hide a Puckish smile when we hear it in future.

The same humour lurks in his " Rules for the Middle-Aged " : " Remember always that to the young you seem much older than you are. The girl in *Sense and Sensibility* who thought that at thirty-five a man needed not a wife but a nurse was excessive, but something of that is always in the youthful mind. . . . Recognise cheerfully that your youth is over, and you will be delighted to find how much of it is left. . . . The secret of middle age is acceptance."

" In general, propitiate the young by insistence on

your age and envy of theirs . . . but you must not be too middle-aged in their society . . . you cannot expect to be an attractive figure in the eyes of youth without some pretence of idealism or altruism. Make that pretence. Avoid it in the society of your average contemporaries; altruism or idealism makes them uncomfortable, even though they are always convinced of its insincerity. Be as material and physical as you like. . . . You need no rules for your discourse with the aged. You have merely to accept . . . their pleasant illusion that you are young."

He writes of a visit to a police court with the tender sympathy of Galsworthy: " . . . the squalid hopelessness, the unspeakable ugliness of the whole affair blighted one's spirit. . . . I left that police court with my nerves quite unstrung—and with a black depression on my mind. . . . A social system which produces such villainies as that of contemporary England is proven vicious, and it is an obligation on those who see that to do what they can politically to change it."

In his essay, "On a Word To Be Dropped," he is back at his game of damning a word. "Except for purposes of ceremony I desire the word gentleman to be abolished."

"There are thousands and thousands of men, otherwise sane, who believe that because their sires were parsons or doctors they are better than men begotten by farmers or chemists. The idea that trade and being a gentleman are incompatible is a piece of very modern snobbishness, and the stress of economics is destroying it, but meanwhile it is responsible for an infinity of fantastic and anti-social arrogance and un-humorous and anti-social resentment. . . . Emotions linger most irrelevantly, and really I believe that by abolishing the word gentleman I shall let a deal of black blood."

In his paper on "Society" he does far more than merely attack a word; he gives us a piece of profoundly

interesting sociological history. "It once was spelled
with a capital S, to be a target for satirists ، . . it
used to be mentioned with a capital S in the voice . . .
old-fashioned people still so use the word. . . . A
hundred years ago there was a compact aristocratic
caste in England . . . it represented political power,
and it was small. . . . It was a large family . . .
mostly related and mutually known. . . . To be in
society meant something quite definite to Thackeray
. . . but now ? The numbers have become so great
and the coherence so slight that a point is reached
when the word ' society ' means nothing at all. . . .
There is a welter of people whose only claim to social
importance is in the possession of titles . . . or . . .
the possession of money. They fill the paragraphs of
fashionable intelligence, but they are not important.
. . . The splitting into sets has produced a small society
more exclusive than the old. . . . Society is not dead
. . . it is often unfairly attacked. Most of it is no
more harmful than money without duties inevitably
implies. If its manners have lost in decorum here and
there, they have gained in ease. It is still better than
merely plutocratic. Only—it does not matter. The
society which does is even more remote from the
average citizen than it was, and not at all at the mercy
of the paragraphist. It is a hard saying for the
aspirant, but it is true."

It really would be hard to find a fairer summing-up
of the existing order than that. Always he preserves
his judicial standpoint.

"If you commit great and serious crimes you are
sent to penal servitude, which all the experts say is
much better than imprisonment with hard labour. Just
so, if you owe half-a-million you suffer little or no inconvenience, but if you only owe ten pounds you may
be sent to prison for not paying it. I suppose the law
has some vague idea of encouraging a spirit of enter-
prise, but it puzzles my old-fashioned morality." He
is talking of the discomforts of the law. "In the way
of mere discomfort, however, as an habitual criminal,

z

I should resent more than anything else the ineffable
air of transcendent virtue which policemen don with
their uniforms. . . . I do wish policemen would look
a little less sainted. They make me feel criminal."

On the subject of "Being Patronised " he shows us
again his very human side : " The other day a young
man of thirty or so, whose aptitudes and abilities
would hardly qualify him to black boots or sweep a
crossing or sit in Parliament, but who is a fashionable
young man in his way, addressed me as follows :—
' How are *you* ? ' he said, with a condescension on
the pronoun no device of writing can reproduce.
' What's *your* news ? ' I was very angry." When the
nefariously rich wife of a Houndsditch tripe merchant
treats him with contempt he merely laughs. He
attempts to analyse the course of our annoyance at
being patronised : " If we are annoyed by patronising
airs, it is not because we think the patronisers our
superiors, but because we are afraid the rest of the
world thinks so. . . . Patronising is half-way between
flogging him and giving him ten pounds."

Very good is his description of the agony of having
to wait for dinner. " You can spoil nothing in a man
that matters so much as his temper."

He pleads in another essay with his brothers and
sisters in buses and Tubes to look as if they were
pleased with his society instead of looking ready to
smash his face in for twopence. " That air of critical
disapproval, that apparent surprise and disgust because
another man walks abroad and goes about his business
—we might trace it to the humours of our climate . . .
one little smile, faint and fleeting, when he meets a
fellow-creature's eyes in public, should not be too hard
of achievement."

On this note we may well leave him. His range is
wide—he even takes us to Bohemia—his mind alert,
his sympathies catholic, his taste fastidious : he is
quite openly anxious to be friendly with all but the
vulgar, the snob and the narrow-minded : he is never
tedious. Everything he says sheds a fresh light on

the subject under discussion, nearly always humorously expressed. He has the lightest of touches. Some of us are hard put to it to define what a prig is. G. S. Street is a splendid example of the type of man that is the exact opposite of a prig.